ELKHORN

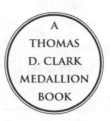

A
THOMAS
D. CLARK
MEDALLION
BOOK

The Thomas D. Clark Medallion was established to honor the memory and contributions of Dr. Thomas Dionysius Clark (1903–2005). A beloved teacher, prolific author, resolute activist, and enthusiastic advocate of publications about Kentucky and the region, Dr. Clark helped establish the University of Kentucky Press in 1943, which was reorganized in 1969 as the University Press of Kentucky, the state-mandated scholarly publisher for the Commonwealth. The Clark Medallion is awarded annually to one University Press of Kentucky publication that achieves Dr. Clark's high standards of excellence and addresses his wide breadth of interests about the state. Winners of the Thomas D. Clark Medallion are selected by the Board of Directors of the Thomas D. Clark Foundation Inc., a private nonprofit organization established in 1994 to provide financial support for the publication of vital books about Kentucky and the region.

Elkhorn

EVOLUTION

OF A KENTUCKY

LANDSCAPE

Richard Taylor

UNIVERSITY PRESS OF KENTUCKY

Scholarly publisher for the Commonwealth,
serving Bellarmine University, Berea College, Centre
College of Kentucky, Eastern Kentucky University,
The Filson Historical Society, Georgetown College, Kentucky
Historical Society, Kentucky State University, Morehead State
University, Murray State University, Northern Kentucky
University, Spalding University, Transylvania University,
University of Kentucky, University of Louisville,
and Western Kentucky University.

Editorial and Sales Offices: The University Press of Kentucky
663 South Limestone Street, Lexington, Kentucky 40508–4008
www.kentuckypress.com

Cataloging-in-Publication data is available
from the Library of Congress.

ISBN 978-0-8131-7601-7 (hardcover : alk. paper)
ISBN 978-0-8131-7603-1 (epub)
ISBN 978-0-8131-7602-4 (pdf)
ISBN 978-0-8131-8717-4 (pbk.: alk. paper)

Manufactured in the United States of America.

Member of the Association of University Presses

ASSOCIATION
of UNIVERSITY
PRESSES

For John S. Palmore (1917–2017) and Carol Palmore (1949–2015), creek dwellers and dear friends who brought light into the lives of many of us and into whose hands I had hoped to place this book.

A Southerner soon as a Northerner, a planter nonchalant and hospitable down by the Oconee I live,
A Yankee bound my own way ready for trade, my joints the limberest joints on earth and the sternest joints on earth,
A Kentuckian walking the vale of the Elkhorn in my deer-skin leggings,
A Louisianan or Georgian . . .
—**Walt Whitman,** "Song of Myself," 1855

Elkhorn Baptist Association, Elkhorn Clothing Room, Elkhorn Campground, Elkhorn Development Company, Elkhorn Heritage Real Estate, Elkhorn Investment Management, Elkhorn Stone Company, Elkhorn Water District, Elkhorn Coal Company, Elkhorn Terrace, Elkhorn Avenue, Elkhorn Hills Lane, Elkhorn Court, Elkhorn Middle School, Elkhorn Securities
—**Yellowbook,** *Greater Lexington,* 2016

Q: "And what church do you belong to?"
A: "My church is the Church of Elkhorn."
—**Scott Robinson,** fly fisherman and songwriter/musician, circa 1980

Water is family.
—**Allan Gurganus,** *Oldest Living Confederate Widow Tells All,* 1989

CONTENTS

AUTHOR'S NOTE

Most of the sections of this book are preceded by italicized narrative vignettes, brief imaginings that attempt to fill in the gaps of history with embroidered facts true to the experience though not delineated in verifiable sources—what today some might call fake facts, others creative nonfiction. Their purpose is to regard the creek's history from yet another perspective in the fuller light that histories often neglect to provide because the sources don't exist or too often suffer from a poverty of lived experience and sensory detail. The other details in the book are as verifiable as I could make them, some drawn from personal experience, some from print sources. The vignettes are intended as a means of looking at Elkhorn from another angle, less as alternatives than as extensions not bound by the limitations of historical sources. Photographs open another window. They arrest light in an instant of time and inventory the scenes they depict. A Paul Sawyier painting creates light and imbues it with the feeling and style of the painter. These windows add to direct experience but don't replace the walk in the woods that wets one's leggings.

HOLT-GILTNER HOUSE   TAYLOR 2017

The Giltner-Holt House. (Drawing by Richard Taylor.)

INTRODUCTION

In the summer of 1975 I took a job teaching at Kentucky State University in Frankfort, where my wife, Lizz, and I began looking for a house in the country. When asked about what kind of house, we said one that was old and that needed some fixing up, hoping it would cost less if it needed work. We visited a variety of such houses and worked with several realtors. None of them panned out. Finally, we called a Berea College graduate named John Hamilton who, among other things, sold one-foot-square pieces of his farm in Bald Knob through an ad in *The New Yorker* for folks who wanted to own a piece of "Daniel Boone country." "I have just the place for you," he said.

We arranged to meet him about four miles northeast of Frankfort at Holt Lane to inspect a barn-like structure known locally as the Holt house. There was a long, stone-curbed driveway bordered by old trees, mostly maples and walnuts. The largest was a blue ash ninety or so feet tall that must have dated to Daniel Boone days. The house with its eighteen rooms had once been a showplace on a large farm. Now it was an over-sized farmhouse that needed a new roof, a paint job, city water, and central heating. John Hamilton, a stocky man to the north of sixty-five wearing a straw panama hat that seemed more at home in Florida or at a used car lot, gave us the tour. The house, he explained, was not technically on the market, but he would talk to the owner if we had an interest. The roof had been damaged by the 1974 tornado, and the ceilings were out on the second floor and leakage had done substantial damage to the fancy plasterwork downstairs in what must once have been a double parlor. One room, ceiling to floor, was half yellow-half blue. We joked that the person painting it had been shot by Indians midway through the job.

Instead of city water, there was a cistern tied to a pump in the dirt-floored basement. Exotic mold adorned the entire wall of the next room. It looked like a sick room, a place where people came to decay. It was clear that the house needed major renovation to be habitable. A family of tenants with a passel of children had lived there last, but not for the past ten years.

We met the owner, Zack Saufley, a trim man in his early sixties who was vice president at a local bank, a former commander of an army reserve unit, an agriculture teacher at the University of Kentucky, and at heart a farmer. He owned a good portion of upland as well as farmland that bordered Elkhorn Creek, some of the richest bottoms in the county. We liked him. He liked us, and that night we bought the house and the accompanying six acres. What attracted me to the Holt house was not only its potential as a place to live but the trees, grand old trees in a yard that was shade filled with patches of sunlight in a pleasing balance. Even then I saw the house as a chance to take something that was noteworthy and restore it over the rest of my life. It would be a great place to raise children, a great place to leave them. What I didn't envision was just how cold it would be that winter as we hunkered around an Ashley woodstove dressed in thermal underwear and multiple layers of clothing. The stove had a hatch top that accommodated whole logs but even then produced only a slim nimbus of heat, most of which rose to the high ceilings or sifted through the porous walls. Still, we loved the place, and we gradually introduced amenities—radiant heat through a hot water system fired by a boiler in the basement, a second-floor bathroom, new paint and patched plaster. Water came off the roof into the cistern, and we supplemented it with hauled water until the water hauler stopped delivering and we had to haul it ourselves, 350 gallons at a time. It was not until over a decade later that we achieved city water through a line that came a mile or so through Zack Saufley's farm. Over the next decade we had three children—Philip, Willis, and Julia—who adapted well to the place since it was the only home they had ever known. An article that Bettye Lee Mastin wrote on the house in 1977 for the *Lexington Herald-Leader* newspaper reminded us that friends initially referred to the house as "Taylor's Folly."[1]

Interested in historic preservation, my wife and I joined Historic Frankfort, a local preservation group, and began to probe the house's past. Though I had a law degree and knew a little about searching titles, Lizz researched the previous owners. After a week or so of digging among deed books at the courthouse, she came up with a complete line of title from the original owner, Judge Harry Innes (1752–1816), to Zack Saufley, who had purchased the property at an auction, I believe in 1960. We realized just how significant the property was to Kentucky history. Appointed to the newly established supreme court for the Kentucky District in 1783 by George Washington, Innes was a prominent early Kentucky settler who also was a land speculator and politician. He was heavily involved in the movement for Kentucky's statehood.[2] When a friend suggested that we apply to have the house put on the National Register of Historic Places, we submitted an application. In July 1977—after a long nomination process—the Giltner-Holt house was officially listed on the National Register of Historic Houses, and we applied a sticker in a corner of the sidelight at the front door. The designation fed our pride more than our pocketbooks.

We soon learned that owning an old house is a battle against time. Over the next forty years or so, the house and remaining outbuildings underwent gradual decay and gradual improvements as summer breaks, teaching career, and money permitted. Systems failed, trees fell, and seedlings were replanted. Occasionally there were discoveries—a hewn stone step buried in the side yard, old bottles in the crawl space, and new historic material regarding the property found online.

The Giltner-Holt House, as it is officially known, was built in 1859 by Henry Giltner, described as a "progressive farmer."[3] In my front hallway hangs an oval photograph of him, bearded in his sixties, billows of hair swept back from a high forehead. His hand is over his heart, looking less like a Kentucky version of Napoleon than a sober deacon about to pledge the flag. While the two-and-a-half-story house was being built, Giltner lived in the log house constructed almost a mile away by Judge Harry Innes in 1792. The house Giltner built was located on higher ground above Innes's creekside holdings, where two of his slaves were captured during an Indian raid. After the deaths of Judge Innes in 1816 and his wife, Anna, many years later, the estate had been sold to Giltner in 1858. The original plan of the house consisted of two rooms to either side of a wide entry hall, with a second floor that replicated the plan of the first. The third-floor attic was divided into three rooms for storage.

In 1863, Giltner in turn sold the farm to Harry Innes Todd (1818–1891), a grandson of Judge Innes. A man busy with civic affairs and local politics, Todd seldom if ever resided on the property, preferring to live in the

Italian Revival villa he built across the street from the Orlando Brown
house in the historic residential district near downtown Frankfort. Todd
previously had been a colorful steamboat captain who had operated several incarnations of a steamboat named the *Blue Wing.* Through his long
life, he also served as a state representative and as keeper of the state penitentiary, then located in Frankfort. We gradually surmised that it was he
who used prisoners to build the matrix of stone fences that bordered and
intersected his farm, because he was sheriff as well as head of the state
penitentiary in Frankfort.

In the 1870s Todd suffered additional financial reverses that forced him
into bankruptcy. A two-story building inside the penitentiary had burned
in 1864 for a loss of $20,000, half sustained by the state, half by the keeper,
Harry Innes Todd. In 1870 the hemp "department," a three-story building, was destroyed, costing Todd another $10,000. When Todd went into
bankruptcy, the Bank of Kentucky kept the property for two years and
then sold it to Todd's wife, Jane. Unable to keep it, she sold the property
to Silas Noel, a local land speculator and leading citizen.[4]

James A. Holt, a prosperous tanner in Louisville, bought the property
from Noel in 1879. In 1880 he added a two-story ell to the house, making
a large house even larger. The addition consisted of eight rooms and four
porches. He also converted many of its details from Greek Revival to the
then fashionable Gothic Revival, adding fleur-de-lis gingerbread to the
eaves and gables, as well as shaped finials larger than cedar fence posts at
the corners of the roof. One of my friends still refers to them as "dragon
fenders." The most sinister addition was iron rings driven into the studs of
the upper back room of the ell to which prisoners from the state penitentiary could be chained when not working in the fields. The severity of this
was tempered by the remains of an enlarged hand-painted checkerboard
on the floor, a first step toward nineteenth-century versions of penal recreation. In addition to a three-bay cottage in back known as the summer kitchen, the outbuildings included a smokehouse, a carriage house,
a shop, and what must have been Franklin County's only partitioned six-
hole outhouse. Unmarried, Holt lived in the house until his death in 1906.
His front bedroom was painted a cobalt blue, and tradition has it that the
old bachelor selected that color because he found it soothing. I have a
photograph of him, taken before his death, sitting on the front verandah,
dwarfed by distance and the monstrous house above him.

Lizz miraculously found a flyer that advertised the sale of the farm at an Internet site selling ephemera. The text described the property in full-blown detail. Up in years, Holt moved to the Masons' Home in Shelbyville in 1905, putting the place up for sale for $65,000. Holt himself wrote the description, stating that only his failing health and age (seventy-nine) induced him to sell the property and that he would not have sold it for twice the asking price had he a son or daughter to whom to heir it. With some puffery, he described the 742-acre farm as "one of the best Blue Grass Farms in Kentucky." He stated that 360 acres of the farm were level "and very rich Elk-Horn Creek bottom" that "never overflows."[5] There is some puffing, yes, but pictures in another sale brochure justified his pride. This eight- or ten-page brochure, copied I'm not sure where, had photographs of the lane running through the farm, scenic vistas of fields in the bottom, the house, the outbuildings. The scenes were idyllic. In its text Holt also vowed that on his farm he had never planted tobacco, knowing its extractive qualities in sapping fertility from the soil. He boasted that the land was enclosed with twelve miles of stone fences, so well constructed "neither a rabbit or a mouse can pass through it."[6]

Our interest in the house eventually extended to curiosity about the neighborhood and its history, and gradually we picked up information from others, gathering what we could here and there until we came to a fuller understanding of the Peaks Mill Road neighborhood—and a greater appreciation. Each day I drive across the little branch that threads along Peaks Mill Road from the west. It runs under the main road and snakes under Holt Lane, eventually flowing under Peaks Mill Road again, ending about thirty yards from where Innes Station once stood. Next to it is a small stone springhouse at which Henry Clay is reputed to have spoken at a political rally held on the grounds sometime after Judge Innes's death in 1816. This nameless feeder creek links the lower and upper farmland that once belonged to Innes. It is all that is left of the wider, deeper waters that once etched out a large portion of the Elkhorn Valley along what is now an abandoned meander.

Somewhere I read that one facet of being educated is an ability to name the things around you, starting with plants and trees and moving to everything with which you share a small sphere of living. When asked of the woods he curated for most of his professional life, a naturalist I know said he could name no more than 80 percent of the plant forms that he passed by each day. Most of us can't name twenty plants. Fuller under-standing extends to the history of a place, the people who lived and died there, everything from its geology to the historical events and human intrusions that shaped it. Such a process is an evolutionary one that comes slowly and sometimes unexpectedly, ferreting out the tragedies as well as the triumphs and the even less apparent patterns of ordinary liv-ing. Such places render up their secrets very frugally. As the pre-Socratic Greek philosopher Heraclitus observed over two millennia ago, "Nature loves to hide." In a gloss to his translation, Guy Davenport, the teacher who influenced me most, explained in reference to nature that Heraclitus noted that "becoming is a secret process."[7] So it is with the unfolding of the secrets held deeper than we will ever know within the bosom of any place, especially the neighborhood along Elkhorn Creek intersected by Peaks Mill Road and Steadmantown Lane.

A friend, innocently or not so innocently, recently asked the purpose of this book. At first I didn't have an answer other than a simple curiosity to know the place in which I've lived for the past forty or so years. That Elkhorn Creek, the neighborhood where I've lived over half of my life, nat-urally interests me is the easy answer. I assumed it would interest others. At root I knew this was a book about place, and I decided to explore its dominant feature, focusing on a portion of Elkhorn Creek, mostly from the Forks of Elkhorn to Knight's Bridge, a distance of maybe eight miles, much of it along the course I and friends kayak during the spring, summer, and early fall when water levels—usually within a day or so after a good rain—make the stream ideally navigable. At the university where I now teach, my class was studying *Earth in Mind,* a collection of essays by envi-ronmental philosopher David Orr.[8] One of them introduced me to topo-philia, a new name for an old concept—the love of place. The etymology is Greek—"topo," "place," and "philia," "love of."

One definition underscores the importance of topophilia intimating a strong association with place, a deep affection mixed with a sense of cultural identity and the love of certain earmarks that identify it. Poet W. H. Auden coined the word and first used it in an introduction to John Betjeman's book of poems *Slick but Not Streamlined.*[9] In an article I ran across on the naming of the Gaelic athletic associations and clubs, another writer, Mike Cronin, cited five metaphors that make a sports stadium topophilic: (1) as a sacred place, especially if euphoric or tragic incidents have occurred there; (2) as a place possessing scenic qualities; (3) as a place that is home for a team and its fans; (4) as a tourist attraction for visitors, "a must-see venue"; and (5) as a place on which local pride and patriotism may be associated.[10] Though these metaphors weaken in the context of a not-so-pure but beautiful stream of water in north-central Kentucky, they hit more often than they miss.

Area residents refer with pride to local impressionist painter Paul Sawyier and his views of the creek from almost every perspective, especially noting familiar landmarks or a typical view. Count among the Elkhorn's fans white-water enthusiasts who mount kayaks on their roof racks and often drive considerable distances to glide along its rough-edged spine. Or the fishermen who wade into sun-lucent pools as they might approach a spiritual or religious experience. And the rest of us, near and far, who love nearly pristine places, land that hasn't been subdivided into suburban citadels with a few acres of tamed lawns or converted into cultivated fields that productively but monotonously generate nicotine or a single food crop to the impoverishment of nature and local soils. Elkhorn is both haven and spa for those who seek the solitary, a place to rekindle a sense of nature and to reaffirm our modest place in it. The hills are indifferent, the strong currents that pull a kayak into the root ball of a toppled sycamore are unforgiving, and every couple of years or so there is a report of someone drowning. The main stem below the Forks is said to drop more than ten feet per mile, creating currents that are both challenging and potentially lethal. When the waters rise, kayakers launch their colorful pods for thrills and a heady flirtation with death within hours of the downpour. Braving the waters at these levels becomes a measure of skill and impetuous courage.

Topophilia plays its part. Geographer Yi-Fu Tuan, in describing topophilia's bonding between an individual and a place, proposes that it includes "all of the human being's affective ties with the material environment."[11] Referring to Yi-Fu Tuan's writing on the subject, environmental philosopher David Orr identifies bonding less with our deep psychology than with our particular circumstances and experiences as individual human beings: "It is closer to a sense of habitat that is formed out of the familiar circumstances of everyday living than it is a genuine rootedness in the biology and topography of a particular place. It is not innate, but acquired."[12] The evolution of my feelings about Elkhorn grows out of the slow accumulation of knowledge of my neighborhood's past and present as well as experiences, not always idyllic, that derive from kayaking its fluctuating and sometimes treacherous waters. Elkhorn, finally, provides a source for contemplation and recreating, a balm for the soul.

Whatever its nature, topophilia entails investing a place in memory and bestowing attention to it, noting both its constancy and its variability as the weather or the seasons—or my own moods and perspectives—change. Over the years the eye grows accustomed to the way water moves in ripples and strands of current, familiar with the craggy profiles of limestone cliffs and the textures and somber tones of bark on bordering trees—the scaling sycamores, the snakelike netting of bark on a venerable black cherry. Though the pebbled beaches in the bends migrate and reassemble themselves constantly, especially in spring, there is a familiarity about them that corresponds to the predictable forces that shape them. Even the quality of light under the towering palisades matches the grooved limestone facings, a pale beige of weathering etched over thousands of years. Antique stone holds its own understated patina. Even the very rare Lucy Braun rockcress sprouting on a steep north-facing hillside, whose flower I have yet to see, takes shape in my mind as part of the surroundings that I'm aware of each time I float at the foot of the steep slope. Ghost blooms. All these things, and more, comprise the anatomy of topophilia. As writer Scott Sanders has said, "We take care of what we love, and we love only what we know, and love begins in paying attention."[13] In a slightly different context, writer Guy Davenport defined art as "replacement of indifference by attention." Overcoming customary oversight and indifference are obstacles to be sidestepped in getting beyond acquaintance to intimacy with a place, just as they are with another person. Attention ultimately means to keep or hold in the mind, i.e., consciousness, memory, and imagination. Such places have taproots that sink deep into the spirit.

For we inhabit three worlds: the natural world, the human-made world, and the world of mind and spirit. The natural world we can honor and imitate through art or degrade and diminish through our indifference and exploitation. We honor it by acknowledging the existence of other species with whom we share the planet. What we sustain sustains us, and art is one means to unite the natural and human worlds. Another is religion, religion in its most basic sense as love and stewardship of the Creation. After all, William Blake affirmed for us that "Every thing that lives is Holy."[14] The mechanism to bridge these worlds of art and the environment is through mind and spirit. What we pay attention to is the measure of what we love and value. Elkhorn is a place where these worlds merge, a stream invested with a degree of residual wildness and a stubborn beauty that draws kayakers, anglers, and all those susceptible to its irresistible pull. What follows is an attempt to redirect our wavering attention to a place worthy of preservation and our fickle notice. For the health of the planet, maybe all of us should devote more of ourselves to knowing such places, by interacting with them and coming to know them as they are as well as engaging our best selves. In so doing, we honor those pockets of wildness that border our dead zones, our trimmed grass, and monocultural fields—those places where the wild has been bent to our will and the random order of nature has been disrupted.

From a state of almost pristine purity prior to settlement, Elkhorn has suffered a dramatic disruption in the linkages that bind its mutually dependent life-forms. Diversity has diminished to such an extent that some species have disappeared from the valley, some driven to extinction. The valley along its banks has undergone its own dramatic changes as the old-growth forest of deciduous hardwoods has been converted to farmland and residential subdivisions, with all the accompanying problems a change in habitat carries. Industrialization along the stream and upstream toward its headwaters has also taken a toll. In many ways, our species intrudes on the normal balances that maintain this vibrant but delicate biosphere. Part of this degradation has been unconscious, part intentional, part a result of our destructive self-absorption and blindness to the complexities that underlie the natural world and its sustaining systems. Though we see an unhealthy foam in eddies around the base of trees by the stream, we thoughtlessly accept it as a norm. After all, the water still flows. There are still some fish in it. Water we are taught from baptismal liturgy both purifies and restores. We lack the perspective to imagine it as it was because we choose to see only what is before us. We can't miss what we don't see, what we've never seen, what we lack the vision to imagine. We see water where there should be water and delude ourselves into thinking it harmless though we are cautioned not to drink it or to eat the fish that swim in its waters.

Elkhorn is a habitat. It should not become a hospice, a place for the terminally ill. As humans, we tend to adapt the world to ourselves rather than ourselves to the world. The result is straining the environment to its limits, creating dead zones and placing it in a state of constant stress. We have become deaf to the environment's cries of enough. These protests are signified by dissolution and quiet extinctions as living things go the way of the passenger pigeon and the Carolina parakeet. In part, what follows is an outline of the changes that have come with conversion of wildness to what passes as civilization to us—mown lawns, bands of asphalt, insecticides, monocultural fields of corn and soybeans, shopping malls, fertilizer run-off, invasive plants that most of us cannot identify unless they are as conspicuous as kudzu. We objectify nature into abstract notions, into flat platitudes, because we are unwilling to give it our attention, unwilling to hold it in our minds in meaningful ways so that we can detect change. We remake the world in our own image, too often regardless of consequences and usually to our detriment. What draws me, and I suspect many of us, to Elkhorn is its relative richness and complexity, a thin strip of wildness in the midst of sterilized immensity, a reserve of the random in a realm of bland homogeneity. It is a corridor of living things, a refugium from the development around it that has yet to fully envelop or arrest its persistent flow. Its slopes are too steep, its lowlands often too mushy to build on. It does not respect private property. It floods. Its history is our history, its burdens our burdens, its well-being our well-being.

Elkhorn is a portrait whose paint never dries—a short run of a small creek that never aspired to be a river. It is the sum of the lives it touched and touches—human, animal, botanical. Its organisms are countless, many invisible to the unaided eye. Someone once calculated that in the inventory of all creatures on the planet the average size is that of a housefly. Unlike a painted canvas on which strokes of the brush are illusions layered one-dimensionally across a stationary surface, I've tried to pry its shimmering lid to excavate a few connections between things as they were and are in space and time. What follows is necessarily an incomplete reconstruction, based on what survives of the documentable past and drawing from printed sources as well as observation and living memory. These are combined with more provisional trowelings of imagination, witnessing, and, I hope, a few informed surmises. The map that emerges, like every other one-dimensional rendering of a place, has its share of distortions, errors, and oversights as well as problems of elevation and scale. Others may fill in the gaps and correct its mistakes to build a fuller picture much as generations of lichen colonize and spread across a bared rock. The hope is to add flesh to the bone, giving voice to the muteness of water, trees, and those who have witnessed, as I do every day, its constant and ever-changing currents. The small findings here acknowledge how puny such reconstructions are since the past and its inscrutable mysteries give up their secrets grudgingly and only partially. Its only memory is genes and fossils imprisoned in rock. The forces that drive nature aim only at what is now, with a view of perpetuating some extension of *now*, not what was or distantly will be. Unlike us at our best, nature does not project. Its future is the consequences of its past. What follows is finally a depiction of a place from basement to attic with as much as one witness can rummage, centering on a living relic that for me and many others is greatly valued.

ELKHORN

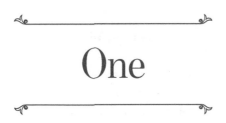

One

Elkhorn. (Photograph by Gene Burch.)

The Feast of Silence

Rounding the bend of Elkhorn
I see the first angler,
solitary, standing motionless,
waist-deep in green water,
shafts of saffron light falling short
of the shade in which
he swishes his fly across the stillness,
air about him laden with an aqua muzziness
in which dust motes seem suspended.

Around the next,
I see more of their number,
a pair in a fishing kayak
drawn off the cove,
another in a floppy hat
hunkered at the water's edge
on a sloping stone
that must have fallen
from the cliffs above
before the first keel scraped Plymouth Rock.
Lost in fisher reveries—
the brief reprieve from jobs,
the raucous levies of family—
they do not seem too anxious for the catch
so much as to feed a patient hunger.

Content to place their lives on hold,
they pause like the dragonfly
lighting on the knuckle

of one paddle hand
to take in the drooping limbs,
the scree of an invisible hawk,
the white knot of roots on the sycamore
whose falling leaves are riddled to gauze
by insects—
these things that can never be summed
but only relished as a meal more substantial
than fish, a stay beyond the creek
against the hard symmetries of the world,
beyond the incessant drone of traffic
and scrapings of famished souls,
as they feel themselves replenished,
feeding on this feast of silence.

Reprinted from *The Feast of Silence*
(Monterey, Ky.: Larkspur Press, 2017).

ELKHORN

Eight miles north of Frankfort, Elkhorn Creek, a little river with two picturesquely mean-
dering branches, the North and the South Forks, empties into the Kentucky which then
pursues its northwestwardly course toward the Ohio without any other large tributary
until Eagle Creek debouches into it just above Worthville in Carroll County.
—**Willard Rouse Jillson,** *The Kentucky River,* 1945

From the lower hill of my small farm in northeastern Franklin County I
can see the craggy palisades that rise above Elkhorn Creek, shelves of gray
limestone slowly being eaten away over the millennia by the erosive force
of flowing water. Between me and the invisible creek stretches a fertile valley whose bordering bluffs and hogback ridges map the contours of the old
flows and meanders of a stream that for hundreds of thousands of years
has gone the way of water seeking its lowest level and the path of least
resistance. The stream sidles east against the hillside at whose foot the
forceful water continues rasping against resistant rock. The valley presents a vast open space confirming the slow but steady hydraulic removal
of vast quantities of topsoil and softer rock to form a flat, fertile bottomland. From where I am standing to the crest of the palisade is about a mile.
Where I stand and where I am sighting share approximately the same
elevation, and in the stream's youth the land between would have been
relatively flat—at least as flat as the rolling terrain of the surrounding Bluegrass. One can sense that the space between the points is the landscape's
ghost, its substance of soil and silt, of less resistant rock and fill, carried off
by Elkhorn to the Kentucky River, to the Ohio and Mississippi, eventually
making its silty contribution to the Mississippi Delta below New Orleans
in the Gulf of Mexico. The valley itself forms irregular swatches of pasture

and cultivated ground, fields and fence lines in rough parallelograms, broken ridgelines, and a few scattered farmsteads as well as a small suburban development of a dozen or so houses. Some things remain hidden. One doesn't see the creek itself or roadways that traverse the bottomland. Roads can be imagined by the tree lines along them. What the water has carved also carves the lives of everything in its basin.

Elkhorn Creek, the second largest tributary of the Kentucky River, drains the central Bluegrass, arguably the richest land in Kentucky, arguably in the country. Within its watershed are four counties: Fayette, Scott, Woodford, and Franklin. Twelve millennia of indigenous peoples lived and hunted here before the first Euro-Americans touched the hemisphere's shores. The creek formed a gateway for surveyors and other land seekers, ambitious to acquire property and a future in the inner Bluegrass. One of those surveyors was a collateral ancestor, Hancock Taylor, from Orange County, Virginia. During the summer of 1773, Robert and James McAfee of Augusta County, Virginia, accompanied by Taylor, surveyed what was to become Frankfort. They also gave Elkhorn Creek its name.[1] The following summer, Taylor and a party of chain bearers and bushwhackers paddled up the Kentucky in dugout canoes, proceeding up the Elkhorn into the inner Bluegrass, where they surveyed thousands of unclaimed acres. The natural boundary of Elkhorn became the measuring point for many of his surveys. Taylor's risky ventures into the Kentucky country came to an end when Indians ambushed him and his companions while they paddled up the Kentucky River in August 1774. Responding to rumors of Indian unrest, they were returning to the more populated portions of Virginia to register their surveys in the names of those whose interests they served.

The land they coveted along the Elkhorn and into its watershed is among the most fertile in North America. One of the region's earliest descriptions appears in Jedidiah Morse's *The American Geography,* published in London in 1792. Called "the father of American geography," Morse was educated in divinity at Yale but had an earthly avocation that soon eclipsed his theology. His textbooks describing the New World became a staple in schoolrooms across the young Republic: "Elkhorn river, a branch of the Kentucky, from the south-east, waters a country fine beyond description. Indeed, the country east and south of this, including the head waters of Licking river, Hickman's and Jessamine Creeks, and

Elkhorn Creek from the Forks to Knight's Bridge. (From *Atlas of Franklin County, Kentucky* [Philadelphia, 1882].)

the remarkable bend in Kentucky river, may be called an extensive garden."[2] Whether Morse actually visited the creek or more likely relied on
information gathered by others, we do not know, but aside from calling
Elkhorn a river he seems to get it right. He notes the deep soils and runs
an inventory of the main species they supported, a wide variety of mostly
deciduous hardwoods—walnuts, honey and black locusts, poplars, elms,
oaks, hickories, and sugar trees. Many were festooned with grapevines
that ran to the treetops, the surface of the land mantled with clover, bluegrass, and wild rye. John Filson, the first to publish a book describing the
Elkhorn land in his efforts to promote immigration, drew on the popular notion that land covered with cane was the most fertile: "There are
many cane brakes so thick and tall that it is difficult to pass through them.
Where no cane grows there is abundance of wild-rye, clover, and buffa-
lo-grass, covering vast tracts of country, and affording excellent food for
cattle. The fields are covered with abundance of wild herbage not common to other countries."[3]

As A. K. Moore, one of my undergraduate English professors, pointed
out in his iconoclastic *The Frontier Mind,* descriptions of Kentucky as
a second Eden were rife around the time of statehood.[4] As the idea of
another fabled Arcadia took hold, another generation of writers perfected
their own hyperbole. A French romantic known only as Father Lalemant,
who had probably never seen Elkhorn Creek, sang its praises excessively:
"Let us speak of Elkhorn Creek: the lands that it waters are so fertile and
so beautiful, the air there is so pure, so serene almost all the year, that
this country is veritably a second terrestrial paradise."[5] As though not to
be outdone, Elijah Craig, the early Baptist preacher, is said to have rhap-
sodized, "O my dear honeys, Heaven is a Kentucky of a place."[6] Bourbon scholars nominate Craig as one of the many putative inventors of
bourbon. Living in Scott County, he doubtless drew his water from Royal
Spring, which feeds into the North Fork of Elkhorn.

There are several popular theories about the origins of Elkhorn's name.
One is that the first explorers noted the great number of shed elk horns
along its banks. Sensible enough. Another says that its name derives from
its crookedness, which appeared to some as being as crooked as an elk's
horn.[7] A third suggests that the name probably derives from its shape
as seen on a map or from a crow's eye, a main stem and two primary
forks. John Filson's 1784 map of Kentucky resembles a matrix of elk horns,

waterways and feeder creeks marking watersheds, understandably the chief feature on a map in which water was critical both for transportation and as a guide for exploration. Though it wound, it formed a relatively fixed natural border for survey lines and settlement. Many streams contribute to the two larger tines of Elkhorn's fork, waterways with such names as Vaughns Branch, Wolf Run, Town Branch, Cave Creek, Buck Run, and Slickway Branch. Names along the North Fork include Goose Creek, Dry Run, McCracken Creek, Blue Spring Branch, and McConnell's Run, each name having a history tied to its owners or some notable feature or denizen.

Geology shapes both the landscape and patterns of human settlement. The physiography of the watershed through most of the Bluegrass consists of layers of easily dissolved limestone that form carbonate aquifers, spacious cavities containing water that underlie the rolling terrain of the area. Groundwater makes its way to creek beds through channels in the limestone, creating a karst geology in which caves and springs are common. Most of the land in the watershed is agricultural, pasture for cattle and horses, or fields sown in tobacco, corn, or soybeans as well as vegetable crops grown in the rich soils of the Elkhorn floodplain. One field, a portion of which is in my line of view from the lower hill, supplies a bounty of garden produce for the Frankfort Farmers Market. The farm belongs to Bobby Hutcherson, whose family figures significantly in the creek's recent history. In late summer when water levels drop, many creekside farms, including Hutcherson's, siphon water from pools in the creek to irrigate their crops with great twirling arcs of silver. Unlike the Kentucky and other waterways in the state, Elkhorn has little use as a means of transporting goods or passengers, a fact that may have contributed to its relative pristineness.

Despite its limited human utility, many people are drawn to the area for its beauty and recreational possibilities. It has been estimated that between 1985 and 1996 the number of visitors for recreational purposes grew from twenty thousand to seventy-five thousand. As the number of kayaks I see on cars and trucks now attests, that figure can only have increased. Estimates indicate that tourism dollars in 1996 ranged from $6 million to $9 million. Perhaps the creek's most notable perennial visitor was the American impressionist painter Paul Sawyier. Toting his paint box and camping gear, Sawyier trekked through the area over a hundred years ago, fixing it in oil and watercolors that he sold or traded simply to subsist. Obligatory prints and occasional originals festoon the dens and hallways of many Frankfort homes, scenes depicting water and rock formations the owners have never viewed either in their natural state nor often in their vibrant first renderings in watercolor or oils. Surprisingly, the pastoral charm of a hundred years ago has not changed greatly, in part because farms still occupy most of the valley and in part because usually at least one bank or the other of the creek has escarpments so steep or remote from roads that building is not practicable. Water soothes, and the arching sycamores, their shadows and dappled leaves, embody the creek's inviting serenity, a sentimental throwback to less complicated times.

About four miles up-creek from where I stand on the lower hill is Forks of Elkhorn, the point where the north and south forks of the creek converge to form the main stem of Elkhorn. Below the Forks, the main stem runs seventeen or eighteen miles before entering the Kentucky. North Elkhorn starts just east of Lexington and flows 75.4 miles through Fayette and Scott counties into Franklin County before debouching into the Kentucky River. South Elkhorn begins in Fayette County and winds through Woodford, Scott, and Franklin counties before joining its sister stream at the Forks, located a few miles east of Frankfort, Kentucky's state capital. The historic Town Branch of South Elkhorn that once flowed through downtown Lexington now lies buried under tons of fill along Vine Street, parallel to Main. It once served as a base line to plot much of the early city. Recently, the area has been developed as a heritage trail, a long-delayed recognition of its importance in the city's history. Many springs spill into the drainage basin of South and North Elkhorn, including McConnell's, just west of the downtown district, and Royal Spring in nearby Georgetown, still the main water source for a city that during the past three decades has exploded with growth. Lexington remains one of the largest cities in the region removed from a major waterway. Though the Kentucky River now provides much of the potable water for central Kentucky, Elkhorn still serves as an important water source for the central Bluegrass region. From the era of the first hunters, lovers of the outdoors have regarded the main stem of Elkhorn as one of the state's most desirable streams for nonmotorized boating and fishing for smallmouth bass. In July 1987, Scottie Sams, a retired firefighter and a fine small-engine mechanic who keeps my John Deere tractor running, caught the record smallmouth bass on Elkhorn. It weighed six pounds, four ounces, and he proudly has it mounted on the wall of his den.

Ironically, though the waters are officially described as carcinogenic and therefore unsuitable for drinking, they contain species of catfish, rock bass, smallmouth and largemouth bass, carp, crappie, and bluegills that are popular game fish. The creek suffers from the effects of sedimentation and chemicals—fertilizers, pesticides, herbicides—that deplete oxygen and poison stream life. Despite the decline in the size and number of smallmouth bass found in its waters, most weekends find anglers along the banks or fishing from kayaks or canoes in water that seldom reaches more than five-feet deep in its pools and much shallower in its riffles. Many simply wear waders or old tennis shoes. The creek is too shallow for outboard engines, a condition that many consider a blessing since rasping engines and canyons of wake would take a toll on stream life and much of Elkhorn's timelessness. That is not to say the creek is boatless. Rainfall permitting, from April through October, recreational kayakers paddle portions of the creek. They range from true-believer thrill seekers to amateurs who rent kayaks or canoes at Canoe Kentucky for a leisurely float. Renters must start downstream at Peaks Mill, a hamlet by the creek whose only going business is the boat livery. But the most challenging white water flows farther upstream, starting at the Forks and running seven or eight miles. This section attracts daredevils and amateurs alike, a winding series of shoals and pools that change constantly with the water levels and tree falls. Erosion steadily undermines many of the larger trees along the mud banks, especially during spring freshets, when the snarled roots of sycamores and other water-loving trees lose their tenuous hold on the crumbling banks. Gravity plays no favorites. Spectacular palisades also add to the appeal of this eight-mile stretch, a wall of limestone rising two hundred or so feet, with tufts of cedars sprouting from the sheer faces and larger trees aproned around the base where soil and mulch have accumulated. These seem not to change, but everything else does. As any experienced kayaker and the Greek philosopher Heraclitus could tell you, no one steps into the same Elkhorn twice.

In addition to its geological past, Elkhorn also holds a human history. Because nature leaves no footnotes, much of its presettlement history is sketchy, as shifty and irrecoverable as its muddy banks. The same goes for the preliterate peoples who fished and hunted the waters before 1750.

Artifacts tells us that Native Americans inhabited the area, probably for thousands of years, as evidenced by the spear points, fractured-flint bird points, and stone implements that still turn up after rains and fresh plowings in the fields or among alluvial gravels collecting by the creek. Remains of prehistoric fauna also have been excavated in the area.

Much of the area's more recent history records collisions of Native Americans and the first Euro-American settlers. The last major Indian foray into Franklin County occurred less than a mile upstream from the vantage point on my hill—the Cook Massacre. Upstream a bit, the cabins of the Cook settlement, at least two of them, still stand stolidly by the creek. The massacre happened near what local historians refer to as the Innes settlement. The neighborhood took its name from Judge Harry Innes, the most eminent person associated with the area. A Virginian who immigrated to Kentucky and was appointed first judge of the U.S. Court for the District of Kentucky, Innes wore many hats—a land speculator, paterfamilias, farmer, attorney, and earliest representative of the federal judiciary in the West. His home doubled as a station, a place of defense under threat in the same year of its construction, 1792. Marauding Indians killed two of his slaves and took another captive. A Jeffersonian Republican, Judge Innes became an important player through the era of early statehood until his death in 1816, and through his home came many notables, including former vice president Aaron Burr, Kentucky's first senator, John Brown, and Governors Isaac Shelby and James Garrard.

The massive limestone walls that form the Elkhorn's banks have withstood water, fires, and winter heaving for over 180 years. This area underwent greater changes during the nineteenth century, when local entrepreneurs discovered the advantages of a ready and reliable source of water to power industry. Across from the cabins of the Cook settlement lie what remain of early millworks. The remains of one of Frankfort's earliest industrial complexes are a mile or two downstream from the Forks of Elkhorn, also marking the site of a now-defunct village whose workers and their families lived close by their work in twenty-five or so houses. The village provided a labor force large enough to operate three mills powered by running water: grist and lumber mills as well as an early paper mill. This mill at one time provided almost all the paper consumed by the nearby state government, and its proprietor made fatal contracts with the government of the Confederacy to provide high rag-content paper for the printing of money. The village was named after Ebenezer Stedman, one of the mill's proprietors from 1833 on. He wrote a memoir in the 1880s in the form of letters to his granddaughter. This memoir gives us one of the clearest pictures of early industrialization in Kentucky as well as the character of the region and the people who followed the first generation of settlers. Stedman's memoir contains one of the richest sources of lore about the creek and the people who earned their livelihoods there.

Distillers also discovered the benefits of the Elkhorn's waters, there being no coincidence that the Jim Beam brand of Old Grandad Distillery, one of the country's largest makers of bourbon whiskey, located just below the Forks of Elkhorn on its main stem. Originally, the water attracted distillers to the area because its reputedly purity contributed to the making of fine bourbon.

At the Forks of Elkhorn just below the Macklin Dam sits the original Buck Run Baptist Church, flanked by an expansive asphalt parking lot coming almost to the Elkhorn's banks. Two empty churches stand on the site, their congregations having immigrated to a megachurch several miles away. Founded early in the county's history, Buck Run's congregation split, not over the issue of slavery as many churches did, but over divisions of personalities and class.

More recently, some of my kayaking friends, several of whom live on property by the creek, created a loose association inspired by a love of the stream, an association we only half-facetiously call the Church of Elkhorn. The name grows out of another local legend, this one identified with the late Scott Robinson, songwriter, musician, and an obsessive fly fisherman in the vein of Norman Maclean's *A River Runs Through It*.[8] When one of his neighbors asked him what church he attended on Sundays—a question often heard in Frankfort and other towns in central Kentucky—he unhesitatingly affirmed, "My church is the Church of Elkhorn," meaning—to him and to many of us—the holy waters in which he fished almost religiously whenever he could. A dozen or so of us who love to relax by and on the creek adopted the name and created several tenets, only partly tongue in cheek, to guide us. First, unlike more institutionalized churches, we dispensed with tithing, hierarchy, and voluntary immersion. All of us, both men and women, qualify now as elders and share a common identity. Adopting a line from the novelist Allan Gurganus, author of the *Oldest Surviving Confederate Widow Tells All*, we held as one of the group's basic tenets that "Water is family," even commissioning the making of T-shirts with this motto printed on the back to accompany a rough engraving of the creek.[9] By the shirt pocket is a Latin motto, *Futue Culpam,* less delicate but also less immediate in its message. Reverence is not the exclusive domain of religion. The spirit also owns market shares in it. One other precept bears repeating, a quotation from the Roman poet Seneca, whose words are as crystalline as Elkhorn on a good day: "Life is a bath. We all paddle in its great pool." Another tenet, more hedonistic, relates to celebrating the intersection of the secular and the religious, "It is never too early or too late to be festive." Finally, the ideal of peaceful coexistence, shared with many other churches, derives from Rodney King's simple and moving dictum, "Why can't we all just learn to get along?"[10]

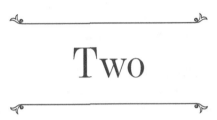

Two

Restoration of a pair of Columbian mammoths by a lake, 1912. (Drawing by Robert Bruce Horsfall, from Berryman Scott, *A History of Land Mammals in the Western Hemisphere* [New York: MacMillan, 1913].)

By the time we got there, I could tell the damage had been done. Around the yellow dozer there were high mounds of dirt, and even from a distance I could see the palish glint of bones. Some of them lay in a pile to one side of what would soon be a pond, but others were strewn about in the black muck as though a cemetery keeper had simply turned a steam shovel loose among the stones. Black water was seeping into the pit, and I knew time was working against us. If only I had been in the office when the call came, a farmer saying he had found some bones in his pond and wanted someone from the state to look at them. They'd contacted my office, geology being the closest thing they could think of to paleontology. I didn't get word until after lunch, and I fetched Byron from his office, got directions, hopped in the state Ford, and made time out Holmes Street and then directly out of town on 127, rising out of what we call the "coffee cup" onto a high bench of land I knew had been a meander of Elkhorn Creek or maybe even an old bed of the Kentucky before uplift. Speeding east on Peaks Mill Road past farms and a long stone fence, we came to Steadmantown Lane two miles or so from the highway. It wasn't a mile after we made the turn that Byron spotted the dozer, a blob of yellow metal in a wide field. We pulled off and cut across the stubble on foot, one of the men, spotting us now, waving us over. We could not see the creek but knew it was close by from the limestone bluffs that were its backdrop. We came straight from the office so I had no time to change from my town clothes, having only tossed my suitcoat in the backseat and loosened my tie. I wish I had thought to bring my boots.

Mr. Hutcherson—a man in his early fifties, I would guess—was friendly enough, he and the mute operator standing by the dozer like they were guarding it in a time of war. The thought crossed my mind that it was us who needed guarding from him and it. The enemies of science take many forms. I was close enough to it to feel the heat rising off the engine, the hotter for the radiant afternoon sun. It was sweltering, the pale blue of Hutcherson's shirt sopping with dark swatches. Sunstroke, I thought. The two of them looked as though they needed to sit in the shade somewhere and drink some water. Instead, Hutcherson, as though just discovering the damage done, said he'd waited as long as he could wait and that the operator—Goins was the last name—was paid by the hour whether he was driving or not. I told him I understood and would just take a look. The two of them stood by, curious, eyes to the ground, as though they were penitent schoolboys and I was their teacher.

It was clear from a glance that the bones were ancient and belonged to a creature larger than anything that had ever slept in Mr. Hutcherson's barn. There was a shattered fibia caked in black mud. It was longer than a pitchfork. Next to it was a joint whose knob was as large as a football. Byron knew to start gathering the bones from the mud, and I rolled up my sleeves to inspect them, mindful that these fossilized bits were older than anything but the rocks beneath them. Handling one and then another, I was sure an answer would turn up, some clue to help me puzzle out what manner of beast had crept out of antiquity to resurface in a floodplain of the Elkhorn Valley. What exactly had these ivory sticks belonged to? Were we looking at something that would change the way we looked at things? At the least I saw another publication. What I did know for certain was that Marie, vexed when she had to hold supper, would have a fit when I came home late, my dress trousers wet and soiled, my shoes off and by the porch door before I dared step onto the parlor rug. From the first I suspected that I was looking at what remained of an ice-age mammoth, though what species, or even what sex, I couldn't say. That, like examining the remains of an exploded skeleton, would take time and study. But I knew even then that it was something truly extraordinary, especially so far from the Licks.

A GLIMPSE INTO THE DISTANT PAST

There neither is or ever was any Elephants in North or South America, that I can learn, or any quadruped one tenth part as large as these was, if one may be allowed to judge from the appearance of these bones, which must have been considerably larger than they are now. Captn. Hancock Lee told me that he had found a Tusk here that was six feet long, very sound but yellow. These tusks are like those brought from the Coast of Africa. Saw some buffaloes but killed none. We found several Indian paintings on the trees. Got plenty of mulberries, very sweet and pleasant fruit but bad for the teeth. One of the company shot a Deer. The loudest Thunder and the heaviest rain I ever saw this afternoon. I got to the Camp well wet and most heartily tired. A Damned Irish rascal has broken a piece of my Elephant tooth, which put me in a violent passion; can write no more.
—*Journal of James Nourse,* "Elephant Bone Lick" [Big Bone Lick], June 17, 1775

It appears somewhat extraordinary, at the first view, that we should discover manifest proofs of there having existed animals of which we can form no adequate idea, and which in size must have far exceeded anything now known upon earth; and those signs too, in climates where the elephant (the largest animal now in existence) is never found.
—**Gilbert Imlay,** *A Topical Description of the Western Territory of North America,* 1797

On the afternoon of August 8, 1945—three weeks before the surrender of Japan—Willard Rouse Jillson, former state geologist soon to head a department at Transylvania College, received a phone message from William Hutcherson, whose farm lay in a deserted meander of the Main Elkhorn Creek about three and a half miles northeast of Frankfort. That morning, Hutcherson discovered the remains of a creature larger than any farm animal he had ever seen as he supervised a hired operator who bull-dozed a likely spot for a stock pond in the soggy ground not far from the creek. Curious and suspecting the bones might belong to some ancient dinosaur, Hutcherson telephoned state government and left a message that reached Jillson asking for help in identifying some bones. In 1920 Jillson had been appointed state geologist and reorganized the antiquated Kentucky Geological Survey. He was proud of producing at least one map for every county in the state. More than a cartographer and geologist, he mined history, focusing mostly on the period of Kentucky's settlement and early statehood.[1] Unfortunately, Jillson could not be reached immediately and didn't receive the message until that afternoon. Excited but half expecting a letdown, he and a friend named Byron C. Graham raced out Peaks Mill Road, too late to stop the bulldozer from reducing much of the articulated skeleton to pieces. The skull was crushed, as were the ribs and vertebrae, as probably were the tusks, which went unmentioned.

Arriving at the site, Jillson and Graham removed most of the exposed fragments, carefully setting them on safe ground. The cavity began filling with groundwater. Working against time, the two men pulled much of what remained from the excavated basin of the pond just ahead of the water spilling in from the surrounding swamp—what today would be described as a wetland. In simpler times, pioneers had referred to such areas as "jelly ground."[2] From the moment he eyed the oversized molars, Jillson knew they had happened on something important to science and something rare. By the next morning, the unexcavated portion of the skeleton—including several of the forward limb bones and phalanges, a portion of pectoral girdle, cervical, central and lumbar vertebrae, a considerable portion of the skull, as well as tusks and other bone fragments—lay submerged under five feet of water. The new pond, now completely full, covered the entire entombment site, making it problematic to recover what was underwater.

Before leaving the night before, Jillson, with the help of Hutcherson and Graham, selected a few of the largest bones, including three well-preserved molars, and drove them to town for preservation and analysis. He also arranged for what remained at the site to be trucked into town. When he had scrubbed the molars, removing the tough blue clay caked around them, Jillson identified them as belonging to a species of mammoth named *Elephas columbi*, which he later footnoted as being renamed by Dr. Henry Fairfield Osborn, in 1936, with "doubtful propriety" as *Paraelephas jeffersono*. During his long career as a geologist and historian, Jillson turned out more publications than perhaps any other writer in Kentucky. His closest rival might be Constantine Rafinesque, the roving botanist and polymath who taught for a time, like Jillson, at Transylvania College in Lexington. Having an appetite for publishing that amounted to obsession, over the span of his adult life Jillson wrote and published more than sixty books and over five hundred articles, including a monograph entitled *The Elkhorn Mammoth,* from which many details of the Elkhorn find are taken.[3] Jillson noted that the mammoth was the first of the species found in Franklin County, though others had been uncovered at Big Bone Lick in northern Kentucky as well as other salt licks in central and northern Kentucky. In light of information he had, Jillson concluded that the animal had probably become embedded between thirty thousand and fifty thousand years ago.[4]

Today, paleontologists refer to this species of mammoth as the Columbian mammoth, *Mammuthus columbi.* According to the *Frankfort State Journal's* story on finding the "great prehistoric monster," its contemporaries included *Megolonyx* and *Mylodon,* the glacial ground sloths; *Bison antiquus,* the giant buffalo; *equus complicatus,* the Pleistocene horse; and numerous other species, like *Casteroides ohioensis,* the beaver that was nearly as large as a modern bear.[5] One of the last in a line of mammoth species, the Columbian mammoth inhabited the northern United States and as far south as Costa Rica, having entered North America from Asia about 1.5 million years ago. It was one of the largest species of mammoth. At the shoulders, it often reached a height of thirteen feet and weighed from eight to ten tons. It had long, asymmetrical tusks used—as we do our hands—for manipulating things, for foraging, and for fighting. The weight of its tusks, which often reached from nine to eleven or so feet, could crush the bones of its adversaries, including man. As Jillson described them, the great ivory tusks at first curved outward and downward and then upward and inward on either side of the trunk. Less hairy than the wooly mammoth, the Columbian had adapted well to a more moderate climate in the post-glacial era. It preferred open areas, for which the Bluegrass region with its park-like landscapes must have been perfectly suited. Though temperatures at the end of the last ice age averaged five to ten degrees cooler than now, things warmed up during the summers, so this mammoth may have been seeking to slake his thirst or simply to cool off. As with modern elephants, the females tended to live in herds; the males were more or less solitary. The sex of the Elkhorn mammoth cannot plausibly be judged by this measure. One telltale characteristic to distinguish male from female mammoths is the pelvic girdle, the birth canal of the female being necessarily larger. This specimen's pelvic girdle must have been crushed by the dozer or lost in the seeping water that poured into the cavity overnight. What is significant is that any remains at all were recovered, a Pleistocene mammoth in Frankfort's backyard! Such a phenomenon links the murky past with the quotidian present. The Columbian mammoth disappeared at the end of the Pleistocene, about twelve thousand years ago, so we know that Jillson's find is at least that old.

Much of what we know about prehistoric life in Kentucky has been collected at salt licks. Sites where mammoths are discovered usually yield only single specimens, though there are exceptions like Big Bone Lick, where the natural lure of salt combined with soft soils and sometimes hunters made for accumulations of remains over a long period of time. At Big Bone Lick, about sixty miles to the northeast near the Ohio River, a site described as "the Tomb of the mammoths," bones have been found of creatures that came to lick salt from springs formed by deposits laid down by the old sea.[6] It is twenty-two miles south of the river town of Covington, Kentucky, just across the Ohio from Cincinnati. The subject of another book by Jillson, Big Bone Lick has been one of the most important sites of American paleontology in the eastern United States since the earliest Euro-American explorers.[7] John Filson, Kentucky's first historian and biographer of Daniel Boone, described the bones he saw "as a quadruped now unknown and whose race is probably extinct."[8] The salt springs there attracted animals, extinct and modern, a kind of mammal mortuary. The remains extracted there for over two centuries, most undocumented and by crude methods, include mammoths, mastodons, giant ground sloths, giant stag-moose, and a forerunner of the modern horse.[9]

What brought mammoths to Kentucky? The answer is simple: proddings of ice. What brought this one to this boggy bottom? Maybe thirst, maybe a desire to escape the heat. Elkhorn has been a major water source for the region for centuries, greening the landscape and slaking the thirst of all that lived along it. What were the mammoths, when did they live, and where did they come from? Among paleontologists a mammoth is any member of the extinct genus *Mammuthus* belonging to the order of proboscideans, animals with an elongate or snoutlike feeding organ, like the modern elephant. It is estimated that their great weight, measured in tons, did much to explain why so many of them died in bogs. Their

weight would have impeded their movement in a soft but viscous substance like mud. In addition to their size, long curving tusks extended
from the region of their maws like spiraling commas. Thomas Jefferson,
incidentally, initiated the change of mammoth from a noun describing a
prehistoric elephant to an adjective applying to anything of an unusually
large size, as in his description of a large Cheshire cheese given to him as
"mammoth."[10]

Mammoths were grazers. They lived in grasslands that had a long
growing season, mild winters, and a wide diversity of plants. They lived
from the Pliocene epoch (around 5 million years ago) until about 4,500
years ago in the Holocene, our own epoch. Informed opinion suggests
mammoths survived on the American mainland until twelve thousand
years ago, dying out around the time of the last glacial retreat as part of
a mass extinction of megafauna in Eurasia and the Americas. What did
them in? Change of climate may have been a factor since forests, in part,
supplanted grasslands during a period of gradual warming. They may
have been hunted out. They may even have been decimated by infectious
disease, though more likely their extinction resulted from a change in
environment and over hunting by our ancestors. In 1857, Scottish naturalist Hugh Falconer first wrote a description of the species using molar
specimens excavated in Georgia sent to him by the eminent geologist
Charles Lyell. He named it for Christopher Columbus. Barring hunters'
spear tips or the kind of misfortune that befell the Elkhorn mammoth,
individual mammoths might have lived as many as sixty years.

As in any small town, word quickly circulated about a huge and ancient
beast being dug up at the Hutcherson farm. A news account appeared in
the August 10, 1945, *Frankfort State Journal*. Another article, separately
written, appeared in the *Louisville Courier-Journal*, the state's largest
newspaper, as well as the *Lexington Herald* the next morning. It must
have been a relief for subscribers to read something other than war news,
especially after the recent dropping of the atom bomb on Japan. As for the
bones, Jillson had them thoroughly cleaned and soon set up a temporary
exhibit in two storefront windows at the *State Journal* office in downtown
Frankfort's business district. The exhibit featured a single toe as large as "a
woman's foot."[11] Jillson properly labeled the specimens, including at least
one of the large molars. For a month or five weeks they attracted large
numbers of people by the novelty of finding antediluvian bones near little

old Frankfort. After the novelty wore off, the bones found a permanent home at the University of Kentucky in the Museum of Anthropology. Within a few months Jillson produced an inventory of the bones of the "Elkhorn Mammoth" and sent them to Dr. Arthur McFarlan of the Geology Department at the University of Kentucky.

On November 20, 1945, after a period of drought, Jillson returned to the valley of the disentombment to properly document the site. He noted that the pond and surrounding swamp lay in the basin that formed part of an abandoned meander cut during the late Pleistocene (ending 11,770 years ago) into the Lexington (Trenton-Ordovician) limestone, some of the oldest exposed rock in Kentucky on what geologists describe as the Cincinnati Arch, an area encompassing most of the Inner Bluegrass region. Using an eleven-foot iron rod one-fourth of an inch in diameter, Jillson probed the north side of the pond at its shoreline. He found soft "valley fill" extending down seven feet below the water level to hard ledges of limestone. The water level, at this time, lay three feet below the level of the swamp surface, indicating that the entire thickness of the swamp fill on that side of the pond was ten feet. Nothing if not thorough, Jillson also probed the south side of the pond, noting a thickness of fourteen feet. He described the three- or four-foot surface deposit as a very dark-colored, clayey earth. He also carefully examined the site for any sign of human artifacts, probably imagining a miraculous stone or flint point embedded in bone, a story that would have astonished the scientific journals of his day. He found none.

Continuing his investigation, Jillson did his best to reconstruct the positioning of the mammoth when it died as well as to surmise the cause of death. As accurately as he could determine, the skeleton faced south into the deeper portion of the swamp. The heavy animal—a mature male might weigh eight to ten tons—apparently waded into shallow water in a deepening, soft-bottomed pond and became mired down. If it faced south, it would have seen to its left the flowing creek, high or low depending on season and rainfall, to its right a couple hundred yards away the spiny hillside now known as the Backbone, the rising timbered spine of bluffs that would have marked the margins of the old channel of flow. Certainly it was not winter. The ground would have been denser, the mammoth surviving to live out its life and wander off elsewhere to lay down its burdening bones. Elkhorn's water level changes dramatically after the right rain and falls almost to a standstill after the rainy season. Around the mammoth, as it starved, would probably have been soft ground and surface waters in the bottoms extending to the deeper channel of the creek.

A mile or so from the site of the Elkhorn mammoth's gradual entomb-ment, I lost a favorite pet—a loveable and overfed Newfoundland named Boo Boo—in much the same way. She had ursine paws and a wooly black hide that grew in ringlets. She weighed as much as most teenag-ers, though her mass lay cumbersomely low to the ground. Seeking relief from the heat during a sweltering July day, she waded into a cattle pond to wallow beneath the algae and bogged down, far enough away from the house that we didn't hear her plaintive barks or find her until two or three days later. The mass of the skeletal material of this less-recent unfortu-nate, as Jillson detected, inclined at an angle between one and two feet in ten feet of horizontal distance. When first found, the Elkhorn mammoth was almost certainly in the position in which it had died, probably from starvation and a nervous exhaustion born out of desperation, as had my Newfoundland, whose remains had to be pulled from the muck by a farm tractor for burial. Had the skeleton of *Elephas columbi* been extracted when first encountered, it would have been more or less complete and a valuable addition to science. But farmers, practical and independent folk, operate by their own lights, and Hutcherson directed that the bulldozer, rented by the hour or day, perform its work. Though the operator com-pleted his task, he complicated Jillson's.

Nevertheless, that day in August 1945 enacted a chain of miracles. Hutcherson called the state, the state succeeded in reaching Jillson, and Jillson, albeit late, was the perfect person to examine what was left and preserve a record of what he found in yet another of his articles. On April 27, 1946—a little over a year after the discovery—Jillson gave an address before the Kentucky Academy of Science in Louisville. Prescient and perennially ambitious, he wrote and printed a version of it, documenting his find for perpetuity, and stored a few fossilized bones for future study.[12] The occasion must have drawn a sizable segment of the scientific commu-nity as well as the curious, each listener seeking clues that might answer imponderable mysteries and shine another ray of light into the opaque-ness of our fragmentary past. Elkhorn had yielded one of its secrets.

Three

An imagined view of an Indian village prior to European settlement. (From John McIntosh, *The Origin of the North American Indians* [Philadelphia, 1843].)

Chin-gash-goochy, the Capering Moose, was a kind of Native American wonder man, young, slim, and strong. He could wrestle, swim, and dive with the best of his people. The arrows from his bow darkened the air and the forest bent before them. Chin-gash-goochy fell in love with an Indian maiden named Ne-me-no-che-char. Her name meant "Sweetheart," and her eyes were brown as the leaves of autumn and tender as the forest pools at twilight. As in every romance, there was a complication. Though she loved Chin-gash-goochy, the young chief, she was betrothed to his father, the old chief. The solution they found was elopement. Capering Moose folded her in his blanket, a sign of protection, and caught a giant elk, Wapita, and they fled to a distant land, Kentucky, to make a new life.

But the old chief, his brow like a thundercloud, his eyes like lightning, pursued them. The roaring of his voice was louder than Ka-bib-on-okko, the North Wind. Wapita carried the lovers through forests and over rivers until they came to the land where the bluegrass grows, and there they rested. The old chief caught up with them at nightfall and shot his last arrow into the heart of Wapita, the faithful elk that had transported the lovers so far. As he was dying, Wapita turned his head toward the enemy. To protect the lovers, he formed a rampart with his branching antlers that was impossible to pass.

Many moons waxed and waned while Chin-gash-goochy and Ne-me-no-che-char dwelled behind the branching antlers, raising a family of brave sons and virtuous daughters before they died in peace. As time passed, the branching horns of Wapita, by their own weight, sank deeper and deeper into the earth, and rivulets formed in the first crevices, and many streams added their waters until a river was formed, branching in the bed made by the Elkhorn.

THE ONES WHO CAME BEFORE

Who those inhabitants were, who have left such traces; from whence they came, and where they now are; are queries to which we never, perhaps, can find any other than conjectural answers.
—**Jonathan Heart to Benjamin Smith, M.D.,** containing observations on the ancient works, January 5, 1791

Elkhorn Creek, unlike most of the waterways in Kentucky, has mythological as well as geological origins, recognizing the succession of peoples that have lived in the valleys along its evolving course. Published in 1938 as a compilation of lore and history relating to the Bluegrass and written by the Federal Writers' Project, a legend tells the story of Chingash-goochy, a Native American living in what was to become Kentucky at some indeterminate time in the state's prehistory.[1]

The legend found a suitable home in Lexington and the Bluegrass country. The source of the legend remains unknown. It, therefore, is difficult to know its origins, though it has little to do with what we know of the presettlement peoples who lived and camped along the creek. More likely, some well-intentioned romantic prepared the confection, wishing to promote Elkhorn and its attributes.

The legend had legs. In 1981, Nettie Henry Glenn, a Frankfort historian and writer, published *Enda Lechaumanne: Legend of the Forks of Elkhorn*, in which she made passing mention of Capering Moose and Sweetheart.[2] Written in the form of a narrative poem, *Enda Lechaumanne*, whose title remains a mystery, is a local version of Genesis, starting with the formation of the creek when the inland waters of the sea receded and God filled the waters with fishes, then created a race of mound builders possessing a superior intelligence in the ancient world. Known only by the artifacts they left behind, these warring people passed on tales of the Dark and Bloody Ground beyond the Caintuck-ee, the River of Blood, where none would build his lodge on the "violated soil." Instead, they came to hunt and fish, arriving by way of Alanant-O-Wamiowee, the Warriors' Path. These wanderers came through the meadowlands to a stream of sparkling beauty but would not build lodges upon its "shoulders" since the mound builders had found it first during "the Pale Moon of Yesterday." Around the campfire at night, the Great Chief recounted the "Sleep Man Tale of its Beginning."

According to this genesis of the Red Man, the Great Spirit brought rain to form sinking springs on the floor of the forest. From these springs came greenness and a single flow of water, the Princess of the Laughing Waters. As the young men paddled their canoes along the waterway, they saw that it joined another stream, "and they marveled at the beauty of their union." During the winter the Great Chiefs gathered their clans around the fires and told the love story of Sweet Heart and Capering Moose—their elopement, the pursuit, the death of the old chief, and the long lives of the surviving couple in "the Happy Valley." The Indians named the waterway that formed where the elk's bones sank into the earth and vanished in honor of Wapiti: Elkhorn.

But the story wasn't finished. For many years, the Red Man roamed the Dark and Bloody Ground alone, and then the White Man arrived. First came traders from the Land of Deep Snows, swapping trinkets for pelts of beaver, mink, and otter. Then, in 1750, the first Englishman, Christopher Gist, crossed the mountains and built a house of logs. Other white men, who praised the Eden Land that lay beyond the Endless Mountains, followed him. Hearing of broken treaties and bloody battles, the Red Man roamed the wilderness to destroy the invaders who built their log houses on the shores of Elkhorn. But their weapons could not defend against the giants named Boone and Harrod, Logan and Kenton. Surveyors staked out farms, and the Red Man turned their horses toward the Place of the Setting Sun and left forever the mysterious valleys of the Cantuck-ee, the waters called Elk Horn.[3]

Appealing as these hybrids of folklore and history are, evidence shows that mound builders did in fact live along the waters of Elkhorn Creek. They formed part of the Adena culture that lived in the Ohio River Valley between 2,500 and 1,800 years ago, during the Woodland Period, dating roughly from 1000 B.C. to A.D. 1000. Adena takes its name from an estate in south-central Ohio where archeologists first excavated mounds with professionalism and some official sanction. Ancestors of the peoples that ranged over Kentucky at the time of settlement, the Adena were a mobile people who sustained themselves from what they could grow as well as what they hunted and gathered, a diet of deer and other small game as well as corn, squash, nuts, and herbs they harvested from the surrounding woods.[4] Their social and religious lives centered on the mounds, where they acted out rituals of life, initiation, and death in ceremonies. We will probably never know the particular content of these life rituals from a people who had no writing and a stream of oral transmission that has dried up.

Because no records document how many earthen mounds existed in Kentucky at the time settlers penetrated the mountains and carved homes out of the wilderness, we can talk with authority only about those at the time they were studied, mostly during the nineteenth and twentieth centuries. In December of 1909, historian Bennett Young and two curious friends visited what Bennett described as the best-preserved "enclosure" in Kentucky. They traveled out the Newtown Pike north and northeast of Lexington about six and a half miles to what was formerly known as the Moore farm. The farm bordered the banks of Elkhorn Creek, and the stream formed the mound's base, the embankment rising seventy-five feet to its top.[5]

Measuring, they found that the outside had a circumference of 750 feet, with an average width of twelve to fourteen feet. A moat dug twelve to fifteen feet deep had been immediately inside of the embankment, and the central elevation had a diameter of 150 feet. They found a gateway that was thirty-three feet wide. Two oak trees crowned the embankment, one thirteen feet and the other thirteen feet, three inches in circumference.[6] Based on these dimensions, they dated the age of the embankment as at least four hundred years, probably five hundred years or older. Whether the mound was used for habitation or burial and other ceremonial practices, or a combination of these, was not clear. Certainly human presence along the creek long predates the coming of Euro- and African Americans. Willard Rouse Jillson cites Lower Elkhorn as one of the areas that served as aboriginal gravesites.[7] In the rock houses along the limestone

cliffs of Elkhorn, Flat Creek, and Lower Benson Creek, numerous artifacts have been found: shells, beads, flint heads for use in hunting and
war, as well as pottery shards.[8]

Elkhorn was only a few miles from an important Indian trail, Alanant-O-Wamiowee, an aboriginal Interstate 75. It was part of a network
of trails followed by prehistoric animals and their successors, including
mammoths, elk, buffalo, and deer.[9] From Drennon's Lick, the trail followed a southerly direction on the west side of the Kentucky and crossed
the river at what became Leestown, where a natural ford provided a
crossing during most of the year. From there, it rose out of the bowl, or
surrounding hills, through a natural gap in the high bluffs, roughly following the course of what is now Kentucky 421 (Leestown Road), which
split off in two directions—one toward what is now Lexington, the other
toward today's Georgetown along Highway 460. It crossed Elkhorn first
at the Forks, where the community of Forks of Elkhorn later formed
around Buck Run Baptist Church. From the split at the Forks, one path
proceeded east to the salt licks located at Stamping Ground and Georgetown toward modern-day Scott County. The other veered off toward Lexington, soon to become "the Athens of the West." The licks were residual
deposits of salt from the time when a vast inland sea covered most of
eastern North America. Some of these trails were one hundred feet wide,
the width of a modern highway, a testimony to the number and duration
of animals passing along them. Buffalo and their predecessors possessed
the knack of following the easiest grades as though their hooves had an
innate sense of engineering. Many of these roadways predate the buffalo
and were grooved by the slowly incising tramp of several species of mammoths, whose undeviating migrations, aided by erosion and dispersion of
dust, gradually cut deep pathways below the surrounding landscape. The
trails also drew hunters who could provision their camps during the great
annual drives of the herds, ranging, Jillson estimates, from hundreds to
thousands as they migrated to the sources of salt. Among the best-known
sources of salt included in this circuit were such sites as Big Bone Lick,
Blue Licks, and Drennon's Lick. The Kentucky River at Frankfort apparently provided a key link in their nomadic circuits because of its accessible ford.

Indigenous peoples lived in Kentucky and along the Elkhorn Valley for over twelve thousand years, according to current archaeological

evidence.[10] Twelve thousand years ago the most recent ice age was ending. With warming of the climate, ice sheets slowly receded to the north,
and an environment similar to the one in which we live began to form.
Botanists describe this central Kentucky on the cusp of settlement as a
park-like land of cane and forests dominated by oaks and hickories, then
gradually by other varieties, including sugar maples, ashes, bur oaks,
hackberries, and other trees still found in patches of forest, along waterways, at fence lines, and in backyards in the Bluegrass today. Indigenous
peoples have lived along Elkhorn Creek and its uplands for all but a short
period during its history, namely the past 250 years. Having no means of
recording their stories but through oral transmission, long broken, we
know them mostly from the artifacts they left behind, flint and stone and
fired clay, natural elements adapted to human uses as weapons, tools, and
cooking utensils.

When Euro-Americans first reached the Bluegrass—mostly Virginians coveting land in this westernmost county of their commonwealth—
they explained the mounds and other remains of previous cultures they
encountered by suppositions that became myths, based more on active
imaginations than either science or history. From their point of view,
"White Indians," for example, built the mounds they saw, descendants of
the Lost Tribes of Israel, Egyptians, Romans, or even, according to some,
the twelfth-century Welshman Prince Madoc. These ideas were similar to
those of Columbus, who 250 years earlier thought he recognized the peoples he confronted as inhabitants of the West Indies—Indians.[11] Another
myth, almost as difficult to dislodge, claimed that indigenous peoples had
never lived in Kentucky as a permanent home, that it had always been
a hunting ground for peoples north of the Ohio or from regions to the
south. Such an idea softened the guilt of those who dispossessed native
peoples of their land. If no one really owned or occupied the land, the
thinking went, Anglo-American law permitted them to claim it for themselves, especially since they regarded themselves as more civilized and
thus superior.

Over this fabled paradise, however, hung a dark cloud—the legendary
"Dark and Bloody Ground" so often cryptically encountered in textbooks
of Kentucky history. Writers about Kentucky often offer its associations with darkness as an explanation of why these superstitious peoples
elected not to live along the inviting waters and hunt the woodlands that

teemed with game. Fight there, hunt there, but don't live there. The Dark and Bloody Ground idea had its genesis in a comment reputedly made by a Cherokee named Dragging Canoe at Sycamore Shoals in what is now Tennessee. There, on March 17, 1775, Richard Henderson of the Transylvania Company bartered with the Cherokee Indians—at least a portion of them—signing a treaty that in fact conveyed a large part of Kentucky to the Transylvania Land Company, a transaction that resulted in Daniel Boone establishing the first white settlement in Kentucky at Boonesborough on the Kentucky River.[12] Richard Henderson planned to establish an independent colony in Kentucky, sell land to those migrating west, and reap riches for himself and those who backed him. Dragging Canoe, one of those reluctant to barter away his tribal homeland, predicted troubles to come. What started as prophecy ended in decades of tragedy. The cloud darkened as newcomers attempted to settle the state, displacing the native peoples, who saw the game depleted and wilderness steadily succumbing to the rifle, the ax, and the plow.

I met Gwynn Henderson on a rainy May afternoon in a warehouse-like building off the main campus at the University of Kentucky. Her job title is staff archaeologist at the Program for Cultural Resource Assessment (a mouthful) at the University of Kentucky. Years earlier, back in the early 1990s, I had heard her make a presentation and had read an article of hers in the *Register of the Kentucky Historical Society*.[13] During our meeting, rain thrummed on the industrial roof like an incessant drumroll. The building's floors were concrete, the offices simple partitions among shelves and drawers that contained artifacts and evidence of Kentucky's undigested but accumulated past. This building plainly contained secrets and the answers to secrets. Having read that the university campus housed the remains of the Elkhorn mammoth, I easily imagined them secreted behind a number in one of the coded drawers. Coming in out of the rain, I asked the first person I saw if Gwynn was around. He gestured me toward the interior of the cavernous building and said, "I think we have one of those," then conducted me to her office. Silver-haired and amiable, Gwynn rose from her desk, happy to talk about the subject that obviously obsessed her. After some polite preliminaries, she gave me a two-hour-and-twenty-minute crash course in Kentucky archaeology, covering indigenous peoples from dawn until their premature dusk when they encountered venturesome and land-hungry Euro-Americans on the eve of the American Revolution. Her enthusiasm was genuine, and I stopped taking notes and simply tried to take in what she seemed so willing to share.

Much of what Gwynn told me dispelled the myth of Kentucky as a place that Native Americans visited but never inhabited. She assured me that Native Americans had lived, fished, and hunted along Elkhorn and the uplands of central Kentucky thousands of years longer than Euro-Americans, who, at best, had occupied this part of the world in numbers for a measly 250 years. Indigenous peoples, by comparison, had lived here for at least ten or so millennia. They left few signs—no large wilderness cities, no monuments beyond some mounds, no architectural ruins as visible proof of their presence. The ancestors of those whom the first whites met dug mounds by hand and carried earth in baskets. Unfortunately, many of these topographical wonders have been flattened by the plow over repeated growing seasons, reduced to anonymity or dug up by pothunters. As for artifacts, the wet climate slowly rotted anything organic. Yet the fields and streambeds render up a steady harvest of arrowheads, chipped scrapers, and flint or chert tools—irrefutable evidence of their presence and period to those who studied them. The occasional shell gorget or effigy turns up too. From 10,000 to 9000 B.C., Paleo-Indians lived in small, mobile groups hunting mastodons and other megafauna and foraging meals from the plant foods in the natural garden that surrounded them.[14] During this Early Archaic Period the climate was cooler, closer to that of present-day Canada. Innovation came slowly as hunters gained an advantage over their prey, utilizing the atlatl, or spear-thrower, to increase the force and deadliness of their projectiles.[15] Essentially, the atlatl augmented the force of the human arm by extending its thrust and penetration. This culture also had an extensive trade network, extending from the Great Lakes (copper) to the seacoasts (marine shells). The proof derives from artifacts buried with the dead as well as excavations of sites where they camped.[16]

As the climate gradually warmed during the post-glacial era, these groups adapted more fully to the changed environment. They became more savvy about available food sources and where to be at certain times of the year to maximize the yield. During part of the year they harvested fish and clams, then moved to a more likely place for hunting deer and elk as well as smaller game, moving yet again in the fall for gathering nuts. There is evidence that the buffalo, or bison, found in Kentucky had migrated across the Mississippi because of overpopulation, though an earlier extinct form at one time grazed on deep-rooted native grasses in the state's meadows and along its hillsides. In the fall, these Native American groups, growing in number, harvested the plentiful hickory nuts and walnuts in certain areas, a food source that kept well during the lean winter months. This period from 7,000 to 1,000 B.C. was designated as the Archaic Period.

In 1976 the Kentucky Heritage Council conducted an archaeological survey of Franklin County. Heritage Council archaeologists found twenty-six sites dating from the early to late periods of the Archaic era. The survey identified at least two of the sites around Elkhorn Creek, one at Switzer a few miles from the Forks, the other near Peaks Mill, a few miles below Knight's Bridge. Both sites, located on high ridgetops overlooking major streams, may have served as base camps used repeatedly over many generations. But most of the sites surveyed were small, temporary camps overlooking streams, though some were found in the floodplains as well as along upland drainage paths.[17]

The Woodland Period (1000 B.C.–A.D. 1000) saw the beginnings of agriculture in small gardens, though hunting, fishing, and gathering remained the primary sources of food. Gardens meant, for some, more permanent homesites, though other groups continued following cycles of camping here and there to exploit food sources. Gwynn dispelled the idea of the "three sisters"—squash, beans, and corn—providing a stable food source at a relatively early date. Rather than rising at one time as a convenient trinity, they were domesticated consecutively over a longer period, squash followed by beans followed by corn.

Gardening gradually emerged alongside traditional hunting and gathering, diversifying food sources and revolutionizing the culture. Reliable food sources, derived from fertile ground surrounding encampments, created larger and more stable populations, bringing more people together in relatively permanent communities. These people devised ever more complex ceremonial lives as their culture evolved, represented in the burial mounds that dotted the Bluegrass. Part of this complexity grew out of their trade relations with other cultures, ranging from the copper regions of the upper Midwest to the seacoasts, where shells were prized for ornamentation and purposes of ritual.[18]

During the Late Prehistoric Period (A.D. 1000–1750), two distinct cultures developed in the region. In the lower Mississippi watershed, including western Kentucky, groups formed that archaeologists designate as Mississippian. In the uplands of the Bluegrass and the mountains of eastern Kentucky lived a people described as Fort Ancient, ancestors of those who first encountered settlers during the period preceding Kentucky statehood. Though the Mississippian group lived in large, fortified towns, the Fort Ancient group congregated in smaller towns only during the summer months. During the winter they broke into smaller groups to hunt deer, elk, bears, and wild turkey, as well as a menagerie of smaller game. Both groups eventually relied primarily on farming, living on crops from the cultivated fields surrounding their camps. In addition to such staples as corn, squash, and beans, they also grew tobacco and sunflowers. They supplemented these crops with fishing and gathering edible wild plants, the net sum giving them a healthy and varied diet.[19]

Physical evidence indicates that a group of these Fort Ancient people occupied the Kentucky River corridor a few miles from Elkhorn Creek, in the uplands close by the river. Capitol View is now the name of a city park along the Kentucky River just a mile or so south of the state capitol. Part of the floodplain by the river has been converted to soccer fields, where all three of my children played on local YMCA and school teams. Beyond these flatlands rise hilly ridges and ravines still heavily wooded and relatively undeveloped, a haven for deer and other wildlife that seem to sense their privileged status, living in a posted area where hunters cannot make them targets. Dense cover begins a few yards from the soccer fields, intersected by only one small, isolated road, an area that is easily imagined as a throwback to its wilderness past. Not far from this area, a small group of indigenous peoples chose a site for their encampment nearly a mile from the river. They formed it on a ridge now occupied by a large box-like building with a sign outside identifying it as the "Centralized Laboratory Facility," a laborious name for what most refer to as the state crime lab, the place where forensic studies are conducted. In the early 1990s, the commonwealth of Kentucky decided to build a new crime lab on the East-West Connector a mile south of the state capitol. As required by law, the site was examined for artifacts worthy of preservation. Archaeologists at the site uncovered objects that indicated that prehistoric peoples had occupied this relatively flat ground atop a ridge on what until recently had

been farmland. The study delayed construction until trained investigators had thoroughly tested and sifted the soils, after which the Kentucky
Heritage Council issued a report of the findings. Though I had somehow
found and read the report twenty or so years ago, I looked at it this time
with a new perspective, thanks to the synopsis of native peoples living in
Kentucky that Gwynn had given me.

Seven hundred years ago, around A.D. 1400, a group of Fort Ancient
people lived at the site for a period of ten or so years, roughly between
the late 1300s to mid-1400s, contemporaries of Geoffrey Chaucer. The
report described the encampment as a "small, semicircular Fort Ancient
settlement located on the northwestern edge of the Inner Bluegrass . . . in
southcentral Franklin County."[20] Hardly possessing great archaeological
significance of the magnitude of Nerfertiti's tomb, the diggings provided
tangible proof that indigenous peoples occupied the area 350 years before
Boone. The evidence of habitation consists of artifacts, charcoal, burnt
clay, and charred limestone rock. More specifically, this means "ceramic,
lithic, botanical, and faunal remains."[21] Excavation uncovered shards of
baked clay, including four non-vessel clay objects: a ceramic disk, a portion of a spoon or ladle, a fragment of a tiny figurine, and a section of a
fired piece of rolled clay.[22] The lack of variation in the design and ornament of the ceramic pieces suggests that the duration of encampment
was relatively short.

The earlier archaeological study of 1976 had identified twenty-two
sites dated from the Fort Ancient Period. Four were camps, fifteen
were villages, and one was a rock-shelter site. Sixteen of the sites were
described as "multi-component" because they were also occupied during
the Archaic and Woodland Periods. Ridgetops as well as bottomland
along major streams and springs were popular sites for these people, as
they had been for their forebears.[23]

The lithic remains at these sites take the form of what is called deb-
itage, fragments from objects shaped by the hands of these faceless people. These bits and pieces become a metaphor for what has been lost, the
shapes of tools and utensils as well as of individuals who had personalities and characteristics that made each inhabitant of the encampment
distinct, with distinguishing features, characteristic habits, and frames of
mind unique to them. Missing too is a key, the relationships on which
they all depended—mother, son, daughter, father, grandparents. Though

the evidence of these relationships is scant, we can see it in the care with which they buried their dead and the prized objects often buried with them. Among the lithic remains at Capitol View were a cannel coal palette and a siltstone pipe. These help us understand the ancestors of those who later resisted white incursion as fully human, susceptible to ornament, seeking to engage in the pleasurable and social activity of smoking. Parents loved their children and respected the elderly.

Among the faunal and botanical remains the sifters found seeds of such wild fruits as sumac, grape, blackberry, raspberry, and plum. In addition to bones of the larger game they ate, the site held remains of smaller mammals, such as bobcat, raccoon, squirrel, opossum, skunk, rabbit, and muskrat. These people ate everything edible. They also ate such amphibians as box, softshell, snapping, and painted turtles, reptiles, fish, and freshwater mussels.[24] A large dog skull was also found, though investigators found no signs that it had been butchered. More likely, its owner regarded it as a pet. The human remains were few, almost all of them adults and adolescents. No infant or child remains were discovered. Were they buried elsewhere? Did their incomplete bone formation make them more subject to decomposition? The answers to these questions are elusive. Most of the adults were buried in a semi-flexed position and showed evidence of tooth decay. One showed lesions associated with endemic syphilis.[25]

The eight structures in which these people lived were square to rectilinear and had rounded corners. They had no internal walls and few interior supports, as indicated by post molds. The posts themselves consisted mainly of hickory and white oak, woods dense and sturdy, long-lasting enough to tell the story. Inhabitants dug some of the structures into basins, with evidence of hearths and fire pits used both for heat and cooking. Based on the floor space of the structures, thirty to seventy people inhabited the site.[26] What covered the structures is uncertain since organic materials and exposure made it succumb to the weather over time. The structures formed themselves in an irregular semicircle, with one area devoid of any cultural features to serve as possible space for community activities. The diggers found trash pits among the structures, earth ovens for outside cooking, and burial sites. Two small creeks nearby offered a ready source of water.

This sketchy portrait leaves us with more questions than answers. Because these people had no written language, we cannot know their feelings, their sense of themselves, their philosophical view of the sylvan world around them. We do not know the name of a single one of them, nor do we know a word of their spoken language. Only remnants of their art or ornament survive as well as their utilitarian tools. The clothing they wore, some perhaps woven but mostly fashioned from the skins of animals, does not preserve well. That they cared for each other is clear from their graves. Their burial practices show evidence of this care and suggest belief in an afterworld. Despite what we perceive as impoverished lives, they tied themselves intimately and necessarily to the world in which they lived. Unlike most of us, they recognized themselves as a part of nature rather than apart from it. If they possessed little of what we call science, they had an intimate practical knowledge of the natural world and its workings, their very survival tied to the seasons and natural processes around them. Theirs was a world of subsistence with few frills, but there must have been some aspiration toward art. They also carried out a tradition of storytelling that added perspective and meaning to their lives and some relief from the austerity of the conditions in which they lived. They had some useful knowledge of medicines derived from wild plants, untested by the measures of science but relying on the tradition and simple empiricism. Today we would call this folk medicine.

They also lived shorter lives in which death, whether by accident or physical illness, often came suddenly and inexplicably. Whether they were warlike, we do not know, though their small numbers would have made organized military efforts a challenge. Overpopulation and lack of resources did not burden them, and their environment could comfortably support, as it does to a degree today, great concentrations of people. Outsiders who could threaten their space were few, and almost unlimited territory was available around them as their patterns of living testify. With only slight variations this pattern and mode of living must have persisted for millennia until the last quarter of the eighteenth century, when they began to encounter pale strangers with a more advanced technology and a hunger for land that would displace the natives' descendants and, in many cases, eradicate them through violence and disease. Seminomadic, their very lives depending on intimate knowledge of their surroundings, they probably knew every fishing hole, mussel shoal, and campsite on Elkhorn Creek. They certainly knew the nearby Kentucky River that provided fish as well as a means of travel. Where did they go? We do not know, but theirs must have resembled many such encampments along waterways in the Kentucky country, a region with more creeks than any other state except Alaska. With its advantages of navigation and variety of food sources, they or their like would surely have lived and fished and hunted along Elkhorn's waters.

The collision of cultures that came with the settlement of the Elkhorn Valley—and all of Kentucky—would be dramatic and irreversible. Though most of the indigenous people had moved north of the Ohio prior to 1750, Kentucky remained a favorite hunting ground. Had there been substantial numbers permanently settled in the Kentucky country, resistance would have been more immediate and more determined. As it was, the land and the wildlife it supported soon showed the strains of a new presence. Game was depleted not just through increased harvesting of the deer, buffalo, and elk on which native peoples depended but also through deforestation that destroyed their habitats and diminished the number of animals the land could sustain. The elk would disappear, and by 1820 the buffalo were hunted almost to extinction. The land would be transformed, much of the native forestland cleared for pasture, crops, a network of roads, homesteads, and cities. To plant tobacco, wheat, corn, and other vegetables, those who came to Kentucky cut or burned large areas of forest to provide tillable ground, replacing a complex system of diversely interconnected plants with large-scale farming: a single plant in rows or mounds occupying a large field. Instead of small groups living nomadically and following the food sources—four-legged animals, nuts, fish, berries—the newcomers built permanent dwellings of logs or brick or stone, erecting fences not only to pen their animals but also to symbolically assert ownership and segregate themselves from nature and their neighbors. Such divisions broke up the old fluidity, the ancient unbroken unity of field and stream and woodland.

These new people had come to stay, and their impact on the environment radiated from fixed points until patchworks and treeless plots intersected the natural environment. They brought domesticated animals with them: cattle, hogs, horses, chickens, and sheep. They hunted to near extinction anything that threatened them, including buffalo, bears, and wolves. Escaped hogs, turned loose to feed on mast, upset the intricate plant systems that had evolved over millennia. The last sighted buffalo in Kentucky died about the time of Boone's death in 1820.[27] The forests suffered almost as much as the fauna. Industry such as E. H. Stedman's paper mill on Elkhorn Creek gobbled up cords and cords of firewood, in a few decades deforesting much of the Elkhorn Valley and contributing as one of the first of many industries to the fouling of the creek's pure waters. And finally, starting in the seventeenth century, the newcomers introduced smallpox and other diseases for which native peoples had little or no resistance, decimating whole villages. An altered environment could not fail to alter the Native American culture that had lived in relative harmony with the natural world around them. The Industrial Revolution, imported from Europe with improved technology and seemingly endless energy sources, accelerated this process of suppression and eradication until native inhabitants of the Kentucky country had all but vanished, only to reemerge in distorted form in dime novels and popular historical fiction.

Four

Charcoal sketch of pioneer and surveyor John Floyd (circa 1890s), attributed to Xantippe "Tip" Saunders and based on descriptions from historical perspectives. (Courtesy of the Filson Historical Society, Louisville, Kentucky.)

The surveyor Hancock Taylor, his cousin James Strother, and the Dutchman Abraham Haptonstall (or Hepenstall) were paddling up the Kentucky to retrieve some supplies they had cached at one of their camps. Their surveys for the summer completed, they planned to cross the mountains through Pound Gap and return to Virginia's more civilized counties. They had successfully surveyed thousands of acres of the choicest land in what was to become Kentucky, including its soon-to-be famous Bluegrass region. Now they were returning to register surveys for the parties in whose interests they acted, many of them family and friends. Living on what they could shoot or forage, they had toted transit and heavy chains as well as the record book in which Taylor made his entries. The weather was muggy, and there were dark swatches on their tattered clothes as they labored to move the laden dugout along the pathway of green water. On either side of them ran a ragged wall of green, trees along the banks perilously bending over the water in a competition for available light. As they made their way, they kept alert and silent, uncertain what lay around the next bend in a country that seemed indifferent to them when not overtly hostile. They spoke only when necessary, all of them bone-tired but motivated by the prospect of going home. The date was July 27, 1774.

Suddenly, from the dense undergrowth along the river came a volley of shots that disrupted the fidgety wilderness silence. Strother slumped over, killed instantly, and Taylor flinched, instinctively pulling both hands to his abdomen, mortally wounded. Realizing their peril, Haptonstall ducked and paddled away from the shooting as quickly as he could, a few balls thunking into the sides of the dugout or raising little geysers in the water around them until the shooting stopped and they were able to reach the far bank, where they felt, at least temporarily, safer. Poor Strother was lifeless. Though shot in two places, Taylor with Haptonstall's support was able to walk for two days before dying in what is now Madison County at the headwaters of Taylor's Fork of Silver Creek, the former named in his honor, near what is now Richmond, Kentucky. Before his death he was able to sign and validate several surveys, giving them the force of law. Haptonstall soon met with other members of the party, including Taylor's cousin Willis Lee, and they buried him under a cairn of stones to mark the site and protect his body from wild animals.[1]

COMPASS AND CHAINS

Passed two riplings [*sic*]. Dined at a good spring, proceeded to a place that is an island when the river is high. [In] getting around it, [we came to] a Considerable rippling, [which is] above a creek on the upper side. [It is] supposed to be Elkhorn Creek, [and it is] where we emcamped [*sic*].
—*Journal of James Nourse,* 27 May 1775, Saturday.

As Hancock Taylor's and two other surveying parties prepared to leave Kentucky in the spring of 1774 after surveying thousands of acres of the Bluegrass, reports of Indian hostility on the frontier had been growing, much of it a result of the gratuitous murders of several members of the family of a friendly Mingo named Logan. On April 30, 1774, a Virginian named Daniel Greathouse and a band of Indian haters had lured a party of friendly Mingoes across the river, plied them with rum, and unceremoniously murdered them, one of the darker acts visited on Indians during a dark time. The dead included Logan's brother, a sister, and a female relative who was pregnant. Logan, previously a friend to the whites, set out on a mission of revenge that broke an uneasy peace and spread throughout the Ohio River Valley as others went on the warpath. Realizing the imminence of danger to the whites remaining in Kentucky, Colonel William Preston sent two able scouts, Daniel Boone and Michael Stoner, to warn those they encountered. Though Boone and Stoner succeeded in bringing out some of the surveyors, including several members of Taylor's party, they missed Taylor, Strother, and Haptonstall. Logan's call for revenge and renewed hostilities in the border country, in part, may have led to the ambush of Taylor and related incidents at Fort Harrod. This escalation of hostilities on the eve of the American Revolution also precipitated Lord Dunmore's War.

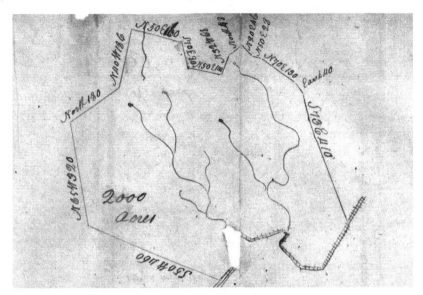

John Floyd's 1774 sketch of the two thousand-acre tract bordering Elkhorn Creek for Bartholomew Dandridge that accompanied his surveyor's notes, twelve hundred of which were later purchased by Harry Innes. Floyd was killed by Indians in 1783, years before Innes became the owner. (Courtesy of the Office of the Secretary of State, Commonwealth of Kentucky.)

The larger complement of surveyors, fewer than thirty, had been in Kentucky since April, part of an organized effort to satisfy a growing appetite for valuable land in the West. The party included John Floyd, James Douglas, and Isaac Hite. They embarked from Smithfield, Virginia, and traveled down the Kanawha and Ohio rivers, stopping at the future site of Louisville, where they conducted twenty-eight surveys consisting of about forty thousand acres. Then they traveled farther down the Ohio, coming up the Kentucky to the area bordered by Elkhorn Creek. On June 3 they broke into two groups. Taylor's visited the fledgling settlement at Harrodsburg, then began surveying near what would become Frankfort and along Elkhorn a few miles downstream.[2] The other party, headed by Floyd and conducting its own surveys, rendezvoused with Taylor's near present-day Midway, where Taylor had selected and claimed a choice parcel of land for himself. Here they divided again, creating a third party headed by Hite and Douglas. Elkhorn became their point of departure, as Floyd, who had already run some surveys on the main stem of the creek, surveyed along the North Fork of Elkhorn toward present-day Georgetown, and Taylor along the South Fork, starting along the main stem below the Forks. Floyd went on to discover and claim Royal Spring, which to this day provides most of the water consumed by Georgetown, Kentucky. Douglas moved south, conducting surveys along Hickman and Jessamine Creeks (the latter believed to be named in honor of Douglas's daughter) in present-day Jessamine County. Floyd rejoined Taylor's party at his camp near present-day Midway on July 1.[3]

Taylor and Floyd probably knew they were not first to explore the Kentucky country in search of desirable land. Christopher Gist preceded them by two and a half decades. Beginning his career as a frontier scout, Gist was originally from Maryland. He was living in the Yadkin Valley of North Carolina when in 1750 the Ohio Company of Virginia, a land company with which George Washington had associations, hired him to survey the Kentucky country. Gist later saved the life of George Washington, acting as his guide and protector during the French and Indian War. He served on the staff of General Edward Braddock during the conflict. Not trained as a surveyor, Gist actually did not perform surveys. No one had legal authorization for grants in the western country. Yet he knew the western country as few of his contemporaries did. He and an unnamed black companion set out that fall, traveling down the Ohio to the falls where Louisville would be formed and then through Kentucky and southwestern Virginia, returning to the settlements in spring 1751. Though Gist explored the region near what would become Kentucky's capital as early as 1750 and kept a journal, he does not mention visiting Elkhorn Creek, close as he might have come. Pioneers who reached present-day Shelby County, Kentucky, in 1775 found trees with the name Gist carved on them, and they named the nearby stream Guist Creek in his honor, misspelling his name, a common practice on the frontier, where phonics trumped the few existing dictionaries and variant spellings might occur in the same paragraph. Active on the frontier during almost all of his adult life, Gist preceded the generation that carved up Kentucky into discrete, ownable plats. Like so many on the frontier, he died in middle age, a victim of smallpox in 1759 while on duty guarding Virginia's borders during the French and Indian War.

As an important outcome of the war, Virginia opened the territory he had explored to pay its veterans. Virginia was land rich and cash poor.

Lacking available funds to pay veterans of the French and Indian War and feeling pressure to satisfy their claims for service, Virginia governor John Murray Dunmore opened thousands of square miles of land to the west, beginning what became the first great American land rush.[4] He awarded military warrants to veterans as payment for their often arduous service. By 1773, parties of surveyors, including the McAfee brothers and Hancock Taylor, entered the Kentucky country, searching out the most desirable land and acting as agents in the interest of those who survived the war and those to whom their interests had been transferred. They surveyed land along the Kentucky River in what would become Frankfort as well as other sites within the vicinity of Elkhorn. Because these early birds had no official authorization, William Preston, the official surveyor, refused to validate their surveys, necessitating Taylor's return with others in 1774, this time with authority.

The physical process of surveying has been simply described by frontier historian Neal Hammon, probably the most knowledgeable scholar of land disposition in Kentucky: "To run the surveys, they used a large open-faced compass equipped with movable sighting slits. This instrument was mounted on a wooden leg or legs, and, after being leveled, the sights were turned to match the desired direction. The marker advanced (clearing vegetation as required) as far as practical from the compass, but keeping in its sights. After the marker had traveled as far as possible, the compass was moved to this position and the procedure repeated."[5] The two chain carriers toted a chain of traditionally sixty-four feet (four poles) in length. As they struck a course, the lead man dropped a pebble or other marker at the end of the chain. The rear chain carrier collected the pebbles, and they were later counted and entered into the notes measuring distance. This practice made the process less cumbersome since it permitted them to record their measurements less frequently. As Hammon points out, distances in the surveys tended to be less accurate than direction, always demonstrating an understandable tilt toward generosity. As a result, few surveys came in under the allotted acres. One surveyor that my uncle told me about had the nickname "Big Foot" because the survey he conducted for his property in Oldham County came out almost half again larger than the allocated acreage. Floyd stood guilty of the same practice. One tract he surveyed for himself, supposedly 400 poles square, turned out to be 485 poles.[6] As for fees, the rate that the Fincastle surveyors charged in 1774 was two pounds, one shilling, and eight cents for each one thousand-acre survey, less expenses.[7]

The Fincastle surveyors became the vanguard of droves that would appropriate unmapped and communally owned wilderness of Native Americans. They imposed domestic order on it through the measurements and titles that answered to time-honored practices of Anglo-American law. Originally, of course, the king claimed Virginia and its furthermost county as his royal domain. When the colonies gained independence, they laid claim to vast expanses of vacant land to the west—at least property not settled by Euro-Americans. The native peoples who lived or hunted in this uncharted territory regarded the surveyors as intruders and thieves. They understandably resented this first collective effort to domesticate the land in transforming wilderness to homesteads and farmland on a massive scale. Though few Native Americans actually inhabited Kentucky, they naturally resisted what endangered their way of life through the conversion of forest into farms and the decimation of the plentiful game—deer, elk, bear, and buffalo—that sustained them. They took great offense at the impositions of these aliens from the east.

Surveyors and the first settlers had little regard for the rights of those they displaced. Records show that among the thousands of acres surveyed during the summer of 1774, James Douglas entered a two thousand-acre tract surveyed by authority of a military warrant issued to Turner Southall, a survivor of the French and Indian War that gave us Braddock's Defeat and in which the English and their colonial allies had casualties of nearly two-thirds of their army.[8] Apparently, Southall or his heirs sold the military warrant to Bartholomew Dandridge (1737–1785), a man of some standing in Virginia. As the brother-in-law of Colonel George Washington (himself a survivor of Braddock's Defeat), he moved in circles in which land acquisition became a consuming preoccupation. Martha Dandridge Washington, the future president's wife, was his sister. Elected to the Virginia Convention held in Richmond in 1776, he won a seat in the House of Burgesses, became a member of the Privy Council, and was later appointed judge of the General Court.[9] By virtue of that post, he also served as a judge of the Court of Appeals, a position he held until his death. A prominent lawyer and jurist from New Kent County, Virginia, Dandridge, so far as the record shows, never saw the two thousand acres bordering Elkhorn, most of which would become the Harry

Innes farm. Since he died in 1785 and Innes acquired the property shortly afterward, Innes likely bought it directly from Dandridge's heirs.[10]

The date of James Douglas's survey of two thousand acres on Elkhorn Creek for Bartholomew Dandridge, assignee of Turner Southall, is June 29, 1774. We know the name of one of the three chainmen that accompanied James Douglas: Jacob Sodowski. Douglas did this survey just prior to the split of the two surveying parties to cover unclaimed land along the courses of Elkhorn's two main forks. It is likely that Douglas, Taylor, and Floyd worked near one another when the survey was done since they came together the next day. In fact, Floyd surveyed the adjacent property for an individual named Adam Stephens, probably another veteran.[11]

A copy of the official descriptive notes for Batholomew Dandridges's, later Innes's, property can be found in the Innes file at the Kentucky Historical Society in Frankfort. Though written in a clerk's hand, portions of the survey require some guesswork in deciphering: "Survey for Bartholmew Dandridge, assignee of Turner Southall by virtue of the Governor's warrant, 2000 Acres of land in Fincastle County on Elkhorn Creek, a north branch of the Kentucky River lying about 70 miles from the Ohio & on the south side thereof."[12] With only Elkhorn as a physical baseline, the notes earmarked boundaries by natural features on the landscape:

> Beginning at three double sugar trees on the south Bank of the Creek by a large Buffalo Ford 360 poles above Cove run and runneth (?) thence 150 west 460 to 2 poplars by a Draft & meadow at the foot of a Hill along the same N 65 W 320 to a white oak hickory & walnut on the side of a flat ridge North 180 to a Honey Locust Ash and Elm N 40 186 to a Walnut black oak and Poplar N 50 E 160 crossing a branch to 2 Hickorys & a Spanish oak on a hillside S 70 E 80 to Walnut Hoopwood and white oak N 50 E 104.[13]

Not all the penmanship is legible, though the record contains a field drawing of the property. The journal of Thomas Hanson contains the following entry of the Dandridge survey for Wednesday, June 29, 1774: "Mr. Douglas made a survey of 2000 acres which joins Mr. Floyds survey. Mr. Floyd went out to examine land."[14]

According to Hammon, notes to the Dandridge survey refer to a large buffalo ford on the property designated as Cove Run as well as a small creek running along Peary's Valley to the Main Elkhorn.[15] The piddling creek, dry most of the year, still winds and weaves its way through the valley before emptying into Elkhorn. The Peary's Valley he mentions is probably the Elkhorn Valley itself and its abandoned meander through which the small creek runs, its erosive force that shaped the valley then now reduced to a trickle. We may never know the Peary of Peary's Valley. Perhaps the name belonged to one of Floyd's chainmen since firstcomers often named places after themselves. We just don't know. Douglas also mentions an adjacent island in Elkhorn Creek, now washed away, located opposite a "high hill." The high hill located on the property is almost certainly the Backbone near whose foot the remains of the Elkhorn mammoth would be uncovered 171 years later. Innes, the first federal judge west of the mountains, would purchase twelve hundred acres of the original two thousand acres soon after Dandridge's death in 1785.

Thomas Hanson's journal provides much of what we know of the whereabouts of Douglas, Floyd, and Taylor as they hopscotched their surveys up the Elkhorn toward the inner Bluegrass. When the parties split into smaller groups, Hanson accompanied John Floyd. Like most other frontier journals, his seems almost telegraphic, summarizing with a kind of Spartan frugality that presents at best a rough outline of the group's activities. One suspects that conditions, lack of time, and sheer exhaustion, in part, account for the short, businesslike entries. Seldom did a single day merit more than a few sentences. Yet, at times, he allowed himself more than simple accounting. Two days after, on July 1, he noted Douglas running the Dandridge survey. He evaluated the land about eight miles up the "river" where Taylor's party set up camp at a large spring: "Mr. Floyd & Nsh went in search of Taylor & Co., whom they [met] in a short time, & who took us to their Cap about 8 miles up [Elkhorn] river at a large spring. All the land we passed over today is like a Paradise it is so good & beautiful."[16] A week later, on July 7, proceeding with Floyd up the North Fork of Elkhorn, Hanson gave a fuller picture of the area bordering the creek: "We continued our Surveys, the lines all running parallel with each—running in length N 20 E. in breadth, S. 70 E. The lands is [so] good that I cannot give it its due praise. Its under growth is Clover, Honey Locust Pea vine Cane & Nettles—intermixed with Rich weed. Its timber is Honey Locust, Black walnut, Sugar tree, Hickory, iron wood, Hoop wood [hackberry] Mulberry, Ash, & Elm, & some Oak."[17]

As Hammon points out, all three parties must have been working long days as rapidly as they could, sensing that they exposed themselves to attack. He calculates that each group surveyed several thousand acres a day, "an incredible feat" considering that two adjoining one thousand-acre tracts require a boundary of about nine miles.[18] He points out that each group, on at least one occasion, managed to survey four thousand acres in a single day in what must have been a satisfying but Herculean expenditure of effort.

When the three parties of Taylor, Douglas, and Floyd had completed their surveys during the summer of 1774, they planned to rendezvous at Fort Harrod and return to Virginia in one body, but on July 8 an Indian attack prompted the parties to return by separate routes. Floyd's party, which had followed the North Fork of Elkhorn and surveyed fifty thousand acres, followed a trail up the North Fork of the Kentucky River and returned through Pound Gap.[19] Douglas's took the longer but perhaps safer water route, following the Ohio and Mississippi rivers to New Orleans. They then booked passage on a ship that sailed around Florida to Virginia. Fate deprived Taylor and James Strother of a choice.

In fact, surveyors in Kentucky during these early years suffered a high casualty rate, and John Floyd (1750–1783), one of the most promising young men in the Virginia hinterlands, soon became a second victim.[20] For so short a life, Floyd crammed his with hazardous adventure. Born in 1750 in what is now Amherst County, Virginia, Floyd descended from Welsh ancestors. But he attributed his swarthy complexion and straight black hair to an ancestor who was a Catawba Indian. His father was a small but apparently successful planter.[21]

Though Floyd's educational background remains sketchy, his penmanship and spelling rank him above average for the time. What he lacked in formal education he made up for with native intelligence and pluck. Richard Henderson, leader of the Transylvania Company that commissioned Daniel Boone to establish Boonesborough, described Floyd as a man "with a great show of Modesty and an open honest countenance and no small share of good Sense."[22]

Marrying early at eighteen, Floyd lost his first wife, still in her teens, during childbirth. His break came when he met Colonel William Preston. As a member of the Virginia House of Burgesses and chief surveyor of Fincastle County, Virginia's westernmost county, Preston was a power broker. After Floyd moved to Fincastle County at age twenty-two, he lived in Preston's home and taught school. In 1774 Preston named him a deputy sheriff and surveyor, and Floyd led a party to Kentucky the same year. The prize of a vast expanse of fertile land lay beyond the mountains. As already mentioned, he led one of the first official parties sent to Kentucky to survey the area around the Falls and the Bluegrass. As Preston's trusted assistant, he oversaw the surveying activities of Taylor, Douglas, and Isaac Hite. Though returning to Virginia too late to fight in the battle of Point Pleasant, he reentered Kentucky as surveyor of the Transylvania Company and remained in Kentucky country until 1776. When the Revolution broke out, he returned to Virginia and took to the sea as a privateer, joining the effort to disrupt British shipping. Instead, the British captured him and sent him to Dartmouth Prison in England. Somehow he talked his way out of custody, making his way back to Virginia on a loan of ten guineas from Ambassador Benjamin Franklin in Paris. In Paris, he also survived a bout with smallpox. Returning to Virginia, he married Preston's niece, Jane Buchanan, who advantageously also happened to be Preston's ward. Returning to Kentucky, he participated with Daniel Boone in the rescue of Boone's daughter Jemima and sisters Betsy and Fanny Callaway when a party of Indians kidnapped the teenagers as they lolled along the banks of the Kentucky River.

In 1779, Floyd immigrated with his wife and infant child to Kentucky, settling on two thousand acres that he had surveyed near the Falls when he and others made their whirlwind tour of the area in 1774. He built a station on Beargrass Creek that he called "Woodside." Soon it became popularly known as Floyd's Station, one of six stations along the Middle Fork of Beargrass Creek that defended the fledgling settlement of Louisville. The station offered a center of defense in the region just as, a little over a decade later, the property surveyed for Dandridge would become Innes Station, a place of refuge for settlers on the lower Elkhorn. Rising in prominence, the powers that be placed him in command of Jefferson County's militia on the recommendation of Louisville's founder, General George Rogers Clark. He accompanied the general on his campaign against the Shawnees north of the Ohio River during summer 1780. Clark described him as "the most capable in the country, a soldier, a gentleman, and a scholar." Not simply a soldier, he also served as a judge on the supreme court for the District of Kentucky.

In his capacity as commander of Jefferson County's militia, Floyd knew how exposed and vulnerable the settlements were. Eleven days before his death, Floyd wrote William Preston a prophetic letter in which he anticipated his own passing: "If the war is continued much longer, I can hardly escape, although I am now determined to be more cautious than I have been heretofore, yet every man in this country must be more or less exposed to danger."[23] On April 23, 1783, he received a fatal wound in an ambush while en route with several others from his station to Bullit's Lick, south of what would become Louisville, near present-day Shepherdsville, Kentucky. Near Bullit's Lick, an Indian bullet pierced his upper arm; another lodged in his side. Carried to his home, he, like Hancock Taylor, survived two days before expiring. Just thirty-three when he died, unlike Taylor who was still unmarried at thirty-six, he left a wife and two small children. A third, named after his deceased father, would be born just days after his father's death. The namesake grew up to become governor of Virginia, as did a grandson, another John.[24]

When Floyd's widow, Jane, died in 1812, one tradition holds that survivors buried her in the scarlet cloak he had acquired in Paris for his wedding and which reputedly he had worn the day of his death. Another states that she used the cloak as a shroud to bury her second husband, Alexander Breckinridge.[25]

Seven years earlier, Floyd and his fellow land seekers had surveyed much of the land along the main stem of Elkhorn Creek below the Forks of Elkhorn. Floyd's death in 1783 became the first of several violent deaths associated with the territory.[26] As shown in the deaths of John Floyd, Willis Lee, and Hancock Taylor, perils beset those who paved the way for settlement in Kentucky County. Casualty rates were high, and the number of surveyors relatively small. From the beginning, Native Americans saw such interlopers as harbingers of settlement, not merely intruders but essentially invaders who claimed the land for themselves and those that would follow. Hunters they had regarded as nettlesome, but they saw surveyors as a threat to their very existence because invariably settlers followed on their heels. Far from the relative safety of their homes, these men found themselves constantly exposed while traveling through unchartered wilderness intent on performing their tedious and demanding jobs. Hunters came and went, competing with native hunters for a harvest of meat and hides. But surveyors penetrated the wilderness as forerunners. Great walkers, they covered hundreds of miles on foot over rough, sometimes dangerous terrain, often blazing a trail. After them came a lethal torrent that destroyed wilderness, converting forestland into farms and homesteads, toppling trees, killing the game that provided their sustenance (and much that didn't), fouling waterways and seemingly everything they touched. Not surprisingly, Native Americans regarded the growing number of immigrants as agents of depletion and annihilation. From the East came Virginians, North Carolinians, and Pennsylvanians who combated the land itself as if it were something to be conquered and bent to their collective will. Every Native American who had experience in Kentucky knew from rumors and painful experience that rivulets became streams, that men with chains and transits would be supplanted by men with axes, long rifles, and plows. They came.

Five

Innes Station on Main Elkhorn. (From Willard Rouse Jillson, *Early Frankfort and Franklin County* [Louisville, Ky.: Standard Printing Company, 1936].)

Given his druthers, Harry knew even early in his career that he would rather have his hands in dirt of the Elkhorn Bottom than thumbing through a legal treatise or his tattered copy of the statutes of Virginia and, more recently, the Commonwealth of Kentucky. Yet he also knew that one fed the other, and he relished the company of other deciders who worked to shape a future for their children and grandchildren as they bettered themselves and, presumably, the country. But what occupied his mind just now was where to plant his orchard. He had consulted locals educated in such things as well as his pocket-sized edition of The Farmer's Assistant, *consolidating what he learned into a plan tailored to his holdings. Low ground close by his dwelling house and the creek were not suitable because such places harbored cold during the winter months, putting trees, especially young fruit trees fresh from the nursery, at hazard. Better to plant them on hilly or uneven ground where frost was less likely to linger, especially on a south-facing slope. Northern slopes delayed blooming and subsequent fruit. Authorities agreed that the best site was on small hills above a valley or depression. Ah, he had that. The likeliest soil, he knew from the orchard his father had tended in Caroline County, should be warm, dry, and fertile. He had that too. Stiff blue clays he knew to avoid as they tended to stunt the roots through binding. Nor did he want to plant on windy hilltops, for the damage a storm might do to brittle limbs or fruit-laden branches. Each starter was to be as carefully tended as one of his children for the fruit it would bear, the winter apple, the luscious peach, the tangy-tasting bell-shaped pear, each leaving its distinct legacy, each, like individual children, having its own distinct character and taste. The rows of trees he planted would follow the contour of the slope and not run vertically in ways that might jeopardize their tenure. The rows as he looked up the hill would be staggered to impede erosion. Each day what he envisioned took on more definition until he mapped the ideal place precisely in his mind, until he fixed an image of what it would become. Now he had only to assemble his tools, a hand or two, and get himself to the designated site.*

So on a chosen day he and Peter, the chief man he designated to help with the planting, rode a mule-drawn wagonload of seedlings out of the bottom to the ridge that had formed an embankment for the ghost of Elkhorn where it had flowed ages ago, up the winding wagon road and west to the hillside he'd envisioned as he studied the mental map of his land. The field he chose was mostly cleared. Together, they staked out where the first rows would be planted and how far apart, between, above, and below. Then Harry took shovel in hand to show Peter how each wispy seedling should be implanted. With the long metal tongue he broke the surface, making a rough circle. Then he scooped out the dark topsoil and piled it to one side. He instructed Peter in the principle that the hole for each tree should be three times the diameter of the root ball. Topsoil was set aside and saved to go back to the bottom of the hole, where it would most nourish. He pruned back a few damaged roots he discovered on the first seedling, a jennitin apple, and spread the remaining rootlets across the topsoil, then buried them. From a bucket of spring water, which he knew would be the first of many trips, he moistened the skein of roots to inspire growth. He considered adding barn droppings to form a slurry but let it go, deciding that proper tamping would fill air pockets, and that the water Peter would bring would quench its thirst. He showed Peter, a wiry man whose skin was the hue of his cherry hoe handle, how to leave a depression around the base of the filled hole, a funnel to catch and hold rainwater. He wished he had mesh of some kind to protect its fragility and discourage mice and rabbits as well the host of invisible critters ever vigilant for delicacies to vary their diets. Then he added enough water to soak the roots again. When he finished, he had Peter repeat the process with a second seedling until he was satisfied that the man had mastered the process. This was not a practice Peter would have seen in the encampments where he was held a prisoner of the Wyandotte for six years. Pleased with himself, Harry stood back and imagined hundreds of trees honeycombing the hillside, a legion of fruit trees deployed like ranks of infantry. He imagined the first fruit appearing *in three years, the mature fruit some time later, and the abundance of apples and pears he would pack in straw in the cellar for a taste of summer during the winter months. He could already taste the first sip of cider, could already savor that first noggin of peach brandy suffusing through his vitals as he sat before the fire at some not-too-distant Christmas.*

JUDGE HARRY INNES

As a judge, he was patient to hear, diligent to investigate, and impartial to decide.
—**Lewis Collins,** *Historical Sketches of Kentucky,* 1847

Harry Innes is hardly a household name. I know of no monument to him other than his tombstone in the Frankfort cemetery, not even a street name in a capital dedicated to commemorating its notable dead. Ask the name of the first federal judge west of the mountains and only a handful of local historians can name him. Ask who presided over the first treason trial of Aaron Burr and most will draw a blank. Yet Harry Innes was an important player in the formation of Kentucky, active in eight of the ten conventions that resulted in Kentucky's separation from the mother state of Virginia at its beginning 225 years ago as the fifteenth addition to the Union.

I became interested in Harry Innes when I discovered that I live on part of a farm that once belonged to him and that two of his slaves, cutting firewood in what became my front yard, were captured by a band of Wyandotte Indians during the last major foray into Franklin County the year that Kentucky entered the Union. I became more curious when I learned that Innes's grandson, Harry Innes Todd, owned the house I live in and that Todd's grandfather, Thomas Todd, was raised by Harry Innes, who became his mentor, and that Todd became an associate justice of the U.S. Supreme Court. A pattern began to emerge when I learned that two of my neighbors, Judge John Palmore and his wife, Carol, lived by Elkhorn Creek in a house that contained at least two rooms of what formerly was Innes's fortified log cabin, though most of the original structure had burned in 1961. The owner of the property then, J. B. Marston,

rebuilt on the site, incorporating what remained in the columned, colo-
nial-style house that occupies the site today. The Palmores bought the
property from Marston and named it Innesfail (Innes's place) in honor of
the judge's judicial forebear.

Local sources regarding Innes are often fragmentary, vague, and ellip-
tical. I wondered why the Innes surname did not appear in the Frankfort phonebook. I wondered how and why Harry Innes came to settle
on twelve hundred acres of wilderness along the main stem of Elkhorn.
Where did he come from? What became of his family? Why was there
not more historical attention given to a man so well connected to the
major players in forming Kentucky County into the Commonwealth of
Kentucky, such as the state's first U.S. senator, John Brown, Frankfort's
founder, James Wilkinson, and Humphrey Marshall, the land speculator and combative Federalist, at odds with almost everyone in a country
teeming with Jeffersonian Republicans?

Harry Innes became the most prominent early resident of the Elkhorn
bottom. Born in 1752, in Caroline County, Virginia, the son of a Scottish
Episcopal minister, the Reverend Robert Innes, and Catherine Richards
Innes, Harry read law under Hugh Rose at William and Mary College.
Some sources say that he also studied with George Wythe, who trained
Jefferson and was regarded as one of the best legal minds in the colonies.
James Madison, the future president, was his friend and classmate. The
name Innes signifies "island" and originates in Scotland, where his family for centuries had held the barony of Innes in Moray, an island formed
by two branches of a stream that ran through the estate.[1] The family was
established gentry, as well connected in Scotland as it was to become in
America. His father had immigrated to Virginia before the middle of the
eighteenth century. Harry was one of three sons, each of whom rose to
eminence in his own right. James, also trained as a lawyer, was attorney
general of Virginia and became one of the chief proponents of adopting the
U.S. Constitution. Robert built a lucrative career in Virginia as a physician.

Harry, too, saw his future in the legal profession. On the eve of the
Revolution in 1773, the Virginia bar admitted him, and he started his
practice in Bedford in western Virginia. Coming of age, Harry had married Elizabeth Callaway (1750–1790) of Bedford County, Virginia, in 1775,
and she bore him four daughters: Sarah "Sally" (1776–1807), Katherine
Eliza (1779–1836), Elizabeth (1785–1872), and Ann (1787–?). Thomas Todd

(1765–1826), with whom Harry Innes was to have both a continual family and professional relationship, entered his life while he was still in Virginia. Todd was born in King and Queen County, Virginia, the son of Richard Todd and the former Elizabeth Richards. Richards's sister Catherine had married the Reverend Robert Innes, Harry's father. When Todd was eighteen months old, his father died, and Harry, his older cousin, took charge, seeing to the boy's education. Starting at age fourteen, Todd served two brief enlistments in the Continental Army during the Revolution.

When the Revolution began, the Virginia Committee of Public Safety selected Innes to administer lead and powder mines in the foothills of the Blue Ridge Mountains. In 1779, Governor Thomas Jefferson appointed him to adjust land claims in western Virginia. Soon he became a tax commissioner, promoted by Governor Benjamin Harrison to district commissioner of a special tax. His climb up the bureaucratic ladder reached a plateau when he was appointed assistant judge of the newly established Supreme Court of Judicature for the Kentucky District of Virginia. This promotion caused him to move to Kentucky around 1783.[2] Thomas Todd followed and lived with the Innes family. He studied law and surveyed with Judge Innes. At the same time, he tutored the Innes daughters. By day he taught the daughters; by night he studied law.

The reality behind Innes's grandiose job title as assistant judge for the Kentucky District of Virginia was holding court in a log cabin at Crow's Station, a rude clearing in the wilderness ten miles south of Harrodsburg, the second oldest settlement in Kentucky though less than a decade old. Crow's Station would later become Danville, one of the most prosperous satellites of Lexington in the Bluegrass region. Though his court held jurisdiction over civil and criminal cases, most of his work was tied to competing land claims. When Indians killed the court's attorney in 1784, Innes resigned his judgeship and was elected attorney general for the western district of Virginia. He served in this role until 1789, when President George Washington appointed him as first judge of the U.S. Court for the District of Kentucky. This was the pinnacle of his career. Until 1792 Kentucky still answered to Virginia as the state's westernmost county. Innes's appointment added another dimension to the political mix, and Indians supplanted competing land claims as an issue that greatly occupied his attention. From the beginning, Innes associated himself with the most powerful and influential among the earliest generation of Kentucky settlers: "His name is identified with every chapter of the early history of the district and state. Among the men who figured in the movements that led to the separation from Virginia, to the establishment of the commonwealth, and who gave direction to her domestic policy, he was one of the most prominent and influential."[3]

Though the job had its demands, his judicial duties did not prevent the thirty-seven-year-old from continuing to practice law. Like many professional men of his time, he made investments with borrowed money, bought slaves, and was highly regarded in the community as a sound lawyer and solid citizen. A multitasker, he also traded in land, farmed, and promoted civic improvements, all the while performing his duties as district judge.

After the death of his first wife in 1790, Innes married Ann Shiel, widow of Hugh Shiel of Philadelphia. Innes also gained a stepdaughter, Catharine Harris Shiel (1785–1841), from Ann's previous marriage. In 1796, Ann gave birth to another daughter, Maria Knox Innes (1796–1851). On Elkhorn, Innes, therefore, lived in a household dominated by six daughters. It was said that "he was a kind father, although of somewhat irascible temper, and a strict disciplinarian."[4] If in public life Harry Innes worked in a world dominated by men, at home he constantly felt the brush of skirts. In fact, none of the three sons born to Harry's father, Reverend Robert Innes, had any boys, so the Innes name in the line of Robert Innes lasted only so long as their daughters remained unmarried. Following the strong tradition of patrimony carried over from Virginia and England, Innes must have been desperate for a son to carry on the Innes name, intuiting perhaps that in his branch of the family it would die out. His relative freedom and the duties of his judgeship, speculations, and law practice must have kept him in almost frequent contact with other males, and Thomas Todd may have been the son he never had. Leaving the Innes home when he entered legal practice, reputedly with only his horse, a bridle, and 37½ cents, young Todd, as the judge's protégé, quickly rose in the profession, moving from clerk of the Federal Court of the District of Kentucky to being appointed clerk of the Kentucky Court of Appeals after statehood in 1792, becoming judge of the court of appeals, and eventually being named chief justice.[5]

Kentucky's most renowned early portrait painter, Matthew Harris Jouett (circa 1788–1827), whose portfolio covers a virtual Who's Who of early Kentucky, painted both Harry Innes and his second wife. Jouett's portrait

Ann Shiel Innes (1760–1851). (Painting by Matthew Jouett.
Courtesy of the Speed Art Museum, Louisville, Kentucky.)

of Ann Shiel Innes conveys an air of privilege and matronly aplomb. Bon-
neted, the neck of her dark garment wreathed in diaphanous white ruffles,
she stares out at the viewer through two centuries and makes no apolo-
gies for the quaintness of her dress that may have seemed old-fashioned
and overly formal even then. From a well-to-do family in Philadelphia,
she had come to Kentucky equipped with luxuries that few on the frontier could even dream of: green window curtains, expensive carpets, and
thirty pounds' worth of silver. All were regarded as extravagances in frontier Kentucky and must have set the family apart from their neighbors.[6]

Behind the formal apparel, her Sunday best, stands a woman of strong
character. Though she had household help and later her daughters, her
hands were not unaccustomed to cooking, sewing, washing, and other
activities of domestic life in a rural setting. She many times must have
been called to step out of decorum and into the barnyard, treating the
sick, all the things a frontier woman might be expected to do. One wonders if Innes taught her to shoulder a firearm or if she straddled a horse
when riding. Her resilience must have been tested in adapting to maladies

without doctors and acting as the household's medical and medicinal authority. She also served as its main provisioner, in charge of the larder and seeing that her family and help were fed and cared for. What she did was gather, store, prepare, and dispense food for her large family as well as seeing to the needs of hired help and her husband's slaves. Her duties as quartermaster and keeper of the commissary would have overlapped with her husband's, along the sketchy divide between indoors and out-doors. The creek just over the bluff must have been a reliable source of fish, especially the smallmouth bass for which the area was becoming so famous. Ann must also have been a dispenser of practical and emotional advice, the primary source of her daughters' moral instruction. Though the family had been Anglican in Virginia, there was no Anglican con-gregation in Frankfort during the first years of settlement. It is possible that the family conducted their own services at home. Sometime later, Ann and her daughter Maria joined the First Presbyterian Church in Frankfort.[7]

Quinn's Bottom—as Innes's section of the creek has been called—must have been a lonely place beyond the unexceptional faces of family and slaves they rubbed shoulders with almost constantly. Raised with all the amenities, Ann's life on the frontier would have required adaptation. Deprived of refined adult company, she may have been prone to depres-sions and anxieties beyond the ordinary stress of being a mother, a house-wife, a companion to Harry, especially when her husband was called away or when she heard the cry of a bobcat at night or sensed the onslaught of storms or the presence of Indians, all of which were fears with which isolated settlers lived during the early years. For Ann Shiel Innes and the Innes daughters, John Brown's wife, Margaretta, and her small circle must have been welcome though infrequent confidantes. Through the rigors of childbirth and the hardships of scrabbling in rural isolation, the frontier indiscriminately ate up women of every station. But this reality was per-haps not quite as brutal for women like Ann Shiel Innes and Margaretta Brown as it was for the less-privileged women in the area who lived in their own isolation. Though her urban upbringing would not have pre-pared her to live in the remoteness of the Elkhorn, a place with few neigh-bors and fewer amenities, Ann apparently thrived.

In addition to establishing his farm and new home, Innes spent much of his time in civic affairs. During his first year in Kentucky he was

Senator John Brown (1757–1837). (Painting by Matthew Jouett. Courtesy of Liberty Hall, Frankfort, Kentucky.)

appointed a trustee of Transylvania College, a position he held until 1793. Beginning in 1787, he served for a time as chairman of its board of trustees. In Danville, Innes formed friendships and new contacts that would help place him among Kentucky's small but energetic political elite. The Political Club in Danville recruited him as a charter member. This progressive group of frontier intellectuals was interested in the development of Kentucky as a sovereign entity with both national and local autonomy. Members of the club included Joshua Barbee, Christopher Greenup, Thomas Todd, George Muter, James Speed, John Brown, James Wilkinson, and Benjamin Sebastian, leading lights of the day. In 1789 a society for the encouragement of manufactures was organized in Danville, and Harry Innes was appointed as its chairman. The club became a clearing house for ideas of how to promote Kentucky, a debating society that met each Saturday evening to discuss issues facing the District of Kentucky and the nation.[8] Once Innes moved to Elkhorn, his attendance would have been spotty, if he attended at all after statehood. His services always seemed to be in demand in Frankfort as well as Danville. He was added to a list of prominent citizens entrusted with holding a lottery to build the first house of public worship in Frankfort when a bill that Kentucky governor Christopher Greenup (1750–1818) drafted authorizing it became law in 1808. Built on the west side of the capitol, the "Publick Meeting House" was "open to any religious sect which should perform service in an orderly manner."[9] As an early resident of the Elkhorn bottom whose interests ranged beyond farming to politics and professional life, he stood taller and more prominently than most of his neighbors.[10]

Early persuaded that Kentucky's future lay in separation from its parent commonwealth, Virginia, Innes served as a member of eight of the ten conventions toward statehood. He negotiated the means to create a new government consisting of officials elected by voters within its own borders. Innes and other members of the convention regarded distance, mountains, and layers of bureaucracy between the Kentucky District and Williamsburg as obstacles to progress, especially when many problems, notably defense of the frontier from the British and Indians, urgently needed attention. More cumbersome was the application of justice. Authorities in the capital had to ratify decisions of Kentucky courts before they became law, a complicated process that delayed justice and must have created great frustration among those seeking legal relief. Nor did anyone in Kentucky possess the authority to activate the militia.

In Danville, Innes enthusiastically joined the movement to organize the Commonwealth of Kentucky. A progressive with his eye fixed on the future, as early as 1789 he became a member of another forward-looking group that organized a cotton factory in Danville, using machinery brought from Philadelphia.[11] Increasingly aware of the region's needs, he soon joined the movement for immediate and unconditional separation from Virginia. Though many gave fellow attorney George Nicholas credit as sole author of the state constitution, correspondence "in existence proves that Innes aided him." With statehood he became president of the first electoral college that selected Isaac Shelby as first governor under the newly drafted Kentucky constitution. Shelby, in turn, appointed Innes first chief justice of the newly established state, but Innes declined.[12]

Political division in Kentucky that mirrored the national debate on the role of government in civil society both preceded and followed statehood. Following the Republican ideal of decentralized government championed by Jefferson, Innes joined those Kentuckians wary of a strong central power. At the other end of the political spectrum stood the Federalist party, identifying itself with George Washington and Alexander Hamilton nationally. Innes, his hand on the political pulse of the country, noted the vigor of the debate over party and the proper relation of the states to a federal government. In a letter to Thomas Jefferson in 1791, he wrote, "The people of Kentucky are all turned Politicians from the highest in Office to the Peasant."[13] More locally, the family of Thomas Marshall represented the Federalists in Kentucky, including future first chief justice of the Supreme Court John Marshall and his irascible cousin Humphrey Marshall. Other Kentuckians who sided with principles of Republicanism included John Brown, Thomas Todd, George Nicholas, John Breckinridge, and Henry Clay—Republicans all. Through correspondence with Jefferson and Senator John Brown as well as the occasional newspaper, Innes could keep apprised of national affairs, but as one writer has commented, Innes was "first a Kentuckian, and secondly, an American."[14] During the vociferous political debate to separate Kentucky from Virginia, he stood out as a leading advocate. The issues that absorbed his time involved land claims, slavery, taxes, law, and lawyers, all relating to fundamental questions of the distribution of property and the locus of power.[15]

In his own interest, Innes purchased the tract of twelve hundred acres along the Elkhorn that belonged to Bartholomew Dandridge in 1791. The land, located about four miles northeast of Frankfort, was the basis of the military survey that John Floyd made in 1774. Over a period of twenty-five years, Innes transformed much of the forestland he owned on Elkhorn into a prospering farm on some of the most fertile land in what would become Franklin County in 1795. Harry Innes took to rural life. He shared with fellow Virginian Thomas Jefferson a "common interest in grape culture, moldboard plows, merino, shepherd dogs, and Indian artifacts."[16] The Elkhorn Valley must have suited his predecessors too, for bird points and other worked flint belonging to dwellers in the Elkhorn bottom turned up each spring in the blue clods of newly plowed ground.

By the banks of Elkhorn, his slaves built a sturdy oak log cabin that many later regarded as Innes Station. The original cabin reflected the typical building pattern of the time, one and a half stories built on a stone foundation. The stone suggested permanency, something more than a temporary convenience. Later, he added improvements, including a storeroom, basement, and an additional wing, covering the logs with clapboard. Intending to defend his property, he had beveled portholes cut, through which a flintlock could be fired. The cabin consisted of two rooms with a hall below and two rooms above.[17] From the abundant timber on his property he selected rot-resistant oak for the logs. The chinking consisted of sand and lime mortar. The storeroom and basement he added at the east end, a frame wing on the west side with clapboarding.[18] Innes Station became one of several forts—places of refuge and defense—built outside the capital in the county, giving settlers confidence that they could claim the property they owned with relative safety.[19] The cabin he built remained essentially intact though neglected until 1961, when a fire gutted most of the original structure.

As Indian troubles increased, Innes must have worried about the safety of his family. His house stood conspicuously by the creek banks, situated as it was in the Elkhorn Valley with few other homesteads to distract passersby. After the adoption of the U.S. Constitution in 1787, the judge became an official voice for conditions on the frontier and shared his concerns with other representatives of the new government as well as contacts he had in Virginia counties to the east. Part of his unofficial duties became keeping tabs on Indian depredations in the backcountry, and he must have been relieved when President Washington's secretary of war, Henry Knox, authorized him to call out scouts to protect the frontier. The judge wrote Knox that, since 1783, he estimated that fifteen hundred people had been killed or captured and that more than twenty thousand horses had been stolen.[20] As might be imagined, settlers on the frontier highly prized their horses as necessities for work, transportation, and, ultimately, survival. Fleet horses served as primary engines of defense during a time when Kentucky became an armyless battleground in which the hit-or-miss tactics of small parties of Indians took a steady toll on isolated settlements and cabins throughout the region. Some few, like the raiding party that was to attack the Innes and Cook settlements, played a larger, more strategic role.[21] As the number of deaths owing to Indians mounted, Innes and his neighbors had no option but to go about their lives under a constant threat of attack. Though Virginia made some token efforts to protect its westernmost citizens, Innes had to rely finally on his neighbors, who formed a combination of neighborhood watch and impromptu militia to protect his large family.

Beyond building the cabin that became known as Innes Station, the judge's slaves played an important role in the history of life along Elkhorn Creek. It is difficult to determine precisely how many slaves Innes owned in Kentucky because the British army destroyed the census records for 1790, 1800, and 1810 when they burned Washington during the War of 1812. Surviving records indicate that on November 13, 1779, Innes, still in Bedford County, Virginia, purchased a slave named Peter for eight thousand pounds of tobacco, probably at Williamsburg. We know Peter accompanied Innes when he came to Kentucky in 1783 because of the ordeal the man experienced as a captive among the Indians, part of the same band that attacked and killed the Cook brothers in April of 1792. At the time of the ambush, less than a year after the cabin had been built, Innes owned at least three slaves of whom there is any mention, but there were probably others. Ironically, Innes lobbied long and early for Kentucky's need for protection against the tribes that increasingly resisted the invasion of their homeland and the depletion of its wild game, ironic because the lack of protection cost him and his own neighborhood dearly. Less than a year after building his station, his personal interests suffered from Virginia's lack of political will or ability to protect its remotest citizens.

We also know that during the attack of 1792, Indians captured Peter on Innes's property at what in 1886 was known as the Holt farm (where I presently live).[22] One account states that members of the raiding party captured Peter and an unnamed companion as they chopped firewood. They gratuitously murdered Peter's unnamed companion on their journey north when he made some indication that he could read: "The unfortunate man picked up a slip of paper at one of their halts on the journey, and being able to read to some extent was spelling out the words printed upon the paper when one of the Indians said to Peter, 'Him read pape [sic],' stepped behind the negro and buried his tomahawk in his brain."[23] His death may have resulted from superstition, the ability to extract meaning from so many paw prints on a smooth surface interpreted by preliterates as a fearful demonstration of the magic to communicate with the dark powers without speaking.

Peter's story had a more fortunate outcome. Because his skin was a "bright copper color," the Indians took a fancy to him and adopted him into the tribe. His captors later confided to him that several times they had drawn a bead on him when he was cutting wood with the intention of killing him, but each time he had jumped down from the log he was chopping, preventing them from firing accurately. Persuaded that he was meant to live, they decided instead to take him with them.

During his captivity of six years, the Indians schooled Peter in wood-craft and tried to bring him to adopt their way of life, but he harbored a fear of being unceremoniously tomahawked, as his literate companion had been, especially during the drunken revels following their trips to the English trading posts for whiskey. Despondent and homesick, he constantly looked for a way to escape and find his way back to the settlements. On one occasion an Indian gave him a tomahawk and told him to kill a rattlesnake that coiled on the trail. Despairing of making his escape, he placed his foot near the snake, hoping its bite would put him out of his misery. The snake, however, seemed too sluggish to strike, and Peter felt obliged to chop off its head, winning the approval of his captors.

Two conflicting accounts of Peter's escape come down to us, one necessarily false. The first—the less likely—parallels the famous escape of Daniel Boone from the Shawnees during the winter of 1778. Gradually, as in Boone's case, Peter gained the confidence of his captors, who permitted him to hunt on his own—away from their village. Exploiting the opportunity, he ran away, losing himself in the woods. According to this account, being less schooled in woodlore than Boone, he wandered around the wilderness for weeks, finally managing to cross the Ohio River and make it back to the home of his master. When he hobbled into the dooryard at Innes Station, no one at first recognized him. We can only imagine him, his hair wildly tangled, his body scrawny, his skin caked with dirt and striped with lacerations from the underbrush. He could hardly speak, having neither heard nor spoken any English for the better part of six years. Like Rip Van Winkle, his children had grown to adult-hood with only a vague memory of their father.[24]

The second account appears more plausible—more detailed, more realistic, and ultimately verifiable. As in the first scenario, Peter accompa-nied the raiding party north across the Ohio and was held prisoner in one of the Indian towns for six years, freed finally through the "instrumental-ity" of Senator John Brown, who somehow induced the Indian chiefs to bring him when they visited "the Great Father" in Washington. From the capitol, Brown or other interested parties sent Peter home to the Innes farm. The piece in which this account appeared stated that Peter had a number of grandchildren and great-grandchildren living in "this section" in 1886.[25] Harry Innes Todd, the judge's grandson, found the bill of sale for Peter's purchase among Innes's papers after his death.[26]

What happened to the other members of the Innes household? At the time of the attack on Innes Station in 1791, Harry Innes had the good fortune to be elsewhere, probably on business as part of his judicial or civic duties. Details of the attack are sketchy, eclipsed by the more dramatic account of the Cook Massacre a mile or so upstream. Some of the Wyandottes apparently surrounded the Innes cabin, killing one slave who was sick and bedridden. The attack, occurring at approximately the same time as that on the Cook cabins, was the last large-scale Indian foray into Franklin County from the north. The trail down which the marauding party came is now known as Indian Gap Road. This trail wound between the ridges that look down on the valley near Peaks Mill eight miles or so from the Innes and Cook settlements.[27] One can deduce that the Innes place lay on their line of march to the Cook cabins a mile or farther upstream. The raiding party also captured Innes's overseer, Ambrose White, taking him prisoner on the trail near present-day Stedmantown as he returned from Virginia with a load of powder. As with Peter, the raiders took him far north of the Ohio, into the Wyandotte villages in the Great Lakes country. Adopted by the tribe, he lived among his captors until able to escape nearly two years later.[28] Where Innes's wife and daughters were is unclear—whether, like the Cook women, they survived the attack by taking refuge inside the station or whether, more likely, they were away, with or without the judge.[29] Most references to this side event suggest that the raiders attacked the station and that it was successfully defended. One wonders by whom.

It is easy to assume that the station and the Innes residence were the same, but it's also possible that one or the other stood at another site, and there is authority to support that view. Most of those of who have considered the matter believe that Innes located his house—which many also regard as the site of his station—in a low divide between two deserted meanders of Main Elkhorn Creek four or five miles northeast of Frankfort. Authorities, however, dispute its precise whereabouts. Nancy O'Malley, an archaeologist at the University of Kentucky, acknowledges the discrepancy in her study of frontier stations, *Stockading Up*: "Two possible locations for the Innes Station were identified. According to

Jillson's location the site is on a divide between two abandoned meanders of Elkhorn Creek. This description places it north of Peak's Mill Pike
where it crosses Innes Bottoms. A road [Holt Lane] diverges from Peak's
Mill Pike and runs north across the divide to a low area which contains
one of the abandoned meanders. This location agrees with Morton's 1908
map, Darnell's 1946 map, and fits the descriptions of Thomas (1939), Cole-
man (1967), and Lewis (1921)."[30]

My own belief, confirmed by archaeologist Nancy O'Malley, places the
station, or at least a very early building on the Innes property, at what
Jillson referred to as the uplands of the Bradburn farm (originally Innes
property, then Holt, then Bradburn, then Saufley land) on Holt Lane about
two hundred yards or so north of the Holt house.[31] This agrees with the
earlier account of two slaves chopping wood in the yard of what became
the Holt house when the Wyandotte raiding party captured them. If they
were cutting wood for the station on Elkhorn Creek, it made little sense
for them to come so far when woods with suitable firewood blanketed
most of the area in 1792 and the creekside house was nearly a mile away.
Common sense would suggest they cut wood to be burned in a nearby
structure, such as the one O'Malley and Jillson describe. The previous
owner of the Holt farm—part of the original Innes property—Zack Saufley, told me that he had taken down a structure at the site. He mentioned
some stone, though I can't remember whether he meant a stone building
or simply a stone foundation, and he is not alive to confirm or deny it. This
would have probably been in the 1960s since he purchased the property at
the beginning of that decade. Though the field mostly lay fallow after 1975
when I bought adjacent property, occasionally Zack Saufley would plant
the field in corn or perhaps tobacco, the latter despite the injunction of
former owner James A. Holt never to sully the richness of his farm with
extractive tobacco. To prepare the ground, Saufley had it plowed. On at
least two occasions I found shards of pottery, dishware, and bits of rusted
metal turned up by the plowshare.

More conventional local tradition places the house or station south of
Peaks Mill Road on Elkhorn. At the creekside site stands a very old stone
springhouse near which Henry Clay, the Great Compromiser, reputedly
delivered a speech at a political rally in the early decades of the nineteenth
century. We know that most settlers built their houses close to a reliable
water source, almost all springs, a stream like Elkhorn or a spring like

the one a short distance away. On Innes's property a squat springhouse, constructed of hewn limestone, was possibly built later because the finished quality of the masonry indicates more refined workmanship, not a structure erected for simple convenience. To devote that much care and attention to a springhouse suggests available labor and a leisure that the early years could not afford. At any rate, the spring would have provided an ideal source of water to supply a homestead or fortified house. The site of the stockade opened into a wide, abandoned meander of Elkhorn, sheltered from the north by a high, timbered bluff that I can see out my window as I write. The soils in the lowland, though soggy in some places during periods of rain, are fertile and easily accessible.

Though safety on the frontier was a persistent concern until the Battle of Fallen Timbers in 1794, when the Indian menace in Kentucky slacked off, Indians were not Innes's sole preoccupation. During his professional life he never strayed far from the arena of politics. The new nation in postcolonial America experimented with federal courts, especially in the West. Understandably, westerners distrusted a strong central power, and many on the frontier had left the East to escape the long hand of any government, with exceptions for local militias and other efforts consisting of people they knew, their neighbors and their neighbors' neighbors. What they wanted from government and too often lacked was protection from Indians, a way to get their agricultural surplus to market, and the means to convert wilderness to farmland.[32] What they received was an ill-conceived whiskey tax to fuel a debt-ridden federal government, an imposition on their freedom and resources that resulted in the Whiskey Rebellion. Citizens and farmers living in the Kentucky District felt fortunate to get Harry Innes as their federal judge, a man who identified with them, though a little better informed and educated. People generally trusted him, and he generally deserved that trust. According to one often overly generous historian, Innes was a fair, evenhanded judge: "he was patient to hear, diligent to investigate, and impartial to decide."[33] During his judgeship, he treaded a razor-thin wire between upholding federal law and serving the best interests of his constituents. He served the public interest in his fair settling of land disputes. Though an appointee of Washington's Federalist administration, he was at heart a Jeffersonian Republican, willing to overlook the imposition of an unjust tax on whiskey and anxious to promote the economic interests of the region. His accomplishments included organizing the federal court, promulgating rules, and swearing in qualified applicants to the bar. He convened grand juries when needed and presided over trials, at the same time "serenely ignoring" the strictures of the federal taxes on distilling. Interestingly, many of the distillers who left Pennsylvania to escape enforcement settled in Kentucky, imparting new life to the distilling industry in a corn-based beverage called bourbon.

Two portraits of Judge Harry Innes survive. Both are painted by Jouett. One of the portraits was said to have been copied from the other, a request of his grandson Harry Innes Todd. Jouett's portrait arrests the judge in late middle age. From a somber background stares a respectable countenance whose dominant feature is dark, appraising eyes that look as though they see little that surprise him. Portly, nearly bald, with a long, sharp nose, he wears a dark frock coat set off by a startlingly white cravat. One senses that Harry Innes seldom strayed from his dignified persona as judge, leading citizen, large landowner—an important man in frontier Kentucky as it inched slowly but steadily toward statehood. What the portrait couldn't tell you was that he was of medium height, suffered perennially from asthma, and stuttered when he was excited or under pressure.[34] Nor did it catch the vibrations of his temperament, which one writer has attempted to portray: "Innes had a capacity for justifying whatever he wanted to do to his own satisfaction and that of almost everyone else, mixing indignation and propriety in convincing measures whenever his activities were questioned. He liked comfort and was seldom inclined to work harder than necessary to achieve it; later, when he was a judge, Humphrey Marshall heard him 'vow to God, he would never take the responsibility of finding facts in a chancery suit upon himself.' Like other members of the district court, he was a planter at heart."[35] None of this reflects greatly on the soundness of his decisions, and self-justification seems a quality that is standard to judicial temperament and goes along with rendering decisions that affect the lives of litigants.

The two individuals who exerted the greatest influence on the career of Harry Innes, both ultimately for ill, were General James Wilkinson and Humphrey Marshall. The first was a tempter, the second a slanderer and would-be nemesis. Soldier, physician, entrepreneur, opportunist, intriguer, and founder of Frankfort, General James Wilkinson (1757–1825) was an actor who performed many parts. Savvy and opportunistic, he

Judge Harry Innes (1752–1816). (Painting by Matthew
Jouett. Courtesy of the Speed Art Museum, Louisville,
Kentucky.)

played a hand in every available game. The man possessed an excess of
ambition and charisma, two qualities that would eventually undo him.
His charm aided him in rising through the military hierarchy during the
American Revolution, serving on the staffs of several generals. In 1791,
after the war, President General Washington appointed him command-
ing general of the army. He and his wife, Ann, joined the tide of land
seekers immigrating to Kentucky after the war. His dream was to repair
his wrecked fortunes and build a commercial empire. Credited as the
founder of Frankfort, Kentucky's capital, he laid out and named its main
streets—tellingly after himself, his wife, and other generals (St. Clair,
Montgomery, Washington) of the Revolution. He also participated in the
statehood conventions preparatory for Kentucky becoming a state.

Innes must have met Wilkinson either in Danville or soon after arriving in Frankfort. At this time land fever in Kentucky spread like a con-
tagion, and soon the judge himself ambitiously speculated in real estate
when he wasn't settling disputes of rival claimants before the bar. Innes's

General James Wilkinson (1757–1825). (Engraving by Charles Balthazar
Julien Févret de Saint-Mémin. Courtesy of the Library of Congress.)

proximity to Frankfort permitted him to lead a double life, becoming
active along with Wilkinson in developing the little town on the Kentucky River as capital of the state. He involved himself in building and
other civil enterprises in the new state capital while he raised a family on
the banks of the Elkhorn and as he carved a farm out of the nearly pristine landscape. Perhaps Innes saw in Wilkinson a way to his own fortune.
They had a close association for at least twenty years. Perhaps too close.
Wilkinson not only promoted his own goals, but also played an important
role in shaping Harry Innes's destiny.

Wilkinson laid out the town of Frankfort, mostly on land he owned,
hiring Harry Innes beginning as early as 1789 as his "attorney in fact"
and his confidant, the ideal person to negotiate and formalize his many
land deals. Innes put advertisements in the local papers for the sale of
Frankfort's first city lots. As Wilkinson's attorney, he sold a large portion of downtown Frankfort to Lexington businessman Andrew Holmes
for thirty thousand pounds of tobacco—tobacco serving as a medium of

exchange due to the scarcity of currency.[36] In August of 1792, Holmes, engaging Innes, donated the property on which the state's first capitol was to be built. Holmes practiced this stratagem as a means of inducing commissioners to select Frankfort over other cities. Borrowing Holmes's idea of donating land now to benefit the community in the long term, Innes himself donated two lots to Kentucky's second governor, James Garrard (1749–1822), to build the state penitentiary across the street from the newly constructed governor's mansion on High Street. Harry Innes became a trustee and oversaw the building of a "Penitentiary House" with walls high enough to prevent escapes.[37] One of the benefits that local landowners received was the hiring out of prisoners for labor. The record does not show whether Innes availed himself of the cheap labor, but he likely did. The penitentiary across from the old governor's mansion was the primary site of Kentucky's state prison until the flood of 1937 forced its demolition and a relocation in Eddyville.

Wilkinson, as is now clearly known, did not always work to advance the public good. Always with an eye on the dollar and aggrandizement, Wilkinson the entrepreneur foresaw a fortune in opening the Mississippi River to markets to the south, especially New Orleans, which until 1803 was under Spanish rule. The Spanish controlled a vast expanse of territory west of the Mississippi, including New Orleans, a vital market downriver for agricultural goods from Kentucky. In a time when roads were either crude or nonexistent, water offered a ready means to transport goods. No one acted on this insight more forcefully than Wilkinson, who did not let scruples prevent him from realizing his conspiratorial goals. He enlisted anyone whom he thought could advance his interests. Now a major western power broker, he envisioned an eventual bonanza for himself and his supporters. Wilkinson entered into a secret agreement with Spanish official Esteban Miró to represent Spanish interests in Kentucky. For his efforts in promoting Spanish interests, Wilkinson received secret payments that then, as today, would be recognized as treasonable, though Kentucky had not yet entered the Union as an independent entity and its relationship with Virginia was growing tenuous enough to place its future in limbo. Quickly grasping the benefits to Spain's interests, Miró agreed to accept Kentucky agricultural products in New Orleans, everything from flour and hams to whiskey, especially goods that would not perish easily. Wilkinson audaciously named a Frankfort street for Miró, though the

Humphrey Marshall (1760–1841). (Courtesy of the
Kentucky Historical Society, Frankfort, Kentucky.)

spelling was corrupted into Mero. Frankfort has the distinction of being a
capital whose founder named a street in honor of the foreign agent with
whom he was colluding to establish his own empire. Profitable as this
arrangement was to be for all parties, a cloud began to form over Wilkinson's involvement with the Spanish, many believing that he wished not
only to separate Kentucky from Virginia but from the Union. His and the
efforts of a few others have been referred to as the Spanish Conspiracy.

If the courtroom served as a forum to settle disputes among adversaries, political conflicts complicated Innes's life more personally in other
forms on other fronts. The great nemesis of Harry Innes's life became
the Federalist partisan Humphrey Marshall (1760–1841), one of the most
controversial and colorful citizens of early Kentucky. Born in Virginia to
a political family, Marshall served in a regiment of artillery during the
American Revolution and moved, like Innes, to the Kentucky District
of Virginia, where he quickly accumulated wealth as a farmer and deputy surveyor of Fayette County. In addition to claiming four thousand

acres granted him as a veteran, he began acquiring property unclaimed in recorded plats and became one of Kentucky's wealthiest citizens.

Humphrey Marshall's antipathy for Harry Innes initially grew out of politics. Like Innes, he participated in the Kentucky conventions for statehood. An ardent Federalist in a state where most citizens identified themselves as Jeffersonian Republicans, his neighbors elected him to a seat in the newly constituted state legislature and then to the U.S. Senate in 1794. Though his federalist principles cost him his senate seat, he served additional terms in the state legislature, fighting a duel with Henry Clay in which both men were wounded, neither fatally, though Clay suffered a limp for the rest of his life. Never reluctant to express his opinions, he insisted on his voice being heard in the shaping of Kentucky and its relations to the fledgling Republic. Unlike most Kentuckians, Marshall opposed separation from Virginia. When both Innes and Marshall settled at Frankfort, they exchanged vituperative attacks through their respective partisan newspapers. Often Marshall's jeremiads in the newspapers appeared under the name of Coriolanus, the Roman hero of Shakespeare's political tragedy. Writing under the pseudonym of "Farmer," Innes dismissed his Federalist critic in the *Kentucky Gazette* as early as 1792: "If he was a man of character, I would adopt proper measures to punish him for insolence . . . but as Coriolanus is that abandoned man Humphrey Marshall, of Woodford County, I shall take no further notice of him."[38]

The personal feud between Marshall and Innes began in the years preceding statehood, perhaps when Marshall was initially blackballed from the Political Club in Danville, the group of movers and shakers who supported separation from Virginia and served as a clearing house for ideas to promote the western country. The feud lasted nearly two decades. Though he was acknowledged as brilliant, Marshall must have been distrusted as a political outsider. From the outset, Marshall was suspicious of Wilkinson and his plan to secure free navigation of the Mississippi and maybe withdraw from the Union. Marshall tried to implicate several prominent Kentuckians, including Innes and Judge Benjamin Sebastian, in Wilkinson's scheme to remove Kentucky from the Union and into an alliance with Spain. Writing under his pseudonym of Coriolanus in Frankfort's *Western Argus*, Marshall also accused Innes of receiving funds from Spain. Despite legal and societal bans against dueling, Innes must have many times considered challenging his adversary. Weighing the fallout and risk, he must have opted for a judicious restraint. A legislative investigation finally forced Judge Sebastian to resign from the bench when it was revealed that he was receiving a pension from Spain. Intrigue has its costs.

The last and most challenging case of Innes's life took place in 1805. Causing seismic disruptions, the case was tied to the contest to convict a former U.S. vice president of treason. After killing Alexander Hamilton in a duel in 1804, Aaron Burr (1756–1836) was forced by public censure to resign as Thomas Jefferson's vice president. Facing ostracism in the East and a charge of murder in New York, he came to the West in 1805, organizing a plan, commonly known as the Burr Conspiracy, to lead an expeditionary force and establish an empire in the Southwest Territory. Joseph Hamilton Daviess, the federal district attorney for Kentucky, a staunch Federalist who adopted the Hamilton middle name to honor his hero, brought charges against Burr, claiming that he intrigued with the Spanish and planned to establish an empire in the Southwest Territory. Daviess was also Marshall's brother-in-law and doubtless shared many of the political views of his vituperative in-law. Contrary to customary legal practice, Daviess submitted a deposition of his own, charging that Burr was "now engaged in preparing, and setting on foot, and in providing and preparing the means for a military expedition and enterprise . . . making war on the subjects of the King of Spain."[39]

As federal district judge for Kentucky, Harry Innes had jurisdiction and presided over the trial. Bringing the disputants together must have been touchy for him because he knew all the parties and was privy to more about the efforts to create an independent entity than he could publicly admit. Concerned about the unusual nature of the proceedings and the requirements of due process, he moved cautiously. In a written opinion Innes dismissed the proceedings, saying that Daviess's beliefs were no substitute for incriminating legal evidence.[40] Burr was in the court to hear Innes's statement and must have felt tremendous relief because much of what Daviess accused him of was true, though as yet no criminal action had been performed. Subsequent efforts to convict Burr of treason must have embarrassed Innes since such persistence called into question his judgment—and perhaps his connection to the secessionists, some of whom were his close friends and associates, including James Wilkinson, whose polished armor was beginning to show some tarnish.

Prosecutor Daviess elected to convene a grand jury. When it met, Daviess said he could not prefer an indictment because a key witness was absent. Forced to discharge the grand jury, Daviess later learned that his witness was back in the state and moved to impanel another grand jury. This grand jury met but did not issue an indictment against Burr. Burr's attorney, no less a defender than Henry Clay, made an impassioned argument for Burr's innocence and questioned Daviess's tactics in presenting himself to testify before the grand jury. The next day Daviess brought the indictment before the grand jury, and it found that the indictment was not a "true bill," pronouncing Burr innocent of any criminal acts. No longer on the hot seat, Innes must have been relieved; Burr's supporters were ecstatic. His friends in Frankfort held a ball for him to celebrate his victory. Because he had presided over the proceedings, it is doubtful that Innes attended, but it is likely many of his associates did.

As others have pointed out, all the parties were eventually vindicated. Judge Innes upheld the law by refusing to sacrifice due process and embarrassed himself when later trials revealed the depth of Burr's scheming. Clay served his client well, effectively warning against the misuse of public office by its servants. Daviess himself was vindicated because Burr was later charged with treason and tried. Burr was vindicated by Chief Justice John Marshall's strict interpretation of what constituted treason and the subsequent acquittal.[41]

The feud between Innes and Marshall continued. Pushed to the limit, Innes finally sued Marshall for defamation, and the parties did not settle the case until shortly before Innes's death in 1816. Oddly, this attempt at truce came at the end of Innes's life, after feuding for over twenty years. Perhaps Innes, older now and wiser, was trying to clear his accounts. Their agreement, a copy of which is found in the Innes files at the Kentucky Historical Society, is worth quoting for its quaintness: "Whereas Harry Innes and Humphrey Marshall have compromised the suit depending between them in the Mercer County Court: It is agreed that all matter and things of a personal nature which existed prior to the compromise shall be buried in oblivion between the parties. And they pledge themselves each to the other that they will not write or publish or cause to be written or published any matter or thing of and concerning the other which shall be disrespectful of the character of the other on any subject existing prior to the compromise. Witness our hands the 17th day of February 1816."[42] Essentially, the parties agreed to stop vilifying each other and to bury their differences in their longstanding feud. Here the matter should have ended.

But, true to his reputation, Marshall got the last word. After Innes's death, Marshall violated the agreement in his *History of Kentucky*, hitting below the belt since Innes was unable to defend his reputation from the grave. Mud-slinging in Kentucky is not a new phenomenon: "Nevertheless, to this day, it is a matter of doubt, whether the head or the heart of this man [Innes] is not to be pitied, censured, or despised. Some supposed him not only weak in reasoning, and in judgment, but corrupt and debased in principle; while others think, that the imbecility of his intellect, the prevalence of his vanity, and the importance of his office as criminal prosecutor, exposed him to flattery."[43]

Marshall's appraisal of Innes years after his death gives a taste of partisan venom, a denunciation that sought to poison Innes's legacy in print by impugning his judgment and character. Attacking his opponent when he was beyond defending himself, Marshall attempted to paint Innes with the same brush with which he had characterized Wilkinson, accusing Innes, in effect, of being a co-conspirator, an allegation that has never been proved. At worst, Innes failed to come forward with knowledge he possessed of the misdoings of others, perhaps thinking of the lawyer/client privilege that prevents an attorney from divulging what has passed in confidence between attorney and client. These spirited exchanges between partisans must have amused readers of the local papers during a time when politics offered diversion from the harsh world of work and worry, as it does today. Marshall believed Innes to have been close to the heart of the Burr Conspiracy. Innes believed that Marshall had played fast and loose with the law in his insatiable appetite for land. Both instigated attempts to have the other impeached from public office. Neither succeeded.

Though historians have cleared Innes of legal complicity in the Spanish Conspiracy, encrypted documents recovered from the Spanish Archives in Madrid long after his death established that he was a confidant of those who planned the conspiracy, Wilkinson being the most notable. Though Innes never fully entered Wilkinson's schemes, he knew them and maintained a lawyerly silence, even as many of Wilkinson's actions bordered on treason, acts that continued through his later involvement in the Burr

Conspiracy. Juries acquitted Wilkinson of all charges growing out of his activities in the Spanish and Burr conspiracies, but his questionable activities eventually put the general's name under a cloud.[44] Though always more circumspect, Harry Innes initially shared Wilkinson's desire for western autonomy, but he neither compromised his loyalty nor took what amounted to bribes. Although the Spanish government offered Innes a pension in its efforts to win the support of influential figures, he never accepted payments.[45]

In defense of a man whose names bears a whiff of scandal, it should be recognized that Innes did not have the benefit of historical hindsight. Life in the West was precarious and lacked the consistency of established agencies of government. In looking at all options, he was, as the good lawyer, examining every possibility, perhaps even hedging his bets. The new republic was itself a gamble. He perceived that his first loyalty was to his countrymen, his fellow westerners. He did his best to protect them from Indians, to settle their land disputes fairly, and to uphold the rule of law. History does not paint in black and white but in hues and shadows. There is much we cannot know because we cannot enter the minds of the actors except through the fragmentary accounts of what they said or did, both subject to qualification.

Busy as his civic and agrarian life must have been, the family had few available diversions other than outdoor activities, living as they did in a sparsely populated settlement four miles from Frankfort. Beyond records relating to his activities in the multiple conventions held to work out the details of statehood and official documents connected to his work and many civic commitments, we know few details of his daily life on Elkhorn Creek, which must have doubled both as a refuge and a place of relaxation for him as he oversaw the operation of farming operations and the upbringing of his large family.

Besides the Jouett portrait, two relics from Innes's belongings come down to us intact. One is a monstrous stone bathtub that measures about eight feet and has a cavity deep enough to drown a calf. It reposes, unused, in the basement of a house in Franklin County belonging to one of the judge's descendants and must have taken a half dozen burly tobacco cutters to move. The stone resembles soapstone, gray and smoothed, soft enough to carve. It seemed at first to consist of modeled clay, but molded clay of those dimensions would be extremely difficult to fire and easy to

Bathtub belonging to Harry Innes. (Photograph by Gene Burch.)

fracture. One end of it slopes like the mouth of a pitcher so that the bather could half recline. Some mystery enshrouds the tub itself, especially since only an undocumented family tradition holds that the judge or his family ever lowered their bodies into it to bathe and renew themselves. One other oddity is that it contains no drain, perhaps because it was too early for manufactured pipes.[46]

The second item also betokens Harry Innes's high station as a federal district judge in Kentucky, a jurist appointed by no less than President George Washington. It is a large stylized initial "I" that must have been mounted on his coach as a badge of his individual identity, his class, and his station. The only photograph I have seen suggests that someone skillfully worked brass into an ornate shape, perhaps a Frankfort jeweler or silversmith, or even a versatile blacksmith. The stylized letter has curlicues at top and bottom, giving it the appearance at first of an upper case Old English "t." As a practical matter, the elaborate lettering identified the owner of the coach and its occupant, as if to create an acronymic message: "Four Eyes" (i.e ., "It Is I, Innes"). The letter, fixed to the side of the judge's coach, also served an aesthetic purpose as well as representing a form of conspicuous consumption in the eighteenth century—before the term, but not the impulse, was created. As it rolled along the unpaved streets of Frankfort or bumped along the rougher country roads with their mud and gullies to stop at its destination, it stated, quite literally, "I am passing" or "I have arrived."

Written records are housed in a few libraries, such as the Kentucky Historical Society and the Filson Historical Society in Louisville. We can only attempt to reconstruct his daily life, to flesh out what is stated, what can reasonably be supposed. Where did he find relief from the political turmoil in Frankfort? Though Frankfort became the capital of the new commonwealth the year he married Ann Shiel, it consisted of little more than an assembly of crude cabins along muddy and untenanted streets. Town itself offered few amenities beyond visiting associates like the Browns and Wilkinsons. Closer to home, he must have cherished his house and family on Elkhorn as a refuge from courtroom cavils and political turbulence, especially after the threats of another Indian attack subsided.

Since there is no indication that the Inneses played musical instruments, they must have been deprived of music beyond their own voices except on special occasions when they found it in church, at funerals, or in the homes of Frankfort's elite. The Browns, it was well known, owned a piano. Beyond cockcrows and lowing cattle and birdsong, the sound that must have pulsed through the Inneses' sensibilities most reliably was the creek itself, ranging from a highwater rush like the sounds of wind passing through trees during a storm to the more soothing trickles of water negotiating the rocky shallows outside their open windows.

The farm offered him a much-needed diversion from the pressures of the times and the stresses of wielding power. It also gave him a physical outlet for stress since he was an active manager of his property. Reading must have offered him some relief from the dry legal documents that provided his livelihood. As a surviving book order from 1785 shows, he amassed an impressive library, ordering books from Manchester, England. As might be expected, the order contained standard legal treatises, law reports, and other law-related books—the backbone of his professional life. But, in addition, it contained works of contemporary fiction and poetry that might interest him and other members of the family, including works by Alexander Pope, Daniel Defoe, Henry Fielding, and Tobias Smollett as well as classics like *Aesop's Fables* and *Plutarch's Lives* in eight volumes.[47] One can imagine him sitting under a shade tree by Elkhorn amusing himself with Henry Fielding's *Tom Jones* or Laurence Sterne's *Tristram Shandy,* head full of fictions, ears full of the sounds of rushing water.

Another window into his less-public self is in his correspondence. For example, a letter from former president and political ally Thomas Jefferson survives in which the former governor endorsed the virtues of the shepherd dogs he was raising and offered Innes a pair out of friendship and to see the breed extended to the western country:

> Your information is correct that we possess here the genuine race of Shepherd dogs. I imported them from France about four years ago. They were selected for me by the Marquis Fayette, and I have endeavored to secure their preservation by giving them, always in pairs, to those who wished them. I have 4. Pair myself at different places, where I suffer no other dog to be, and there are others in the neighborhood. I have no doubt therefore that from some of these we can furnish a pair, or perhaps two, at any time when Judge Todd can send for them; he giving me some notice to seek out a litter in a proper state for traveling. There are so many applications for them that there are never any on hand, unless kept on purpose. Their extraordinary sagacity renders them extremely valuable, capable of being taught almost any duty that may be required of them, and the most anxious in the performance of that duty, the most watchful & faithful of all servants But they must be reasonably fed; and are the better for being attached to a master. If they are forced by neglect & hunger to prowl for themselves, their sagacity renders them the most destructive marauders imaginable. You will see your flock of sheep & hogs disappearing from day to day, without ever being able to detect them in it. They learn readily to go for the cows of an evening, or for the sheep, to drive up the chickens, ducks, turkies every one into their own house, to keep forbidden animals from the yard, all of themselves and at the proper hour, and are the most watchful house-dogs in the world. I shall be happy in an occasion of being useful to you by putting you in stock with them, and avail my self of this occasion of renewing to you the assurance of my high esteem and respect.[48]

No evidence has been found that Innes ever requested or received the dogs, though the Innes family had a history of dog lovers on the property.

To the east of the Innes house and its later incarnation as a planta-
tion-style mansion with a high portico, the Innes family placed its graveyard. It contained not only members of the family but, remarkably, some
of their slaves, perhaps the loyal Peter—and their dogs as well—an equally
unusual arrangement. The early markers have been replaced by newer
ones inscribed with names and dates from those still legible. One wonders if in fact the dogs' graves include a pair of shepherds that Thomas
Jefferson sent to the Innes farm. Not likely, since such a gift would have
excited some recorded publicity. Though Innes himself initially lay in
the family resting place, descendants reinterred him closer to his seat of
power in the scenic Frankfort Cemetery, not far from his contemporaries
Boone and Thomas Todd, as well as that later denizen of Elkhorn, artist
Paul Sawyier. The Innes gravesite presides over Frankfort on a high bluff
on a dogleg bend of the Kentucky River.

Thomas Jefferson's letter to Harry Innes acknowledges the parties'
mutual membership in the fraternity of agrarians who regarded farming
as the foundation of civilized and productive living—even if it relied on
brute labor performed by slaves. The letter also shows Jefferson's wide
reach as well as his acceptance of Innes as a fellow Virginian and peer.

The Kentucky Historical Society houses the surviving "Notebooks"
that belonged to Harry Innes. Filed in storage boxes, they contain a mis-
cellany of household accounts, business dealings, and incidental mental
notes as well as columns of expenditures and debts that in their fragmentary way flesh out his daily life on Elkhorn. As might be imagined,
many of his expenditures went for items associated with his wife and
children. A random look at his accounts reveals such items as knitting
needles, ladies' hats, a cravat, one funnel, one yard of gauze, one dozen
buttons, three yards of "broad, dark lace."[49] Not surprisingly, items associated with farming accounted for many of his purchases—for example, a
pair of hinges, "pop. [poplar] plank [ing]," and "X gallons of whiskey." The
notebooks also contain fuller notations relating to activities on the farm:
"I hauled all the corn home with my waggon and cart." Maybe he means
that he instructed others to haul the corn, but maybe not. Living on the
frontier required a variety of skills and did not always permit divisions
and classes of labor. The list of persons with whom he dealt contains a roll
call of prominent Kentuckians of the time: Green Clay, Elijah Craig, Isaac
Hite, Simon Kenton, Thomas Barbee, Isham Talbot, Hubbard Taylor, and

Christopher Greenup. Several have counties named for them. Though I didn't read every name, every accountant's entry, I did not encounter a single woman's name. Men dominated Innes's world, even if women undergirded that world and made it manageable and civilized. Occasionally, in the vein of *Heloise's Helpful Household Hints,* Innes steps out of his masculinity to enter the world of household remedies. One finds on the end page of one of the notebooks a testimonial and recipe for a stuffing or dubbin for leather in shoes and boots. His endorsement, one of the longest texts in the notebooks, reads as one might imagine an eighteenth-century sales pitch: "The New England fisherman [*sic*] find great benefit from serving their boots with the following composition; which excludes water, and preserves boots and shoes. The same advantages are applicable to the shoes of husbandmen. My shoes have been served with it constantly for seven years; and in no instance has it let in any water or dampness through the leather nor does it stiffen the thinnest calf leather. One pint of boiled linseed oil; half a pound of mutton suet; six ounces clean bees wax; four ounces rosin: melt and mix over a slow fire."[50]

Innes goes on to give precise instructions about preparing the leather, especially seams and the joining of the "soal" and upper leather. Clearly, he didn't trust others to perform this procedure: "I use a painter's brush for laying on the stuff." And he means "stuff" literally: "This stuffing fills the pores of the leather and excludes water."[51] As this recipe and its application indicate, Innes was exacting and thorough, traits that probably carried over to the courtroom. The notebooks function as his computer, his calendar, and data bank. They give us insights not so much into his professional life as a jurist but to his home and farm economies on Elkhorn.

Not all the entries are so practical or so sanguine. The following notation appears on a detached sheet in another of the notebooks: "1 negro girl purchased by my brother, 50." The line below it contains the notation, "1 iron gray Horse sent you by Mr. Todd," revealing that farm stock and slaves occupied similar mental spheres, interchangeably. We see an orderly man, a practical man, who kept careful accounts, starting before the Revolution and lasting until his death. At any given time, he could give a fairly accurate approximation of his monetary worth as well as his cash on hand. More officially, the notebooks also contain reports and summaries of all his cases, dating from 1785. The entries in the notebooks, which range in size from the palm of one's hand to a ten-pound ledger book, appear neatly in

Memd. Between the fruit garden and orchard, are four apple and other Trees,

Beginning at the So. Est. end,—

1 Quince	2 Peach	3 Do.
4 Cherry	5 Red Streak	
6 Golden Pippin	7 Red Streak	
8 Priestly Apple		

1st Row

Beginning at the So. Est. End,—

1 Red Streak

2 Do.

3 Do.

4 Seedling

5 Do.

6 Do.

7 Do.

8 Ralsdens Gennitins

9 Red Streaks

10 Seedling

11 Redstreaks

12&13 Seedling

14 Ralsdens Gennitins

15&16 Seedlings

17 Red Streak   18 Seedling

Other trees

Pound Pippin	Newark King Apples	Priestly Apple
Common Bennett	Bell Flower	
Golden Pippin	Queen Apples	Bans Summer Pear
Hughes Crab	Cheese Apples	Pearmain
Colo. Munhall's Pears	Codlin	
Hubbard Taylor's W. Pears	July Apple	
Gray Bennett		

Harry Innes's 1807 plans for an orchard on his Elkhorn property. *Gennitins* is a folk etymology, a corruption of "June-eating," meaning probably that the species ripened for eating in early summer. (Orchard Records, folder 9, box 1, Harry Innes Papers, Kentucky Historical Society.)

a schoolteacher's hand, measured with occasional flourishes and abbrevia-
tions. The ink has browned, as has the paper, though it contains a high rag
content, more durable than the standard anemic and highly acidic paper
used today, paper that would not hold up so well as his has done.

Innes, like many of his class and generation from the agrarian South,
took an active interest in matters agricultural. He had an abiding passion for horticulture, bringing slips of fruit trees and packets of seeds to
sow on his newly acquired property. He also had an appetite for learning
the best methods and economy of agriculture, ordering seeds of various
kinds from Europe, keeping himself informed of market prices for the
commodities in the seaboard states, and watching with interest the burgeoning development of the region.[52] Among his papers, one surviving
document sets forth his very specific plan in 1807 for an orchard on his
Elkhorn property. He probably selected a site for it on the higher ground
of his twelve hundred acres along one of the south-facing ridges and hillsides above the Elkhorn bottom. One of the storage boxes in the Harry
Innes Papers at the Kentucky Historical Society contains a meticulously
detailed plan of his orchard, the pride and practical application of any
serious farmer on the frontier. The memorandum is dated January 1, 1807.

Clearly, Innes took the project seriously, both in the specificity of his
plan and its breadth. Many varieties he lists are heirlooms no longer available today. Many derived from graftings of individual farmers, such as
Hubbard Taylor, one of the early settlers of Clark County, Kentucky. Ironically, the range of available tastes in apples especially was much wider
and more local than today's narrow and homogenous commercial varieties. Innes knew what he wanted and meant to have it. He, like many
amateur horticulturalists of the day, could identify not only individual
varieties by taste but the specific tree in his orchard from which a given
apple came. In the letters he wrote for the *Kentucky Gazette*, the first
paper west of the Alleghenies, relating to political issues separating the
Kentucky country from the mother state of Virginia, one is reminded that
he identified himself as "A Farmer."[53]

Vestiges of a similar old orchard and a few very old fruit trees survive
on my own property, though the chances are slim that any of the originals, planted over two hundred years ago, survive. In my sloping side
field not far from his grandson's house are a few old pear trees. The fruit
is hard and gnarly, bitter to the taste, all but inedible. The largest and

best preserved of the old fruit trees seems to have been dying for the for-ty-plus years I have known it, its top long ago a storm victim. Each year I expect it to simply withhold itself and give up the ghost. But each spring it still leafs and sends up life-seeking suckers. The scabby bark sheathing its punky core seems more dead than alive, but somehow it hangs on, a collar of weeds and shoots around its base, brittle limbs so low it's protected from mower blades. How long it has been hanging on is hard to estimate. But this pear tree and at least two others of similar girth might well be what remains of seedlings planted on the site of Innes's earlier orchard on upward-sloping land nearly a hundred feet above his creekside house. If they are his, Innes—"Farmer" in another sense—made a good choice of sites. Frost in the bottom is common; frost in the uplands more a rarity and thus less of a threat to budding fruit.

Harry Innes's blood and even his name lived on to a third generation through his only daughter by his second marriage, Maria Knox Innes. The year after Innes's death, in 1816, she married John Harris Todd, the son of Innes's "adopted" son Justice Thomas Todd. Over the duration of their careers the families remained close. In letters to his sons as they grew up, Thomas Todd often recommended that they seek the advice of "Uncle Innes."[54] These interwoven blood relationships between the Inneses and the Todds recall the story of one of my neighbors, who confessed that in digging up her family's genealogy in the library of the Kentucky Histor-ical Society she discovered its interconnectedness. "Richard," she joked, "I found that my family tree is a wreath." Such families intermarried in part because they sought their peers and, though they might not say it, found their choices among others of their class few.[55] One is reminded what one wag said despairingly of the highborn Todds—that even God himself was content to spell his name with one "d." Thomas Todd's asso-ciation with Harry Innes never hurt him. Recognizing that the West was growing, President Jefferson extended the judicial system, appointing Thomas Todd an associate justice of the Supreme Court in 1807, a posi-tion he held until his death.[56] After his first wife died in 1811, Todd mar-ried Lucy Payne Washington, the sister of Dolly Madison. Theirs was the first wedding performed in the East Room of the White House. When he died in 1826 after a long and spotless career, his family laid him to rest in the Innes graveyard, and he was later reinterred with his benefactor in the Frankfort Cemetery.[57]

Thanks to Matthew Harris Jouett we have a portrait of Maria painted in her youthful prime. Jouett had profited from the Innes family, securing several commissions from the Todds and Inneses to paint family members. As befitting a proud father and husband, the judge commissioned portraits of Maria, his only daughter by Ann, as well as Ann herself. Thirty years younger than her mother, Maria was arrestingly beautiful, with fashionable ringlets on her forehead and wearing a stylish high-waisted dress. She would turn heads in any crowd. The story goes that Jouett painted her portrait in trade for a white horse that the painter hitched to his carryall for transporting painting equipment.[58] When he set up shop in Lexington in 1816—the year of the judge's death—Jouett charged $50 a portrait, not an inconsiderable sum at the time.[59]

Maria Knox Innes had three children with John Harris Todd: Harry Innes Todd (1818–1891), Elizabeth Ann Todd (1820–1898), and Catherine L. Todd (1824–1895). The couple named their son Harry Innes Todd in honor of the judge. Maria met John J. Crittenden (1787–1863) as she was traveling in the procession that buried her husband John Harris Todd in 1824. Coincidentally, Crittenden was returning to Frankfort in a funeral procession after the death of his daughter Eugenia. Like Maria, Crittenden also had just lost his first spouse, Sarah O. Lee (1787–1824), Eugenia's mother. Two years later, Crittenden and Maria married. Their union produced two sons: Eugene Wilkinson Crittenden and John Jordan Crittenden Jr., who tragically died with General George Armstrong Custer and his command at the Little Bighorn in 1876.[60] Maria's youngest daughter with John Harris Todd, Catherine L. Todd, married Thomas Leonidas Crittenden (1819–1893), her stepfather's son, who was appointed consul to Liverpool by President Zachary Taylor and who later served as a general in the Union Army during the Civil War.[61] There were other Innes-Crittenden entanglements. In 1822, an Innes granddaughter, Ann Innes Morris (1799–1888), married the brother of John J. Crittenden, Robert (1799–1834), whom President James Monroe appointed first territorial governor of Arkansas.[62]

At his death in 1816, Harry Innes left a wife and grandchildren as well as property, real and personal—and human. The cause of his death isn't mentioned, but at sixty-four he had outlived many of his contemporaries. He died, for the time, well fixed. He made every effort to treat his children equitably. In his last testament he instructed his executor, John

Morris of Frankfort, who was the husband of his daughter Ann, to sell eleven hundred acres that he owned on Panther Creek in Ohio County to pay off his debts. Innes directed that the remaining funds be distributed equally among five heirs. Morris received one part. Another portion went to Samuel G. Adams of Richmond, Virginia, who had married Katherine Eliza. Thomas Casson Alexander of Stafford, Virginia, the husband of Elizabeth, was another heir. One daughter, Sally, the wife of Francis Thornton, predeceased Innes in 1807. Her share of the inheritance went to her son, Henry Innes Thornton. His youngest daughter, Maria Knox Innes, received the last part of these funds. The latter two were held in trust until each turned twenty-one or Maria married. He left the remainder of his estate to his wife, Ann. Innes also left slaves whom Maria was to inherit if she married before her mother died: "Sally and her children, George Lewis Alexander, and Fanny and any increase which may in the meantime accrue."[63] Innes emancipated Peter, the slave who had been captured and returned from Indian captivity, for his perseverance and loyalty. He also directed that Peter be provided with $20 to be "laid out in clothes." After the judge's death, when members of the family discovered that Peter could not care for himself comfortably, the executors of the estate, per the judge's instructions, made provision for maintenance until his death. He directed Morris to also make provisions for two other slaves, Isaac and Lucy, too old to be emancipated. He also ordered that if his wife as coexecutor of his estate elected to sell the farm, the one acre containing the family gravesite was to be excepted.

History places Harry Innes as a transitional figure, half in the untamed world of the frontier, half in the technocratic world that was emerging in Frankfort and dozens of other nascent townships in the West. The attack on the Innes settlement marked a transition from the dominance of the wild and ungovernable to the ascendance of civil society controlled by Euro-Americans settling in Kentucky. It meant the eradication of the hunting and gathering culture of the woodland tribes, so painfully evident in the ferocity of their resistance. Innes served as an architect in the formation of the state of Kentucky as well as in the emergence of a constitutional national government. He and thousands like him came to symbolize the doctrine of land ownership that transformed wilderness into thousands of freeholds and farmsteads in central Kentucky that thrived as an agricultural economy, fueled in part by slavery, supplanting the old cycles of nomadic hunting cultures that had formed its past. He witnessed two early attempts to draw the Kentucky country away from its eastern roots in the conspiracy for the West to secede and create an autocracy. If he was the first to bring the federal impress of law and order to the western country, he brought structure in carving a settled place from the wilderness along a segment of Elkhorn Creek.

Ann Shiel Innes outlived her husband by thirty-five years, dying May 12, 1851. One biographical account properly glorified her as "one of the pioneers of Kentucky" and "the pride of her State and an ornament to the country": "Her early days were spent in the wilderness, and yet in the society of such men as Clarke [George Rogers Clark], Wayne, Shelby, Scott, Boone, Henderson, Logan, Hart, Nicholas, Murray, Allen, Brecken-ridge, and all the great and heroic spirits of the West."[64] A local paper, the *Frankfort Commonwealth*, even more extravagantly praised her, wheeling in the standard clichés that project her reputation excessively beyond the human and into the realm of hopeless hyperbole:

> Her tenacious memory retained all she had seen, and she became the chronicler of her own times, and interwove her narrative with traditions of the past. Providence had been kind in all his dealings with her. He had blest her with a strong mind and constitution, and with great cheerfulness and courage. He had blessed her in her "basket and her store." He had blessed her in her children, and at last when the message came, having borne all the trials of a long and eventful life with heroic firmness, she died in the full communion and fellowship of the Presbyterian Church, of which she had been long an exemplary member.[65]

Ann Shiel Innes spent more time on Elkhorn than her ever-ambling husband, and as a widow was one of the few women who had a voice in the destiny of Elkhorn. Unlike the men who lived along its banks in the nineteenth century, Ann refused to desecrate the landscape by sell-ing timber. Why? What put Ann's stern expression in the portrait that Jouett painted? Hers would have been the woman's perspective to com-plement the male-centered and sometimes narrow interests of Elkhorn's male recorders, illuminating the feminine worlds as Dr. Lyman C. Draper and Reverend John D. Shane had included in their rich interviews of late survivors of the Kentucky frontier. Sadly, Ann's read on the austerity of life on the frontier, childbirth, sickness, the threat of marauding Indians we can only imagine and portray in platitudes. Too often Elkhorn speaks only in a masculine voice, lacking the testimony of perceptive women.

The creek itself, aside from increased but largely invisible pollution, changed little in its physical appearance during Innes's lifetime, though settlers cleared or thinned the timber along its banks that had stood undisturbed for millennia into pastures and farmsteads. Axmen chopped and toppled the valuable old growth stands along its course into the water and dragged it to the maws of sawmills or, more typically, simply burned it where it fell. To get a sense of what the Elkhorn Valley looked like in the early years of settlement, consider the specifics that George Hunter gives in his description of the farm of one of Innes's neighbors, B. S. Cox, whose property included the palisades that were within a mile or so of the Innes farm. This Cox was likely a member of the Cox family that intermarried a generation later with the family of a more visible neighbor, Ebenezer H. Stedman. Traveling from Frankfort, Hunter may have been attracted to the landscape because he was interested in acquiring the property. He described the area in his journal entry of September 29, 1802:

> The Land is beautifully situated on the river Elkhorn a few miles [more like twelve or so] from its junction with the Kentucky river. It contains four hundred acres of very rich land, near 100 acres cleared; has 50 clear acres of meadow in a rich bottom—Has a few Log houses or cabins built such as dwelling house, barn, stable, workshop (he is a Sadler) &c. Before the house is a gradual descent to the river & on the other side are prodigious high, steep, and romantic Cliffs at the foot of which, almost level with the bed of the river is a Salt lick or spring where the Salt water runs out of the bottom of Cliff between two horizontal strata of Limestone in small quantity, about as strong or rather stronger to the taste that the water of blue Licks.[66]

The reason for the visit was professional. Mrs. Cox was down with a "Deep consumption" and was not expected to survive the winter. The poor financial straits of the Coxes put them in imminent danger of losing the property. "I believe that if I was to order the Land to be sold now," Hunter concluded, "the shock would cause [Mrs. Cox's] immediate death."[67] The source of salt bears noting, but most surprising is how quickly the valley had been transformed to farmland. Hunter's description comes just ten years after the Wyandotte raiding party had terrorized the first settlers.

Generations came and went, a few retaining the land on which their forebears settled, starting a pattern of development and degradation that has continued for over two centuries. Though altered by dams and bridges, by villages and farmsteads, Elkhorn itself retained much of its pristine appearance as well as its customary autonomy, responding to rainfall and periods of drought as the region's primary drainage system. Beyond geographical features like the Backbone and the time-worn palisades a little farther upstream, little is left of the farmstead Innes loved and knew so intimately. The surviving hearth in the Palmore house would have seemed somehow familiar to him, though the structure around it would seem alien, another enigma in a world transformed and fraught with wonders.

If each of us has an emblem to identify us with the world, Innes's would be the tulip poplar that must have been prominent in the woods that honeycombed his property. Designated as the state tree, it's appropriate for Harry Innes to be associated with the tulip tree, as it was called, because of his efforts to usher Kentucky County into statehood. A fast-growing tree, its limbs rise in balanced tiers, the lower ones eventually giving way to new growth, shaping itself toward a loftier crown. Its grains are straight and thus easy for craftsmen and carpenters to work. Its four-lobed leaves are described as "squarish, firm, and lustrous," attributes that might be applied ideally to the judiciary.[68] Overall, its aura is virtue. Its presence among trees with uneven grains, gnarly bark, and less-gainly shapes accentuates its own impulse toward order. Highly valued, its wood built much of nineteenth-century America, vertical forest converted into studs and siding on houses, the building stuff of America's towns and cities. Somehow this tree, which Aristotle never saw, embodies the early Greek values of logos: order, symmetry, and balance. These apply in nature as well, ideally, as in one's character and judgment. The soul of judgment is rationality, a governing principle for any aspiring culture, especially one shaping itself on democratic values. I plant at least one each year in the field where I imagine Innes rooted his orchard. Someday I hope to walk in the shade of the most recent seedling. Its unfurling new growth throughout the summer, its flowering drawing honeybees, its healthy appearance becomes an emblem of harmony and communal health. It has a certain willowy quality in the upper limbs when the wind blows, some give. It does not lack dignity.

Frontier hero to some, conspirator to others, Harry Innes remains a shadowy figure in the state's history, dislocated and indistinct in the morning mist that hovers over what remains of his homestead on the Elkhorn. To my knowledge, there is no full-blown biography of Harry Innes. The person who appears to have studied him most closely and evenhandedly is historian Mary Tachau. Her assessment of him is balanced and, in the final measure, positive: "The records of the federal court in Kentucky reveal a man whose competence, conscientiousness, and devotion to the process made his court a respected institution in the life of his state. He may have reconciled his countrymen to the authority of a government that was at a distance and out of sight."[69] By most measures he was a Kentuckian first, an American second. Many Kentuckians understand and still hold that profession of allegiance.

Six

"Indian Raid." (From Colonel Frank Triplett, *Conquering the Wilderness* [New York, 1883].)

From their chosen hiding spots along the banks of the creek and behind a screen of trees, they primed their rifles—those that had them—and studied the two men in the field as though this was a lesson they could not fail to learn. One man, taller than the other, sat on a felled log in the shade of a giant sugar tree, wiping his brow with a dirty red rag. The other had been swinging his crooked knife on its stem in long sweeps against a wall of green as though he would bring the entire valley low. They supposed he was clearing the ground to plant corn. The cutter was stripped to his waist, his arms and back wet with his efforts. The sitter still wore his rough, cream-colored shirt. Behind him were a few bundles of bound stalks unlike any bundles any of them had yet seen. They would later discuss what was to be done with the bundles, what they could be used for, since they seemed worthless as fuel and did not look as though they would be agreeable to taste. Maybe they were to put on the cabins to keep out the rain. The two cabins were close by, but they were not concerned because they knew that neither contained more men but only two or three women busying themselves with the things that their women busied themselves with, the selfsame things their own wives busied themselves with, cleaning and mending and cooking and caring for children.

So as the sun rose higher, they concentrated on the men, whose long rifles were close by, as if they once had expected trouble but had somehow forgotten. Now one was collaring a sheep. The men held several of these animal prisoners in a pen that was close by. The pen had a gate from which one of the men had fetched the animal. The other was somehow shaving hair down to the wrinkled pink hide. They continued to watch, fascinated yet a little impatient as the time grew heavier. Others of their band, they knew, were choosing points from which to attack still other cabins in this small settlement, and they knew these men needed time to seek out their targets and secrete themselves. Everyone seemed confident that this raid would reflect well on all of them, one that would strike fear and reward each of them with things that would demonstrate their mettle—all they could carry, and if they were lucky, horses to carry still more. It would also win them honor in the eyes of those who stayed behind. The day, the time, the weather—all seemed perfect. The sounds of flowing water made it possible to inch so close the men could be heard talking in the way men at work talk, a desultory give and take broken by long pauses as they either worked or rested, both of them adopting the mood of water which knew no hurry, the ground about them an even balance of sunlight and shadow. Whatever they said made no sense to any of those who waited, though a few guessed at words they thought they knew or had heard among those people in one place or another. Though it was spring, there had been no rainfall for a week, and the dryness made it more difficult to move in silence, the trees creating a leafy chamber, like an enormous gourd, that contained all sound but the riffling from up the creek. Everything was still but the man in the field again with his crooked knife on its bent stem that resembled the long neck of a heron. So they watched, each pondering in his mind what might happen next, their rifles cocked, black powder dry, their senses honed to pick up anything out of the ordinary as they waited for the first shot that would be their signal.

THE COOK MASSACRE

The sorrows of maidens, wives, and mothers in the border wars of our colonial times, have furnished themes for the poet, the artist, and the novelist, but the reality of these scenes as described in the simple words of the local historians, often exceeds the most vivid dress in which imagination can clothe it.
—**William F. Fowler,** *Women on the American Frontier,* 1880

In a letter to John Brown dated December 7, 1787, Judge Harry Innes complained of the defenselessness of Kentucky from Indian depredations since 1783, the year in which he crossed the mountains into the Kentucky country from Virginia: "I have lately been endeavouring [*sic*] to make some estimation of the Persons killed & taken & the horses which have been stolen from this District since September 1783 to the present period, & I think without exageration [*sic*] the following Statement would bear the Test—Killed 300—Prisoners 50—Horses Stole 2000 say of the value of £10 each £20,000—in my last Letter I think I informed you particularly of the ravages of the Indians for about 3 weeks—4 Persons killed & 65 Horses taken, and this happened since you left us."[1]

Judge Innes's message was prophetic, because the Indian menace would soon take more immediate form in an attack in his neighborhood that affected him and his neighbors palpably. In 1792, the year that he had his cabin built on Elkhorn, a mile or so upstream in what is called Quinn's Bottom, Hosea and Jesse Cook and others erected cabins at what was to become Cook Station. The Cook brothers were sons of William Cook II and Margaret Jones and had immigrated to what was to become Franklin County from Henry County, Virginia. Hosea was born about 1769 in Pittsylvania County, Virginia, and Jesse about 1765 in Halifax County.

Cook settlement from a distance. (Photograph by Gene Burch.)

Jesse married Elizabeth Bohannon in 1785, and Hosea married Elizabeth Edrington in 1791. Both Elizabeths were called Betsy. Hosea's Betsy had a son, Hosea Jr., who was born several months after the attack, indicating that she was pregnant and showing at the time the attack occurred. Jesse and Betsy Bohannon Cook were the parents of William B. Cook (about seven at the time of the attack) and Seth (who would have been about six).[2] They built their cabins on a portion of a large grant of land awarded Robert Church for his services in the Revolution.[3]

Young and hopeful, the Cooks and other newcomers established their settlement by Elkhorn, a little below where the Stedman mill would operate forty years later on the opposite side of the creek. Clearing fields for planting and stockpiling logs with which to build their cabins, the brothers situated the settlement on crescent-shaped lowland about three miles below the Forks and twelve miles from the Kentucky River.[4] Their cabins were built about four hundred yards apart. Upstream, the small community at the Forks had a meeting house, located several miles south of the settlement where the South and North Elkhorn met. Others settling in the area included their brother-in-law Louis (sometimes spelled Lewis) Martin (sometimes appearing as Mastin), Lewis Bledsoe, William Dunn, and a man named Farmer. Dunn's wife, Margaret, was a sister of the Cook brothers. A single man named McAndré also resided in the settlement. Other sources indicate that a man lived with Bohannon, his wife, and child in the neighborhood.[5] Within some proximity was a cabin housing three of Harry Innes's slaves and their overseer, Ambrose White. More cabins rose closer, three or four hundred yards apart in a loose cluster in the woods for convenience and defense. Cane and undergrowth provided extra privacy and camouflage. Because so many of the inhabitants were related by blood or marriage, the settlement could almost be regarded as a family enclave.[6]

Estate inventories for Jesse and Hosea Cook and for Louis Martin provide a window into the daily lives of those living in the settlement. In comparison to the Inneses, the people of the Cook settlement were of relatively modest means. Yet some households contained slaves. Hosea Cook and Louis Martin each owned one "girl slave" who helped the women with their many chores. They appeared in the inventories along with livestock that included small herds of sheep, as well as a few horses, cows, and hogs. The settlers also grew flax to make clothing, as Hosea's estate inventory listed a flax wheel among his possessions. The appraiser, John McAndrew, probably the single man McAndré, also recorded one bedstead; a pair of saddlebags; two axes; one pail; one piggin; one pot; one Dutch oven; and six knives, forks, spoons, and tin plates belonging to Hosea's estate. The inventory of Jesse Cook's possessions included two beds, one bedstead table, one chest, five chairs, two pot hooks, a pot, a frying pan, a bell, and a hackle. Books were rare, but Jesse Cook and Louis Martin each owned a Bible.[7]

Isolated as they were, church membership offered one of the family's few social outlets. Many Cooks and their relatives joined the Forks of Elkhorn Baptist Church, established in 1788 by noted minister William Hickman, the first church in what would become Franklin County. At the time, its meetinghouse, the site for which shifted over the years, took root several miles south of the settlement close by the Forks. Records reveal that the church served as a vehicle of social discipline and control within the community. Early church minutes not only report reception of Cooks, Bohannons, Martins, and Jones into membership, their deaths and baptisms, but also dismissals and excommunications for misconduct. Others, including Jesse Cook's son Seth, for unknown reasons became dispirited with Forks of Elkhorn Church, requesting their own dismissal.[8]

Surviving cabins, Cook settlement. (Photograph by Gene Burch.)

The tragedy that occurred at Cook Station began with an ominous sign that may have triggered the attack. No one paid any special attention to a lone Indian who had passed through the settlement on horseback one cold winter night.[9]

As the Cooks and their neighbors prepared to put in their crops, clear the ground of trees, and split rails for fences, a party of about one hundred Indians made a simultaneous attack, firing from fallen trees and brush piles that had accumulated along the banks. One of the brothers was shearing sheep, the other looking on from a nearby stump. The first fell dead immediately, the other mortally wounded. Managing to drag himself to the cabin, he died before crossing the threshold. War cries followed the first shots, and most of the raiders probably went on to attack other cabins. The two Cook wives, who may have been washing clothes, rushed to one of the cabins, one of them dragging in the body of her dying husband. Inside were two children, belonging to each of the wives, as well as a slave child. They barred the puncheon door and discovered that they had only one firearm between them. Fortunately, no windows had been cut into the log walls, essentially creating a box with only the door as a means of entry or exit.

Attacking the cabin, the Indians fired at the door, but no bullets could penetrate it. They tried to chop it open, but the door was too stout.

Terrified by the thumping on their door, the two women inside tried to load the rifle. They had a patch with lead balls, but the balls were too large. While one poured in powder, the other reportedly bit a bullet in two and succeeded in loading the rifle. Through chinking in the cabin wall, they could see an Indian seated on a log by the dead Cook brother still outside the cabin. Working the barrel of the rifle between the logs, one aimed at the Indian and fired. Most accounts state that the Indian sprang high in the air and fell dead.

The death of their comrade infuriated the others, and two climbed onto the roof and touched firebrands to the shakes. One of the women climbed up to the loft, and the other handed up a pail of water with which she managed to douse the flames. Soon the Indians started another fire, and the besieged women ran out of water. Next, they threw a pan of milk that was on the fire. Casting about, one of them found some eggs that they broke in the bucket, again dampening the fire. Though proprieties of the time insisted on silence regarding such matters, the determined women probably filled the pan with their own water. Undaunted, the Indians touched another torch to the boards, finally burning a small hole in the roof. One of the women inside, even more desperate, pulled the bloody vest from her dead husband's body and thrust it into the smoldering hole.

When the first shots sounded, Louis Martin, in conversation with McAndré at his cabin, took a ball in his knee. As he hobbled toward his house, a second shot killed him. McAndré jumped on a horse and made his escape, carrying one of Martin's small children. After a half hour or so, the Indians realized they were running out of time because they knew McAndré would rally the whole settlement to come after them. Hearing the gunfire, William Dunn and two of his sons—one sixteen, the other nine—escaped to the woods and separated. The father escaped, but Indians discovered the two children and murdered them. Margaret Jones Cook, the mother of the Cook brothers and grandmother of the two Dunn children, apparently always disapproved of William thereafter because he ran to safety without making more of an effort to save his sons.[10] Bohannon, plowing at the time of the attack, was killed and his boy "lost." Long after the attack, bones suspected to be those of Bohannon's son were found in the area.[11] The Indians who attacked the other cabins had done their work and had run off. Some of the attacking party, their ears to the ground, may have heard hoofbeats of the relief party. Realizing that time worked against them, they dragged the fallen Indian to the creek and set him afloat in the current. One, who had climbed a nearby tree, fired a final shot at the upper part or gable end of the house, where one of the women was posted in the loft. The ball zipped near her head, passing through a hank of yarn hanging from the rooftree.

Still, the attack had taken its toll: the two Cooks, Louis Martin, the Dunn boys, Bohannon and his son, and eventually two of Innes's slaves. The raiders mercilessly butchered one of the Innes slaves, who lay sick in bed, taking the two remaining slaves prisoner. No one discovered Farmer's house, sequestered in a thick stand of woods, surrounded by cane and underwood. Elkhorn's current carried the body of the dead Indian down the creek, and eventually it lodged on a rock, which later came to be known as Indian Rock. Others called it Tomahawk Rock for its resemblance to the head of an oversized tomahawk. The outsized rock, half in the water, half out, lies a short distance downstream from Church's Grove near another rock, this one a high, craggy stone formation often painted by artist Paul Sawyier, from which some sources say another Indian had been shot, this one from the second story of a distant cabin, still standing, on the high ground near Church's Grove. Robert Church built the cabin in question. No nineteenth-century accounts that I have been able to find mention the shooting. The alleged incident seems conflated with the Indian shot from the Cook cabin a mile and a half upstream at the Cook settlement. If true, newspapers and local chroniclers would have made more of it. It would have derived from a written record of some kind. So far, I and better-informed researchers have not been able to find a published account of it. The shot would have been the work of a marksman since the high rock, also called Lover's Leap, stands at least 250 yards from the house, separated by a screen of trees that must have been even denser, perhaps impenetrably so, in pioneer times. Most firearms of the time were smoothbore, less accurate at a distance than rifled barrels. None of the many accounts of the Cook massacre mentions a report of an attack around the Church cabin.

Word of the attack spread quickly through the neighborhood and beyond. Daniel Trabue, a Revolutionary War veteran who lived twelve miles away and whose two sisters lived in the vicinity of the Forks, arrived the next morning in the aftermath of the massacre. Trabue and his brother

Stephen witnessed the effects of the "meschief" that had been done.[12] They saw bloody ground where the brothers fell, blood in the cabin where the second brother was dragged, and blood where the Indian had been slain. Trabue noted the black hole that had been burnt in the roof. When he arrived, he found the widows washing their husbands' bloody clothes. Still shaken, they told the brothers what had happened. After the Indians left, they had remained in the house about two hours until Colonel John Finney came to their assistance with a company of men. The women had been so terrified they hadn't cried for their husbands until they felt themselves safe: "The Mr. Cooks was buryed [sic] and the woman [women] was moved off to neigbor's [sic] about 2 miles."[13] As his rich narrative so amply testifies, Daniel Trabue probably had greater accuracy as a marksman than he did as a speller, a better witness than grammarian.

Going to the home of their brother-in-law, the brothers joined the party assembled to pursue the Indians. But the company could not "strike their Trail."[14] Trabue relates that the pursuit to find the fugitives failed because this smaller party of Indians cunningly lay low for a few days not far from the murders until the searchers gave up and returned to their homes. Only then did they slip off into the wilderness to the north toward the Ohio. Trabue must have learned this information from sixteen-year-old Jared Demint, who had been captured and managed to escape the raiders before they crossed the river and reached safer ground north of the Ohio. Lurking in the neighborhood and once spotting a large party of pursuers, the Indians had been afraid that in moving they would be discovered. According to Trabue via Demint, they had "hid themselves in the bushes."[15]

More than one early printed account of the massacre identified the Indians as Wyandotte, one of the tribes living in what would become Ohio but which was then a part of the amorphous Old Northwest Territory. Also known as Huron (French, ruffian, rustic), the Wendat (later called Wyandot or Wyandotte) originally lived in southern Ontario, but rival tribes of the Iroquois Confederacy drove them into northern Ohio, mainly in Wyandot, Marion, and Crawford counties. They had alliances with the Shawnees, who regarded them as "nephew" or "younger brother." The Wyandotte had formed an alliance with the French until 1740, when the first British traders ventured into the country. When the French pushed the British out, the Wyandotte again became friendly with the French until they were defeated by their British rivals during the French and Indian War. During the American Revolution they sided with the British and made incursions into the Kentucky country, including the siege of Bryan's Station and the disastrous defeat of Kentucky militia at the Battle of Blue Licks.

The retreating Wyandotte captured another person during the attack on the Cook and Innes settlements. They waylaid Harry Innes's overseer, returning from Virginia with a stock of gunpowder. Sensing something amiss or simply practicing caution, he must have hidden it somewhere before his capture. Despite his precaution, Indians intercepted him on the trail close to the Cook settlement, not far from what would become Stedmantown. He was forced to go north of the Ohio to the Wyandotte villages in the Great Lakes country. The Wyandotte adopted him, and he lived with them nearly two years before escaping and returning to the precious cache of powder and placing it in the proper hands.

In his *Historical Studies of Kentucky*, Lewis Collins notes that the alarm raised by the attack resulted in a pursuit party of a hundred or so men that chased the marauders back to the Ohio. Though most of the Indians crossed the river successfully, a party of pursuers overtook a small group that had lingered behind to steal some slaves and horses from another settlement. When the Indians came into sight, the whites fired and the hindmost Indian fell. When one of the whites imprudently rushed his horse through the tall grass to the spot where he went down, the wounded Indian rose and shot him through the heart. In trying to get away, the wounded Indian was also shot, the wide Ohio ending the pursuit.[16]

One of the surviving Betsys later said that she believed that the notorious border renegade who led the raiding party was Simon Girty. She claimed that she recognized his voice from having heard it during the brief and famous siege of Bryan's Station, when Girty tried to persuade the besieged inhabitants to surrender. If so, she must have had a remarkably retentive ear, for the encounter at Bryan's Station had occurred a decade earlier in 1782. Wyandotte were among the besieging force of Indians and British at Bryan's Station. Girty's earlier association with the Wyandotte, therefore, may have been the source of the rumor that he accompanied the party that raided the Cook and Innes settlements ten years later. Known as fierce warriors, the Wyandotte switched their allegiance to the British and raided along the frontier during the Revolution. In 1782, they

defeated a force led by Colonel William Crawford, a respected officer of
the Revolution who had come to destroy the Wyandotte town at Upper
Sandusky in Ohio. Simon Girty, who engineered the defeat of Kentucky
militia at Blue Licks several days later, accompanied them. They captured
Colonel Crawford and burned him at the stake despite his pleas to the
renegade Simon Girty to save his life.[17] No firm evidence confirms that
Girty in fact accompanied the Cook and Innes raiding party.

During the raid, Indians also captured sixteen-year-old Jared Demint,
who provided another perspective on the main pursuit. A descendant,
Leonna Jett Shyrock, recounted his story in 1916.[18] On the day of his capture, young Demint was making his way to the Innes settlement about
six miles from his home off what is now Versailles Road near Frankfort.
His sister had married one of the Cook brothers, and Jared had not seen
her since before she moved with her husband to Kentucky from "the Old
Dominion." Just after he crossed Elkhorn, about a mile below the Forks,
Indians shot his horse from under him. Then two dozen Indians sprang
from ambush, binding and gagging him. Knowing they would soon be
pursued, they rode toward Glenn's Creek, hiding in a cave so they could
escape after nightfall. The gag removed from his mouth, Demint began
to negotiate his escape. Since some of the Indians understood English,
he told them he knew where they could find some whiskey. Though suspicious, they let him lead them from the cover of the river valley to his
Uncle Easterday's distillery. When they arrived, they discovered that the
uncle was hosting twenty-five or so pursuers.

When the Indians spotted the horses, they decided to get away as
quickly as they could. Before leaving, however, they entered the stillhouse
and found two jugs of whiskey among the barrels. They also managed
to steal all the horses, and Jared knew that the pursuers had little hope
of overtaking the Indians without their mounts. Next morning the men
at the Easterdays' awoke, discovered their loss, and rushed to Frankfort,
where they mustered a large band to pursue the thieves. Since a trail so
pronounced was impossible to hide, the party caught up with the Indians
near a place called Eagle Creek, shooting and killing one of the war party.
The survivors dismounted and scattered in the woods, soon hidden by
the underbrush. Hiding during the next day to ambush any pursuers, the
Indians traveled at night and reached the Ohio River a day or two later at
dawn, fairly certain they had outdistanced the pursuit. Most of the band

wisely crossed the river, but the chief and some of his companions stayed behind to consume the whiskey. That night Jared easily made his escape, running all night with his hands still bound. A settler took him in, removing his bonds, and gave him some food. Then he tramped home, traveling mostly at night, reaching his uncle's exactly a week after he was expected to return from a day's visit to his sister. The family had been mourning his loss, certain he'd either been killed or captured. Only after his arrival did he learn that neighbors regarded his widowed sister as a heroic survivor.[19]

Because the sensational murders and the women's defense of their lives underwent so many retellings, new details kept creeping into the accounts, accumulating as the story was told and retold. Writers variously describe the slain Native American as a large Indian, a chief, a medicine man. Was the blood-soaked clothing of the dead Cook brother a jacket or a vest? Did the party fire the roof with arrows or torches? As mentioned previously, one later newspaper account even suggested that the white renegade Simon Girty led the party. Accounts of the women's heroism found their way into papers and books, including *Noble Deeds of American Women*, edited by J. Clement, based largely on the Abraham Cook version of the massacre.[20] Published in 1880, William W. Fowler's *American Women on the Frontier*, in a segment entitled "the Heroines of Innes Station," tells essentially the same story with only a little embellishment.[21] Into other narratives crept grandiloquent ornamentation with details intended to present one view or another of the incident, much in the way that anonymous folk ballads from the eighteenth century became collective expressions as individuals and generations interpreted events to fulfill a vision that suited them. Over time they evolved, sometimes in preposterous directions.

In the fall of 1837, forty-five years after the Cook Massacre, R. T. Dillard accompanied Reverend Abram Cook to visit the site where his brothers had been killed. The cabin he recognized had fallen, the field smothered in briars. He walked some distance around the site as if reliving the anguish he felt at losing his siblings. Toward the end of the visit he shared his feelings with Dillard. "I am standing within ten feet of the grave of my brothers," he said. Dillard considered that plowshares had often passed over their remains. Abram had arrived at the site within two hours of his brothers' deaths, and he recalled what he saw vividly. In 1843 when the account was printed, Abram Cook was still alive and preaching in neighboring Shelby County. He described a graveyard on a little knoll a few hundred feet from the two surviving cabins. It contained over thirty-five graves, some of them presumably the burying places of those massacred that spring morning.[22]

Legends lack hard edges. The accounts passed down through the survivors' families often attempt to enshrine memory and to shape the apocryphal and vague into historical fact. Biases and preferences of the teller inevitably adulterate and often embellish details of the actual events. The idea that the women broke eggs to dampen the fire and that they bit through lead bullets strains credulity, though desperation admittedly sparks the extraordinary and activates adrenaline. In most of the accounts, certain details perhaps unfairly demonize the Indians, who, after all, were defending the land they claimed from the unbidden encroachment of settlers whose superior numbers would ultimately destroy them and their way of life. Whatever the distortions, at least two of six or so cabins at the settlement site of the Cooks still survive as reminders that exceptional events occurred there in the year Kentucky became a state. One archaeologist from the Kentucky Heritage Council has said that one of two contains cut nails and could not for this reason have been built before 1810. Homes at the time that the Cook cabins went up would have contained earlier hand-forged nails—an anachronism, though it's possible the cut nails may have been added later. No one lives in either cabin, but they have sound tin roofs that in the short term should protect them from further deterioration.

When local historian Nettie Glenn visited the cabins in 1976, she described the site and condition of one of the remaining cabins, the one she identified with the massacre:

> It stands in remarkable good condition in a lush, green valley just above the creek. Its weather-beaten logs lay plumb, unmarked by decay or insects. When confronted with such a genuine, practically untouched link with the past, a nostalgic feeling for the rich challenge of pioneer life is likely to envelope you and the imagination almost becomes the real. Through the humid, noonday heat of the hazy summer's day came the incessant drone of insects, the call of song birds and the distant lowing of cattle. The gentle lapping of Elkhorn's sparkling waters upon the rock shore joined the

refrain, producing an almost mesmeric effect upon the listener. A party of Indians could have sneaked upon this homestead with comparative ease.[23]

Having changed little over the years, the area exudes a sense of pastoral timelessness. Passing it by kayak and spotting the cabins from the stream triggers an immediate sense of entering a time warp in which the Cook brothers are warming to the work, their wives tending children and washing clothes. The raiding party waits patiently under the cover of trees that surround the site. The sound of water flowing over rocks is constant, a medley of sounds English has no proper words to describe. This sound changes only in intensity as water levels change, and the channel is deep enough here that drought has not greatly drained it. Single sounds meld into a symphony, a mingling that resonates in a faltering tremolo. It requires a feat of imagination to visualize all this loveliness—the quietude, the mottling of shade and sunlight, the shimmering water—as a crime scene.

Seven

Stedman Mill. (Artist unknown. Courtesy of Mary Nash Cox.)

When Ebenezer glanced over at his young wife, the mother of his baby daughter, she was crying. Together, rumbling on the wagon seat, they had traveled over fifteen miles to the outer rim of the Bluegrass, from Georgetown to the Forks. Rolling into the village at dusk, the wheels cut little grooves in the mealy roadway. As they approached the covered bridge, Mary had her first look at the main stem of Elkhorn, a broad, silver stripe of water dwindling into ragged edges toward their new home. The water seemed to spill into the darkness like milk over the pewter lip of a pitcher.

What was the matter? She was homesick, afraid, yanked up with so little say-so from the family and friends she loved, removed from the familiar comforts of tight little Georgetown with its steeples and candle-lit sashes, now heading for a place in the backwoods of Franklin County to a mill she'd never seen and to a hovel her husband had bought on borrowed money and said little about except that she would come to love it. Not gifted with an abundance of words, Ebenezer seemed to sense her worry but did not know how to console her except to say that things would be all right, that the place was not the end of the world, but was only a few miles from the capital, after all. And that her people were not so far that they would never find the road to Mount Pleasant. To her, the name Mount Pleasant itself sounded suspicious, especially when she learned its center was the old meetinghouse while hers, such as it was, would be the broken-down mill and buildings on the fringes into which her husband and brother Sam believed they could breathe new life. Hearing her distress, baby Sophie woke up and began to bawl in sympathy, and Mary tried but failed to soothe her. It was as if Sophie, too, envisioned through the wisdom that was a part of her name, Sophy, Sophronia, Sophia, a future the others might not see.

They kept on along the wide dirt road and turned onto a narrow lane a mile or so after crossing the creek and passing a few houses that flanked the road. They followed its winding thread along the ridge over the Elkhorn Valley. Above their heads the dark mass of limbs seemed to clasp and blot out the sky. To their right, they could see rolling pasture that tilted finally into a bank of trees and sank into the hazy blueness of the valley. As the wide sky darkened, so it seemed did the trees, only their tops visible now, their invisible trunks lost in some deep folding of the hills.

When she spied the big cliff above Elkhorn, Mary sang out again, accusing Ebenezer of carrying her to the jumping off place of the earth, saying that the Forks were Satan's dinnerware and that little Sophie would grow up a wild Indian. Then they passed the cabin where brother Sam and his wife had set up housekeeping and went on until they reached the old frame house that she feared would be her life's great challenge. Unpainted and missing some weatherboards, it had bleached to an anemic gray. She noted a sag in the roofline she knew would never straighten, and some of the windows' panes were black. When she asked if this was where they would live and Ebenezer confirmed that it was, she raised her complaint. She had sighted desolation, and it had touched her. No fence around the ramshackle house, only three old locust trees in the yard with ridges of rough bark uninviting to the touch. No fruit trees, not even a garden plot. After a while, Sam's wife, Kate, came over to console her, taking her into the cabin where she and Sam lived. Here Mary berated Ebenezer and Sam for bringing them to this God-forsaken place, protesting that she and Kate were accustomed to society and the busyness of town and could not endure a life of thistles and thorns, a future of wildness and desolation in the mountains.

MILLTOWN ON THE ELKHORN

The Elkhorn lands are much esteemed, being situated in a bend of Kentucke River, of great extent, in which this little river, or rather large creek, rises. Here find mostly first rate land, and near the Kentucky River second and third rate. This great tract is beautifully situated, covered with cane, wild rye, and clover; and many of the streams afford fine millsites.
—**John Filson,** *The Discovery and Settlement of Kentucke,* 1784.

Hear on this Beautiful Stream was made the first Sheet of paper in the Great West.
—**Ebenezer Stedman,** *Bluegrass Craftsman,* [1878–1885], first published 1959.

One finds the Forks of Elkhorn several miles east of Frankfort where the North and South Forks of Elkhorn Creek join to form Main Elkhorn Creek. The community that grew up around this convergence of streams dates from 1783, when John Major Sr. bought a large tract of land between South Elkhorn Creek and Dry Run from Lewis Craig in the vicinity of what became the Dry Run community southwest of the Forks.[1] Major built a blockhouse between the Georgetown and Versailles roads a mile or two from what would take form as Frankfort, the capital of the state. In 1788 he and a group of citizens formed the Forks of Elkhorn Baptist Church near his settlement.[2] Locals referred to the little community that grew up in the neighborhood around the church, the first in the county, as "The Fawks." Soon it had a series of water mills where local farmers could convert their wheat and corn into flour and meal.[3] The settlement also boasted the county's first schoolhouse, which stood at the intersection of the Versailles and Georgetown roads.[4] When the river trade opened in 1787 through the efforts of Frankfort's founder, James Wilkinson, the need grew for warehouses to hold farm products, such as flour, whiskey, salted hams, and tobacco. As early as the 1780s, early entrepreneurs built a warehouse at the Forks for holding these and other goods, the convergence of streams becoming a local storage place for area commodities before shipping them downriver from Frankfort or nearby Leestown.[5] Nathaniel Sanders (sometimes written Saunders) operated a mill on South Elkhorn near the Forks as early as 1789, and others soon followed.

Following on the heels of the first surveyors came several men whose names date among the earliest associated with the Forks: Charles LeCompte, William McConnell, and Robert Haydon. Le Compte and McConnell, both Pennsylvanians, came down the Ohio in 1775, traveling in a large canoe, or pirogue, up the Kentucky and Elkhorn to the Forks, where they camped and sought out good land. All came to the Kentucky country as land claimants.

Firstcomers had the privilege of bestowing their names upon the landscape, leaving their signatures on the planet. McConnell, a surveyor, and his cohorts named several key settlements on or near their holdings in the Bluegrass. He staked claims for members of the party, including LeCompte, who returned to the Forks in 1779 with a wagon train of other land seekers. McConnell then went on to what would become Lexington as well as to Georgetown. LeCompte established a claim at a large buffalo stamping ground along the waters of South Elkhorn.[6] Nearby Stamping Ground and Great Crossing in Scott County apparently owe their names to McConnell and LeCompte, who gave the "ancient herding trail and water hole" of the buffalo its lasting name.

William Haydon settled on a claim of 242 acres near the Forks on the main stem of Elkhorn. He gave his name to one of the stations that offered a place of defense from hostile Indians in a region answering the description of "wild West." In June of 1775, William McConnell and a party of hunters camped on the South Fork of Elkhorn at what became known as McConnell's Spring when news came of the victory of Americans at Lexington, Massachusetts, the battle that launched the American Revolution. To celebrate the victory, they named the settlement that they envisioned Lexington. McConnell and a party of men later went on to build the settlement's first blockhouse. The stone house he built for himself not far from the spring still stands. The house is adjacent to where the Bluegrass Stockyards burned near Lisle Road in west Lexington in early 2016. In 1783, McConnell, a man who seldom seemed to be in one place for long in his hunger for land, established a station at Royal Spring in Georgetown. LeCompte and McConnell both have feeder streams named for them: LeCompte's Run and McConnell's Run as well as LeCompte's Bottom.

Though Reverend Elijah Craig built the first paper mill in the area at Georgetown in 1793, the most lasting and successful one flourished at the Forks. From its earliest settlement, this little community became a commercial center, largely because of the industries that formed at the critical junction of the two forks of Elkhorn Creek. The first settlers early recognized the creek's potential as a site for mills powered by water funneled through races in a fairly reliable stream. Seneca McCracken operated grist and sawmills on North and Main Elkhorn until his death in 1829.[7] Subsequently, a woolen mill joined the grist and lumber mills operating in the area. Farmers would later bring in their wool to be woven into jeans and linsey for slaveowners in the region to clothe their slaves.

With settlement and commerce came churches, wherever communities formed and people congregated. Zealous Baptists built Mount Gomer Baptist Church (later known as Mount Pleasant) in July 1790, locating it a mile or so from Forks on a bluff above Elkhorn, not far from the cliff that begins at the edge of the Ebenezer Stedman's property and drops 150 or so feet to the creek.[8] Whether out of modesty or preference, Stedman himself referred to the area, where soon the community named after him would form, as Mount Pleasant. In 1833, Stedman described the first meeting house, constructed of logs and later covered with weatherboarding, as he first saw it: "It looked at first sight like it had been built before the flood, and had floated and lodged on the hills like Noah's Ark. A look inside showed the seats made of poplar slabs from the sawmill, with legs, and they came through the slabs, which made it quite unpleasant to sit down on. . . . The pulpit was of wilderness pattern."[9] One wonders what constituted "wilderness pattern" beyond being rough-hewn and basic, more functional than aesthetic. Many years later, a landowner took advantage of the high ground where the early church stood as a house site. At some point, J. J. King, a patron of artist Paul Sawyier, lived there. Now this house too has vanished.

Understandably, early churches became community centers, among the few places besides gristmills where people could meet and socialize, exchanging news and gossip as well as worshiping. Ministers and church elders exerted a power over their congregations that was both vigorous

The ruins of Stedman mill. (Photograph by Gene Burch.)

and unequivocal. The rules of discipline adopted by these two churches give a sense of how churches of the day enforced their rigid moral codes. Their leverage included the threat of expulsion from the communion so central to community life and, in the early years, survival. Church records indicate that from 1801 to 1804 church elders brought offending members before the congregation, charged with "lying, tattling, gaming, adultery, pilfering, defrauding in swapping horses, swearing, offering to bet, or playing ball."[10] What playing ball meant is not clear, but such an infraction would clearly be an anomaly today in a state where basketball reaches the level of regional mania. The whole acting as a jury (or was it a committee of elders?), offenders could be expelled or punished less severely. At Mount Pleasant Baptist, offenses for males included "singing carnal songs, nicknaming young ladies, or wearing long hair," while those for females included "wearing ribbons and finery, shearing the hair, or using powder." Authority apparently despised the vanities of the young. Such was the world in which the Cooks, and later the Stedmans, moved—a world of which they approved, at least tacitly.

The remains of the Stedman mill lie north of the Forks of Elkhorn, about a mile or mile and a half down the creek's main stem. You will

Stedmantown, circa 1910. (Photograph by Judge Walter Jeffers. Courtesy of Capital City Museum, Frankfort, Kentucky.)

know it by its ruins that have withstood spring freshets, frost heaves, and floodwaters for 175 years. Floating down Elkhorn with a careful eye to the left bank, you will see a wide shelf of limestone, at the end of which weathered blocks fit into a wall twelve to fifteen feet high. Though ruptures and displacements break its original symmetry, the visitor senses that something extraordinary existed here, and the moss on the stones and trees growing in its interior tell you that it wasn't yesterday. What the eye doesn't tell you is that a town of sorts flourished on this site, twenty or so houses in addition to warehouses, a store, even a post office. Remains of a stone fence and piles of foundation rocks lie here and there. The rest has vanished with the people who lived in those houses and worked in the three mills that once operated in the valley. Approaching from the creek, one can easily miss the spot, especially in summer when foliage tends to camouflage the few remaining signs of human presence.

First named Stedmanville in honor of the brothers whose imagination, know-how, and entrepreneurial spirit made the settlement possible, the name evolved more modestly, more realistically, into Stedmantown. Nearly a hundred years after Ebenezer's death, the Martin family erased

Ebenezer Hiram Stedman (1808–1885).
(Courtesy of Mary Nash Cox.)

its last signature, the Stedman "Hotel," located on the uplands above the creek. The Martins' roots reached back to the years when the Stedmans' three mills provided wheat for bread, lumber for building, and tons of high-quality paper for Kentucky's state government. The appetite of bureaucracy for paper seemed insatiable. Not all business was local, especially as shipping became more reliable. The Stedmans even did business with the fledgling Confederacy in far-off Virginia, as well as providing flour and lumber for local farmers. The name Stedmantown survives today only to designate the lane that flanks the property, and it is misspelled as Steadmantown.

The Stedman mill complex symbolized Elkhorn's—and Kentucky's—transition to the industrial age, harnessing steam and waterpower to produce paper. While the earlier grist and lumber mills simply processed existing plants, rendering grain into flour and cellulose into symmetries suitable for building, Ebenezer Stedman manufactured paper. Using steam technology, he rendered cotton rags into a smooth, fibrous material—reams of blank surfaces compatible with moveable type and lasting ink. Stedman emerged from the frontier as an early industrialist at a time when factories were just beginning to transform the country. Locally, he satisfied the needs of a growing governmental presence in Frankfort, one that required documents, files, and books on which civilization and its bureaucratic underbellies until recently relied, an appetite that only grew. He also provided a source of cheap newsprint to support Frankfort's several papers.

Ebenezer Hiram Stedman (1808–1885) was born in Dorchester, Massachusetts, to a papermaker who immigrated to Lexington in 1816 to work in a paper mill, bringing his large family.[11] The family was said to be of Welsh origin and had immigrated to Massachusetts during colonial times.[12] Isaac Stedman came to Massachusetts aboard the ship *Elizabeth* in 1635. He settled in Scituate and later moved to Brookline, near Boston. After moving to Kentucky, his father, E. H. Stedman Sr., became foreman of a paper mill on Lexington's Town Branch, a tributary of South Elkhorn. In Lexington Ebenezer received some schooling, learning to read. His father had a drinking problem that worsened when he moved his family to Georgetown. There he managed the paper mill built between 1789 and 1793 by Elijah Craig and two brothers named Parker. Ebenezer senior bought a brick cottage in sight of the Royal Spring, whose waters formed another tributary of Elkhorn, this one on North Elkhorn. In Lexington and in Georgetown, and finally on Elkhorn Creek, Ebenezer Stedman learned and mastered the art of papermaking. At the end of his life, he chronicled his experiences for the benefit of his descendants and, unknowingly, for posterity.

He was the third Ebenezer in a line of Ebenezers extending to his grandfather. The name Ebenezer in the popular imagination bears negative connotations. Charles Dickens uses it in *A Christmas Carol* for the miserly Ebenezer Scrooge. More recently, Disney studio writers bestowed the name on Uncle Ebenezer, Donald Duck's tight uncle in the popular menagerie of Disney characters. In Hebrew the name means "stone of help," a biblical reference from the Old Testament signifying the megalithic monument that Samuel erected to commemorate God's assistance in routing the Philistines in battle. God apparently sent loud thunderclaps that panicked the Philistines and tipped the balance in favor of the Israelites. Ironically, stone is all that remains of the structures at the complex of Stedman's mills. The huge stones of the foundation, finally, serve as Ebenezer Stedman's lasting monument, the only evidence that flourishing mills occupied the Elkhorn Valley by the vanished village of

Stedmantown. Elusive and less substantial monuments to his efforts are the surviving anonymous printed pages he produced, in the thousands and tens of thousands, shelved in libraries, public and private, around the state, especially in law offices, where law reports formed part of the stock-in-trade of lawyers and lawmakers. His product constitutes the essential stuff of geological surveys, government publications, and records as well as commercially published books, magazines, newspapers, and handbills.

At the time, the manufacture of paper required tedious and back-breaking labor. Anglo-American mills of the period had a three-stage process. First, workers sorted cast-off linen and ripped it into pulp by hand and later by a "rag machine," a rotating cylinder equipped with knives that reduced the cloth to filaments.[13] Second, the vatman dipped his mold—a rectangular wire mesh framed in wood—into a vat of warm watery pulp. The mesh was then raised and shaken into a customary pattern that ensured that the fibers shut.[14] From dipping, the vatman passed the dripping mesh with its sheet of paper to the coucher, who transferred the sheets from mesh to felt. Once he had a sufficient stack, the coucher applied the press to the moist papers. The layboy then delicately separated the paper from the felt and hung each sheet over cords to dry. Each of these steps required experience, a practiced touch, and an artisan's skill. The papers were pressed more than once. A sizerman then gathered the paper into an emulsion of hides, hoofs, tripe, and alum, a kind of gelatin bath that filled the paper's pores so the surface would not blot when ink was applied. Women and the sizerman then sorted the paper, removing flawed or stained swatches. Then the loftsman wrapped the paper into reams. The process of converting pulp to paper took several weeks, requiring intense labor and skills that were acquired only with extensive experience and training.[15]

If Judge Harry Innes stood more in the public eye than anyone living on Elkhorn during the settlement years, Ebenezer Hiram Stedman's life over a generation later—a near contemporary of Lincoln, Darwin, and Poe—was the more thoroughly documented, the most consummately human, giving us a sense of his likes and dislikes, his struggles, his observations, his outlook and daily routines that mark the highlights and daily challenges of a life. Retiring to Texas near the end of it, he wrote an account of his personal experience and work on Elkhorn Creek in a series of letters to his daughter Sophronia "Sophie" Cox back in Kentucky. The result was

*Bluegrass Craftsman, Being the Reminiscences of Ebenezer Hiram Sted-
man, Papermaker, 1808–1885,* compiled in book form by Frances L. S.
Dugan and Jacqueline P. Bull. The University Press of Kentucky published
the edited but only slightly altered compilation in 1959.[16] Ungrammatical,
full of phonetic spellings (the continent of "Urope," "suxcess," "lafture"), it
brimmed with life, a vivid account of papermaking along the Elkhorn—its
modest beginnings, its boom years, its many trials, its final dissolution.
Out of print for years, Frankfort Heritage Press republished it in 2006.[17]
Charles Hockensmith, who documented what remains at the site, added
illustrations and an illuminating archeological report.[18]

Though gifted as an artisan and entrepreneur with an unrelenting
work ethic, Ebenezer Stedman had received little formal education. Ironically, his memoirs stand as the country's most complete account of early
American papermaking.[19] A plain man given to plain speech, Stedman
wrote pretty much as he spoke, so his narrative has a refreshingly unstud-
ied quality to it, giving us a sense of language as it was spoken by an obviously intelligent man, a member of the laboring middle class unschooled
in literary expression but savvy and perceptive.

Who was Ebenezer Stedman the man? We have a fleshier sense of his
life than that of any other along this stretch of Elkhorn because he reveals
himself throughout his colorful and rambling narrative. His writing confirms his complexity and his humanity. We know him, for example, as
an admirer of the great men whose lives brushed his, including Georgetown's Richard Mentor Johnson, a U.S. vice president who rode to office
on his claim to have shot Tecumseh. Near Georgetown, Stedman once
glimpsed the Marquis de Lafayette, the Revolutionary War titan who as a
hero made his triumphal visit to the young republic in 1825. Though the
general also visited Frankfort, he came to Georgetown by way of Lexington. He, therefore, probably never saw the little community at the Forks,
though glimpses of one branch of the Elkhorn or another at various
stages of his journey would have been unavoidable. During the festivities
in Georgetown, Stedman's future wife, Mary Steffee, succeeded in securing the plate on which the general dined before the ball held in his honor.
It must have been one of her proudest possessions.

In his reminiscences, Stedman necessarily reveals the highlights of his
life. Throughout the rambling narrative he gives testimonials to the firsts
in his life—his first ream of manufactured paper, his first trip to Frankfort,

his first boat trip to Louisville with a load of paper, his first ownership of real property. We know him as an acute observer, as in his description of a wife of a "Celerbrated Hunter" as she prepared a dinner of venison that was "amongth one of the Best Suppers that I Ever sat Down to":

> While she was Cooking the venison I had a good Chance to take a good Look at hur. She was a woman I should think about 35 years old. She had Black Hair [and] Black Eyes. Hur Face was not handsom But Still thare was Something pleasant & agreeable In hur looks That had a tendancy to make a Stranger welcome & feel for the time Being at Home. She was Dressed in a home Spun Dres of a yellowish Coullor. Hur hair was tucked up with a home made horn comb. She was Bare footed & stood on hur bare feet about Six feet high. Freequently She woold stir the Contents of a coffy pot that Set on the coles with [a] wooden spoon.[20]

Equally vivid is his description of the annual county "Maliatia Musters" in Scott County with its "Shuting Mach," hearing "the Keen Crackk" of the rifle: "How ofen have I heard the Sound From Some one near the target, 'Noched Center.' & them Boys Could do it often Eight times out of ten."[21] Stedman takes special notice of the first paper he made and his first sale. Since the original mill on Elkhorn could only be operated during the winter and spring months, when water levels ran reliably higher, for a time he turned peddler and sold the band boxes his mother made for women to store their bonnets. Setting out with a wagon pulled by a blind mare with one leg two inches shorter than the other, he traveled to Lexington and on to Winchester, selling fifteen dollars' worth—a bonanza for him—to the wife of a "Red-faced farmer" who had told him he wanted no peddlers on his place and then relented as young Stedman charmed them both.[22] Stedman mines the details from his encyclopedic memory over a span of sixty years with a vividness and subtlety that is as revealing as it is ungrammatical. Ebenezer Stedman does not suffer from a Victorian reticence about sex, as in his reference to Couglar, a "Jerman" miller who married his employer's daughter and eventually took over proprietorship of a gristmill: "He was sent to the Barn to Frail out Grain with the imployers Daughter & they got Mixt up Amought the Grain & Couglar Had to Marry hur was the way he commenced."[23] Stedman, an old man when he writes, often shows himself thoughtful, at times philosophical:

Sam Stedman. (Courtesy of John Gray.)

"In Memory of those days I look Back & Find that this life is all a—what Shall I call it—a delusion, a Bright Light of Some Metor, [sic] to lead one on & on for happiness & Newer [never] find it."[24]

In Georgetown, Stedman joined the Baptist church, where presumably he met and courted his wife, with whose family he would have lifelong associations. In 1833, at twenty-four, he secretly married his sweetheart, Mary Steffee: "I was at an age now that young men Feel a warm desire to Be with young Ladies, and hear I must Say that I never went to Se But one, never Kept Company with But one, never Walked to Meeting with But one & That one was you dear Mother."[25] At least he thought he had kept the marriage a secret. When the couple came to the Steffees' house, Stedman, "Half mad and half glad," confronted a houseful of celebrants with a wedding supper steaming on the table. The preacher, in on the trick, married them and they all sat down to a sumptuous supper. Wedded first to his work, characteristically, at 2:00 A.M. on his wedding night, he got up to go tend the mill, continuing his practice of putting enterprise and success ahead of domestic happiness. But not entirely. In time the couple had four children: Sophia Stedman Cox, Nelly Stedman Cox, Harmon Steffee Stedman, and George Clinton Stedman.

Ever looking for opportunities to better himself and his family, Stedman purchased the mills on Elkhorn from Amos Kendall (1789–1869), another Massachusetts transplant. In 1820–1821, Kendall, a Dartmouth graduate, came to Kentucky and found employment tutoring Henry Clay's five children. Active in political affairs, he went on to become postmaster general in the administration of President Andrew Jackson. Like so many of his contemporaries, he speculated in land, building the Franklin Mill on the Main Elkhorn a mile or mile and a half from the Forks at the site of what would become the Stedman mill complex. In part he invested in the land as a speculative venture, having learned through insider information that the federal government planned to establish an arsenal in the vicinity.[26] He planned to eventually sell the property to the government for a comfortable profit. Starting in 1820, he began to build a mill, completing it early in 1821. Never able to succeed with it, Kendall put it on the market as early as 1823, eventually selling it to Stedman and his brother Sam in 1833 for $2,300 along with fifty acres of land.[27] Soon Stedman and his brother put the millworks to use. He proudly recalled the first ream of paper he made, having collected all the rags he could find and serendipitously coming on fifty pounds of rags in the ceiling of the mill that had been rats' nests, starting "from the Bottom Floor of Poverty."[28] Both Stedmans had some experience in the mechanical and commercial running of a paper mill, most notably at Elijah Craig's in nearby Georgetown.

In working at the Elkhorn mill before he and brother Sam owned it, Stedman describes conditions of the creek at the time of a cholera outbreak in Georgetown as well as his own tendency toward frugality in scavenging: "After a uncommon heavy Rain which Caused a Big Freshit in Elkhorn I remember The Entire Creek from Bank to Bank was a Continuous drift of Fence Rails & trees & logs. I Caught thousands of Rails until about dinner time I had to quit as the watter Stank eqal to a dead & Rotten carcus."[29] The smell of death was portentous, because the next day his father-in-law became the second victim in the cholera epidemic in Georgetown, a scourge that in a few weeks claimed the lives of a tenth of the population in nearby Lexington. Not until later in the century did scientists discover a link between the disease and contaminated water.[30]

The mill's operation had been suspended for years. How to reactivate the neglected works so he could support himself and his new wife became the newlywed's biggest challenge. When the new husband loaded a wagon to take his wife from the comfortable brick home in Georgetown she'd lived in all her life, she balked. Reaching the Forks with its timbered hills and unshorn wildness, she complained that he was taking her "into the mountains." When they reached their new home, a neglected frame house on the bluff above the millsite, she could not hide her distress, as Stedman related to Sophie: "On top of the hill Your Mother was so full She Could hardly talk. So Shure she was That I was taking Hur to Sum awfull Place. Gest Before we got to the top of the Hill down Below the School house She Spide the Big Clift on Elkhorn & the Cedar trees. She Could hold in no longer & Bursted out Crying that I was Carrying hur to the Jumping of [off] Place of Earth & She & little Sophy Never woold See Anny Boddy again, wood Become wild Indians."[31] Such was Mary Steffee's debut in the Elkhorn Valley, which the couple would call home for nearly the next half-century. Cedar Hill they adopted as the name to refer to the property, though sometimes he interchanges it with Mount Pleasant, the name locals probably used in referring to the neighborhood. When the Stedmans took up residence at the Forks, Judge Innes had been dead for eighteen years, though his widow, Ann Innes, remained very much alive. These neighbors, therefore, must have at least been acquaintances.

To put the old mill back in operation would require Stedman and brother Sam to outlay both labor and money. Labor they had, but money was a problem until A. G. Hodges, the state printer and publisher of two local papers, the *Commentator* and the *Commonwealth*, saw a sample of their paper and stepped up with financial help and easy terms to get them started.[32] Owner Amos Kendall also wanted them to buy the property and did what he could to grease the wheels, so to speak. Philanthropy alone was not Hodge's sole motivation. He and Orlando Brown, co-owners of the *Frankfort Commonwealth*, would benefit from a close and reliable source of newsprint.[33] To get the fiber they needed for a high-quality book paper, the Stedman brothers placed ads for rags in local papers. As a result, many households saved cotton scraps and old clothing in a ragbag that "the rag peddler" periodically came around to collect. When drought and seasonal changes made water power of Elkhorn unreliable, the brothers upgraded with steam. For years, the blowing of the mill whistle at 5:00 A.M. for workers to commence work served as a signal for farmers in the area to get up and go feed. Many who did not possess a reliable timepiece set their clocks by it.[34]

In 1835, James Martin became the brothers' first hire. Martin, a jack of all trades, eventually tended both the saw and corn mills. Ebenezer praised him as an "untiring, industrious & most Reliable man"[35] The mill, which had been built in 1823, seemed in decent repair but had most recently been used as a hog pen and was crammed with corncobs and manure. The undershot wheel and most of the equipment had rotted. They found the other two mills in shambles. Worse, most of the mill dam had washed away in the last flood. As Stedman put it, Mount Pleasant was "no paridice."[36] He characterized the challenge as "the most uninviting desolations that Two young men Ever had the nerve to undertake to Repair & Build up."[37] "To me," he confided, "after living so long in the Blew Grass Regions, the place looked wild & it was wild."[38]

They first needed timber to rebuild the dam so they could ensure a reliable source of power year-round. Hodges assured the brothers that they could purchase sufficient timber from neighbors—Fennick, Church, or the "Widow Ennis" (Ann Innes). Fennick, or Fenwick, refused them, saying Amos Kendall had made similar promises and that they had come to naught. He seemed to distrust the brothers' inexperience and youth. So, they asked directions and made their way through the woods to another neighbor, William Church, the man who owned hundreds of wooded acres across the creek and on whose property the Cook settlement had "died aborning" over forty-five years earlier. He lived in a two-story cabin a short distance from the creek at a spot known locally as Church's Grove. Church hospitably put them up for the night and fed them, finally offering to sell timber from the hill "above his house" at $3 an acre. With this assurance, the brothers left for Frankfort to close the deal with Hodges. They agreed to buy the mills and fifty acres of land for $2,300.[39] When they asked who in the neighborhood could be trusted to deal with them fairly, Hodges gave them names, then cautioned that any dealings with Billy Church be written "in Black & White."

So they returned to Church's and asked for a contract. When they read it, they found they had been hornswoggled. The amount had been changed from $3 per acre to $5. They called the deal off and went on to Widow Innes's place, the once-fortified residence by the creek, now enlarged and improved, though the judge had long been in his grave. Although she owned seven hundred wooded acres, Ann Innes refused to part with any timber. Back to square one, they tried a neighbor named

Jack Birchfield who owned wooded land close by the mill site. For $50 he
offered to sell them five acres of timber from anywhere on his farm, stipu-
lating that the money be paid before they cut any of it. This condition the
Stedmans were either unable or unwilling to meet. Stedman formed the
impression that many of his neighbors suspected the brothers of being
"yound [sic] tramps," "Young Bomerangs." Becoming more desperate,
the brothers again went with extended hands to Frankfort in search of
a loan. They found it in a "Mr. Moore," who willingly gave them the loan
of $50 payable in four months and, amazing to them, charged no inter-
est.[40] Optimistic and bent on success, Stedman resolved "Eather to make
a Spoon or Spoil a horn."[41] At the time of their undertaking, Ebenezer
weighed 122 pounds and was twenty-six years old, so young that a judge
in Frankfort made him swear that he'd reached his twenty-first year the
first time he went to vote.[42]

With a sawmill and a gristmill already on the property when the Stedmans bought it, they started to generate income by grinding grain to flour
and sawing lumber, some of the latter for their own use. With the help
of four or five hired hands, they began felling the trees necessary for a
new milldam. They hauled the logs in two wagons and hired additional
hands to remove what remained of the old dam and to dig the foundation for a new one. Things went well, even the feeding of so many extra
mouths. Stedman notes that whiskey and bacon, flour and meal, could
be procured cheaply. He also recorded the abundance of grey squirrels:
"This was the Great Squirril year. They were very Fat. In frying them the
oil wood Come out like Fat Bacon. After Breakfast, anson wood, with my
little Smothbore shot gun, go up The Creek & kill thirty for dinner. After
dinner He wold Kill Sixty for Supper & Breakfast & he woold not go half
the way to the Head of the Mill pond to kill them. I have often of a Morning Got up Soon & Could Se Hundreds Crossing Elkhorn. . . . They ware
a God Send to us."[43]

Ebenezer, always keen to find a new efficiency, also discovered that he
got more work out of the men when he served whiskey at meals. So he
bought two gallons a week, giving each man a dram at breakfast, lunch, and
supper. The whiskey may have also cut down on sickness, because the water
that was the source of his living was not safe to drink. Almost from the
time of earliest settlement Elkhorn's water must have been polluted with
an increasing freight of toxic substances from Georgetown and Lexington,

though its contamination did not increase substantially until after the Civil War as population and industry accelerated. Elkhorn Creek must have been one of many conduits by which cholera and typhoid spread.

While they worked on construction of a new dam to replace the old one that washed away in 1831, the Stedman brothers confronted a new problem. The neighbor who owned the land across the creek—perhaps William Church—appeared with a gun, saying he would shoot the first man to lay a timber on his property. Undeterred, the story goes, the brothers paid Albert G. Hodges $5 to go over and regale the irate neighbor with amusing stories until he softened his stance so the dam could be built.[44] Before starting, the workmen had to remove about twenty feet of the old dam and shovel out about six feet of accumulated sand.

To construct the dam necessary to harness the power of water, the workmen put in logs and notched them into ties, filling cribs with stone hauled in two rented carts. By the end of the third week they had thirty men working for them, and by October the dam rose to seven feet, high enough that the Stedmans wouldn't have to worry about it during the summer. They also built new head gates and a new head race as far down as the grist and saw mills. Just how far, Stedman doesn't tell us, but the distance must have been considerable. That summer of 1834 they also hired a millwright to build a new waterwheel. By the fall of 1835 they were making paper in quantity.[45] Directing James Martin to operate the grist and saw mills, the brothers concentrated on the paper mill, buying a steam engine and boilers in 1837. They also erected a massive brick chimney as an exhaust for the steam engine used in the making of paper. Clever in their dealings, they arranged with Hodges that payment on their loan would be made in paper, a benefit to both parties. They needed additional help to haul the paper they produced from the mill to Frankfort. For years "Mr. Herrin" worked as their chief teamster. The owner of a horse and wagon, he lived in a modest house on the high ground somewhere above the mill. Transportation changed little for two decades. A generation later, the Midland Railroad Company laid a rail line between Frankfort and Georgetown, passing just south of the Stedman property and crossing the Elkhorn on trestleworks built adjacent to their mill site.[46] By 1886, when the line became operable, Ebenezer had already moved to Texas and died. What an asset reliable transportation that could carry paper in bulk over great distances would have been to his enterprise.

Frankfort, Lexington, and Louisville all had commercial publishers. The West during these years had a growing need for paper locally, especially to satisfy the insatiable appetite for news. Frankfort, a small town of 1,987 people in 1830, had no fewer than five newspapers during the 1820s, each representing various political factions. Then, as now, regular as the tides, the population would swell when the General Assembly convened and then recede when it adjourned. Consumption of paper answered to this tendency.[47] The nature of the consumers was more varied and less predictable. Paper fulfilled a variety of needs. State government needed paper for record keeping and lawmaking. Paper was also in demand to satisfy the fashionable taste for novels. Residents of fine houses began to use printed wallpaper. Before telephones, polite society required paper when people bombarded each other with "little notes, invitations to dinner, thank-you notes, begging notes, scolding notes, and notes for no reason at all."[48] And the Stedmans obligingly stood ready to provide it, shipping their product near and far. The need for rags did not abate. An advertisement that appeared in the *Frankfort Commonwealth* for March 11, 1845, offered to purchase two hundred tons of "cotton and linen rags in any quantity."[49]

Despite their origins in New England, a region where the antislavery movement had always found more agreeable minds, the Stedmans, like many of their neighbors, apparently had no scruples about owning other human beings. Prosperity permitted each of the Stedman brothers to purchase a slave to help his wife manage her household. Ebenezer bought Isabella and her six- or eight-year-old daughter for $500. They worked at Mary's direction in the house, while the brothers used free labor to run the paper mill night and day. Perhaps Ebenezer and his brother purchased household slaves in part out of guilt for neglecting their wives and their domestic duties. Census records for 1860 show that Ebenezer Stedman owned seven slaves:

80-year-old female
40-year-old female
14-year-old boy
9-year-old boy
7-year-old boy
5-year-old girl
1-year-old boy[50]

Ebenezer Hiram Stedman Home. (Artist unknown. Courtesy of Mary Nash Cox.)

The pattern of births suggests that the children may all have had one mother, most likely Isabella. All would have been manumitted by 1866, young enough to make a new start in postbellum America. Perhaps the father of these children worked at the mill. Perhaps he wasn't listed because he was a freedman or lived on another farm or belonged to another family. No whiff of sexual impropriety sullies the Stedmans themselves. Ebenezer seems to have been singularly bent on labor and profit, not philandering.

In one letter, Ebenezer confessed that prosperity compelled him to become his own slave, a "Slave to Buisness."[51] More than once he raised this complaint: "Never was a slave kept as Constant at work Day & Night as i was."[52] In a very real way Ebenezer had realized the ambitions of his father, who also dreamed of owning his own paper mill but had failed due to fire and the distractions of depression and drink.[53] "The gingle of Silver," the son wrote, "has its Charms & often Creates a desire for more."[54] His pursuit of profit he describes cryptically as the chase after "Jack with his lantern."[55] In a darker vein, in the letters he laments how different his fate would have been had he "worked brain insted of Hands!"[56] The routine of his day's work as a layboy entailed freeing 2,520 sheets of paper from the felts and washing the cloths.[57] Both tasks required repetitive labor, mind-numbing and backbreaking.

But Ebenezer's labor harvested its rewards. When a manufacturer's representative from Madison, Indiana, came to Mount Pleasant, brother Sam bought a buggy, and Ebenezer bought a "Silver Mounted Barouch," a carriage that represented a display of conspicuous consumption to impress the Steffees when the couple made their own triumphal visit to Georgetown. Such a display also assured their neighbors of their worth and served to "Surmount all predices against us."[58] With growing satisfaction, he visualized his neighbors anticipating that the Stedmans would be so rich they would belong to the aristocracy, or "upper tens."[59] In fact, Ebenezer and brother Sam had arrived as certifiable members of the Jacksonian *nouveau riche*.[60] After all, they had made a mark on immortality with a community named for them. These, as he puts it, were the "Hay day times."[61] The brothers had a mutually beneficial working relationship. Ebenezer oversaw the operation of the mills, while Sam, who had "business qualities" and was "Sharp in trading," kept clear of the mills.[62] In effect, Ebenezer made the paper, Sam sold it.

As the business began to prosper, the brothers learned painfully that prosperity had its price. They discovered that fires and floods played no favorites. Elkhorn, still their primary power source, had a will of its own, and water, as any kayaker will tell you, is unforgiving. No one learned this lesson more painfully than the Stedmans, whose "new" dam across the creek washed away. The flood of 1847 brought Elkhorn Creek to its highest levels in forty years, sweeping away or seriously damaging dams and other obstructions along the creek. They also lost the paper mill and the machine shop, going into debt to rebuild because they had no insurance. Frustrated with the loss, Sam threw in the towel. In 1852 he sold his interest in the mill to Ebenezer, who stubbornly decided to go it alone. In 1854 floodwaters destroyed the dam again.[63] Suffering an even greater reversal in 1855, Stedman lost the mill to fire. Though uninsured, Stedman's reputation and credit permitted him to rebuild it at a cost of $40,000. Ebenezer persisted, undeterred.

Misfortune turned Ebenezer's latent disposition for romance backward to better days. In his piecemeal narrative, he fluctuates between memories of disaster and a longing for an idyllic, preindustrial time—a natural and recurrent pattern because he is an agent of transforming the natural world into an industrial one. In one of his many digressions he recaptures the joys of fishing Elkhorn, a reliable resource for their table as well as their precious leisure. Along the way, he documents the creek's growing reputation as a place that others visited for recreational fishing: "Thare ware plenty of Fish to Be Caught then. Them days the Bank officers and welthy men woold Come down and Fish, up the Sport. They Brot the Best provisions and alwais The Best of old Burbon not to drink to Excess, But to Make one Feel Renewed after the toils of Fishing. The president of the Bank alwais Kept his Black Bottle in the Spring and the mint grew Rank and Completely Hid the Bottle."[64] Ebenezer himself fished year-round, in winter using a "dip net" that he baited and fetched home with as many fish as he could carry. He also cut holes in the ice, catching his fill of fish, he tells us, with ease. In passing on the fish stories related by others, he became a kind of unwitting folklorist, a collector of tales circulating among those who lived and fished along the creek, some substantially true, some told with obvious exaggeration for the joy of telling. Storytelling passed the time for working men who had not the advantage of books and ready news sources—one of the reasons that so little of what they said or thought survives. An oral culture corrals only a tiny portion of what is heard, just as a writing culture records only a fraction of the wealth of actual experiences that comprise a life.

Stedman represents the partial exception, the unfinished storyteller who simply wants to pass on the exceptional and not so exceptional happenings of his life to his descendants and, unwittingly, to us. In "Old Man Birchfield" he paints one of his most alluring portraits, a character who would be at home in the *Leatherstocking Tales* of James Fenimore Cooper. The unnamed old man is Jack Birchfield's father, a contemporary of Daniel Boone, who, like Boone and Simon Kenton, had left Kentucky, in this case to Indiana, when the game became scarce and people too plentiful. Ebenezer describes him as about eighty and "not much bent," carrying a large "Buxskin" purse full of his pension money. Stedman notes that as this old man came down the road he swivelled his head from right to left, often looking behind him. He explained this odd mannerism as a habit of survival—always on the lookout for game or danger. He told Stedman that he had hunted the valley near the mill and that it was a "Monsterous place for Game."[65] Old Man Birchfield bore memories of "Pionear" life in Kentucky. Among other things, he remembered the beaver dam in the bottom, how many deer he had seen in one drove, the bear he had killed in the Backbone hills, the deer he had killed in Judge's [Innes's] Bottom, and the buffalo and buffalo trail from Stamping Ground to the Salt Licks.[66] He went on to relate his experiences during the ill-fated expedition of Kentuckians at the Battle of the Raisin during the War of 1812. The old man described the course of march northward by Captain Paschal Hickman's Kentuckians as "all a wilderness" extending from Georgetown to Cincinnati. More than anyone else, Jack Birchfield's unnamed father, as reported by Stedman, gives us a fuller sense of the abundance of game that inhabited the Elkhorn bottom.

The Elkhorn Valley itself underwent dramatic changes as Stedman and his neighbors felled large portions of the native forest for firewood and lumber, transforming more of the valley to pasture and cropland or simply denuding it to a residuum of stumps. Stedman himself estimated that the mill consumed two-thirds of the wood standing as far down as the "widow Enis," whose impulse was to conserve much of the natural environment she and her husband first encountered.[67] Over the period of thirty or forty years, what happened to the game? That sportsmen hunted it out is only partially true. Quite simply, the needs of the mill required deforesting much of the valley, consuming great quantities of firewood to stoke the steam engine used in papermaking as Stedman's hardworking employees converted a living forest, a biosphere, into books and records so that state government and the world of law and policy could document themselves. They shrank the available habitat for species of game that populated the valley at the time of first settlement. In the way of the speechless, game simply disappeared or sought pockets of isolation in greatly diminished numbers. As these changes came, Stedman remained aware of the critical need for clean water to produce quality paper. Purity became a necessity, increasingly threatened as the natural filters of landscape diminished and cities grew in population and industrial development.

More than once as an old man, Stedman pondered the woods as they were when he first came to the Elkhorn Valley. In a letter addressed to his daughter Sophie, he reminisced, "I wish you Could have Seen the Bright Scenery Surrounding old mt. pleasant at this time. The Field this side of Jack Churches line on the Creek was Covered with the original Forest. The Finest White ash and as you Come near the hill the Good Big

Shade Shugartree,[68] the glory and delight of the First poineers under the Sweets Shades of the Shugar Camp."[69] Selective memory or simply old age permits him to forget that eighty years earlier the Cook Massacre occurred just across the creek on Church's land, the two or more derelict cabins an indelible reminder of its bloody past. It's possible that the Cooks' successors in the Elkhorn Valley regarded the cabins as jinxed, evoking painful memories of the misfortunes that occurred there. From the Churches and his other neighbors with longer memories, he could not have failed to hear of the tragic killings. Stedman's buoyancy in his emotional makeup acknowledges but doesn't dwell on his or others' misfortunes. Part of this ability resides in his self-deprecating humor, part in his zestfulness for life that sustains him in the face of old age and death. The homespun poem he includes in one of his letters provides a good example. Its theme is appetite:

Jest Below mt. pleasant Hill
Stands the Franklin Papermill[70]
And a little to the East or West
Stands the Saw Mill and the Grist.
When Mary Hangs the Red Rag out,
Then Jack He girks the Bell about,
And all the Hands are to be fed
Then you will Se E H S Go ahead.[71]

Here, Stedman makes light of himself, aware that he makes better paper than he does poetry. Clearly, he does not—at least at this point in his life—take himself too seriously for a man who went from boom to bust several times in a period of thirty or so years. Earlier, he mentions that by the time Jack Birchfield built his cabin in the valley at the foot of Backbone, all the fields had been cleared and one could see a squirrel on the ground five hundred yards away.[72] He doesn't acknowledge, at least explicitly, that the reduction in cover and mast meant fewer squirrels.

Change in the valley at first came slowly. The thunk of the ax, the thundering crash of a falling tree, must have roused attention and curiosity at first. Soon, axes and two-man saws were converting stands of trees to saw logs to be milled into thousands of board feet of lumber to build homes and barns and other outbuildings all over the neighborhood and beyond.

In addition to the sawmill operated by James Martin, another at the Forks that Stedman describes as the best on Elkhorn ate up its share of local timber.[73] With just the slightest hint of envy, Stedman credits one of his neighbors, William Johnes [Jones], with possessing the heaviest stand of yellow poplar he ever saw, some of the logs being six feet in diameter.[74] Never does he acknowledge his part in transforming the value, regarding the changes as a part of the cost of doing business.

The finger of guilt pointed to Stedman himself, his need to make steam for his paper engine requiring him and his workers to scour the hillside and lay the treescape low. He reckons the immense quantities of fuel consumed by the mill's steam engine. From a man named Sanders, Stedman and Sam bought a strip of timber one hundred yards wide that extended to the creek from some distance above it. He described it as "the Finest slice of timber Thare was in the County," for which he paid $300.[75] Standing "thick on the ground," the trees, most of them, made forty feet of saw logs and would amount to many thousands of cords and hundreds of thousands of bushels of coal.[76] Since a full cord of wood traditionally measures four feet high by four feet wide by eight feet, the volume must have been stupendous. Besides the carbon-ladened coal they used, the mill consumed an estimated fifty thousand cords of wood.[77]

Stedman also altered the landscape through quarrying, having worked in one near Lexington early in his career. He blasted much of the stone used for building foundations, races, and dams from limestone shelves on his property. The remains of his primary quarry on the hillside are still visible. He describes placing explosives in the ground to "Blast rock." As he confesses, "I was very fond of powder."[78]

An eminently practical man, Stedman took advantage where he found it, as when he salvaged lumber and other debris after a heavy rain that caused a "Big Freshit" in Elkhorn.[79] One can imagine him, one eye on the creek, scavenging by hook or crook anything useful that providence floated into his grasp. He may or may not have known that in the cliff beyond the site of the Mount Pleasant Church was a "Salt Petre Cave," from which saltpeter is said to have been retrieved to make gunpowder over twenty years earlier, during the War of 1812.[80]

The Elkhorn he knew both gave and took, and his vigilance kept him apprised of its opportunities, its moods and eddies. One of Stedman's Cox neighbors, writing to her son in Texas, mentioned the destructive flood of 1847 that would become a major setback for the Stedman brothers: "We have had a great deal of rain—Elkhorn is higher than it has been for forty years—Stedman's and Church's dams have been carried away besides several others—indeed much damage has been sustained all along the creek."[81] For those living along the creek whose livelihoods depended on its erratic flow, an excess of rainwater from upstream in a short time spelled disaster as the watershed drained more water than its channel could accommodate.

Despite setbacks of fire, flood, financial pitfalls, and the steady depletion of the natural wonders about him, for thirty years the mill produced most of the paper used by printers for the state as well as much of the newsprint for Frankfort's several newspapers. The county's manufacturing census in 1850 listed the value of the paper mill as $15,000, the gristmill at $3,000.[82] The value of 250,000 pounds of stockpiled rags was $12,000, and 4,700 pounds of wheat $10,000, as well as 1,500 pounds of flour at $10,000. Ten men and two women worked in the paper mill, two men in the gristmill. Annual output amounted to 150,000 reams of printing and wrapping paper valued at $27,000.[83] The manufacture of lower-quality wrapping paper and "bonet boards" when the creek ran muddy bespeaks Stedman's sheer drive.[84]

During the 1850s the mill ran at peak production. The village that grew up around it was so bustling that, from 1855 to 1857, it had its own post office.[85] Local newspapers continued running ads for cotton and linen rags to provide fiber to go into its vats.[86] Stedman estimated that for the first twenty-four years of production, the mill produced from $75,000 to $100,000 worth of paper.[87] In addition to the three mills, the complex included a store, a blacksmith shop, a stable, and twenty-five or so log houses for its employees—virtually a company town. The post office must have been part of the general store, operated by brother John Stedman, who in 1855 was listed as the postmaster. Discovering natural gas on the place when a well was being bored for water, Ebenezer applied Yankee ingenuity to light the cabins with gas burners. He pioneered one of the first gas wells in the region. Other physical facilities at Stedmantown included the dam, the millrace, the enormous brick steam engine chimney, and a stone quarry that provided on-site building materials. In one of his letters Stedman boasted, "We built up quite a village."[88] The Stedmans, the Churches, the Coxes, the Macklins, and the Martins dominated the

George Clinton Stedman. (Courtesy of Capital
City Museum, Frankfort, Kentucky.)

valley as the neighborhood's leading families, interconnected through
marriage and longtime friendships. Few, if any, of the Inneses remained
on their forebears' land after Widow Innes's passing, though Harry Innes
Todd, one foot in town, one foot in the country when not on the river, was
a partial exception, a sometime commuter.

Finally, ideology and politics as much as economics played a major role
in bringing Stedman's success to an end. During the years leading up to
the Civil War, his daughter Nelly Stedman Cox described her father as a
neutral or a "union man," though her mother, Mary, had strong sympa-
thies for the Southern cause.[89] Ebenezer's loyalty to the Union did not
prevent him from turning a dollar wherever he could, including a deal
with the government of the Confederacy. In 1861 he contracted with the
Confederate government in response to a substantial order for paper
to print its currency.[90] He delivered the paper for bank notes but never
received payment. Nor did Stedman's neutrality prevent his son, George,
from enlisting in the Confederate Army. To make matters worse, when
the mill failed, Ebenezer faced an indebtedness he had accumulated with
recent building costs and lost revenue. Richmond's defaulting on its

contract further hampered his liquidity. Finally, he would make an even greater sacrifice to the Confederate Cause—his son.

The war claimed Ebenezer's son George just three weeks before armed conflict ended. A captain in the Confederate Army, before the war George, "a scholarly and poetic young man," rose as a promising journalist, his career beginning in Louisville. Working in Jefferson City, Missouri, when the war broke out, he soon served as a reporter—what today we would call a war correspondent—for the *Richmond Enquirer* on the front lines. He was captured during the summer of 1863 and held prisoner for eight months at Fort McHenry in Baltimore. Released, he left the newspaper and enlisted in the Confederate Army as a captain. We can only guess at his motivations. In fall 1864, his superiors ordered him to the Western Department of Kentucky in an effort to sever General Sherman's rail communications. Appointed to the staff of General H. B. Lyon, orders sent him to western Kentucky on a secret mission just prior to Lyon's projected raid. Wearing blue overcoats, he and six comrades met three armed riders in Union County near Morganfield, Kentucky. Captain Stedman ordered them to surrender. Instead, one of the riders pulled out a pistol and shot him at point-blank range. George fell from his horse, mortally wounded. Before his death a day or two later, he dictated a brief but moving farewell note to his parents:

My dear Parents

In company with six companions I had an engagement with a body of Yankees in Morganfield, Kentucky supposing them to be Confederate soldiers. I had a hand to hand fight in the encounter and was shot through the breast and both arms. I am in a dying condition. My wound is very painful. I have no fear to die. My pain is so great I can not say so much as I would desire. I have very much to say. I have the very sweet consolation that I have fought bravely for my country. Do not dear Parents grieve for me since I expect to meet you before a great while. Let me beg you not by any means suffer for me, but with a firm resolution and an unconquerable spirit remember that I die as a true soldier and as one you will not be ashamed to own as your son.[91]

A local paper indicated that survivors found a set of black whiskers and moustache in his haversack. The letter indicates that he was a victim of

mistaken identity, taking the riders for fellow Confederates, a fatal miscalculation. Though we may never know the goal of the mission, Stedman
and his companions practiced deception in wearing blue overcoats. In
effect, he acted as a spy, an offense that both sides regarded as punishable by death. His devotion to the Confederate cause prompted him to
take the risks such a mission entailed. George's death must have grieved
the Stedmans deeply and, accompanying financial setbacks at the paper
mill, dealt a crippling blow to his father's long-persevering will. When
George's remains were shipped home for burial, Nelly Stedman Cox
experienced the shock of seeing her first dead person, looking on his
"dear dead face . . . in the sleep that knows no waking."[92]

At least one other Stedman, Howard, fought in the Civil War. Ebenezer's
nephew, the son of his younger brother A. T. (Anderson Turner), Howard
Stedman weighed 120 pounds when he enlisted as a private in the 1st
Louisiana Cavalry on October 5, 1862. He, like his ill-fated cousin George,
fell captive. Unlike George, he survived the war and returned to Forks of
Elkhorn, where his father lived. Taken at Somerset, Kentucky, he eventually received a parole and returned to the fighting, surrendering in May of
1865 in Alabama as part of General Richard Taylor's command. Returning to Kentucky, he became proprietor of the Elkhorn Woolen Mills at
Forks of Elkhorn, dying around 1905 or 1906 and buried in the Frankfort
Cemetery.[93] Near the Forks his house still stands, a large frame structure,
the name "H. Stedman" still engraved on the stone gateposts across from
the nondescript building that housed the woolen mill. Military records
indicate that during the war he also served in Company C of John Hunt
Morgan's 9th Kentucky Cavalry, fighting alongside many of his neighbors,
including A. W. Macklin Jr., A. J., W. H., and Robert Church, and others
around the Forks and Peaks Mill Road areas.

The Civil War touched Stedmantown in one other instance, this time
more lightly. On August 22, 1864, guerrillas raided the Stedmantown store,
owned by Ebenezer's brother, John. A raid on the store would have been
another blow to the Stedman family's shaky economic equilibrium, adding
to Ebenezer's Job-like trials. Reports of the robbery identified one of the
members as Hugh Harrod of Bald Knob on the west side of the Kentucky
River, a deserter from the company of R. B. Taylor, and probably everyone
in the company had deserted from the Union Army.[94] Guerrillas preyed
on the county's defenselessness. When the Confederate Army's threat to

the capital had ended, the governor disbanded the Capital Guards, leaving Frankfort and Franklin County virtually undefended and vulnerable, ripe for plucking. Guerrillas quickly took advantage of the area's sparse protection. They killed a Union man named Robert Graham in nearby Peaks Mill, a murder for which Union troops retaliated by executing four Confederate prisoners a few blocks from the current state capitol, then a farm pasture. An historic marker on Shelby Street in South Frankfort commemorates the spot. The reprisal executions followed an infamous order by General Stephen Burbridge, Military Commandant of Kentucky. This and similar executions greatly contributed to the growing public disillusionment with the Union presence in the state. Robbings and shootings in Franklin County occurred almost daily, the guerrilla menace not ending for months after the Confederate surrender. Guerrilla bands, uncommitted to any cause but plunder and survival, contrasted sharply with the laudable though perhaps misguided motives of Ebenezer's son, George.

For some reason Ebenezer Stedman doesn't mention the raid in his letters, though, as he admits, his powers of recollection, though strong, often occur in spotty and random patterns. They may also have been selective. He may have blacked out events relating to the war because they included the death of his son at a time when his own fortunes had fallen to their nadir. He may never have recovered from the default of the Confederate government on monies owed for paper to produce its currency, throwing him into insolvency.

Stedman and the community he built also underwent decline. During the 1870s Stedman experienced more misfortunes. The ruinous economy of the Civil War and its aftermath were the final burden that brought the mill down. Ebenezer had no direct male heir to pass the business on to after George died. His daughters had married and had lives of their own, one in distant Texas. Though Stedman resolutely tried to revive the paper business, the accumulated effects of fires, floods, and the economic downturn caused by the Panic of 1873 finally brought him to bankruptcy. As he put it, "Fire, war, intrest Eat me out."[95] He neglected here to add flooding, ironically, to which he had directly contributed by timbering the wooded slopes that bordered the creek, an act that exacerbated the effects of runoff. The big trees whose deep roots held the soil and absorbed rainwater no longer offered protection from runoff. These misfortunes persistently gnawed at his success and must in some ways have seemed to him a conspiracy of nature. Finally, his money woes got the best of him. Forced into a financial corner, he declared bankruptcy in 1874. Pressed by creditors, he sold the mill equipment and then the contiguous property. With the mills idle, the workers left and the village he created gradually fell into ruin. Even the Stedman house went up for sale.

For a time, Leonard J. Cox, Sophia's husband and Ebenezer's son-in-law, attempted to revive the mill by producing butchers' wrapping paper made of straw. When this venture failed to return the necessary revenue, the mill closed. In 1870, the gristmill belonged to Stedman and Martin, the paper mill to Cox. The Dupont firm in Louisville salvaged the machinery from the paper mill, marking the end of papermaking on the Elkhorn. Former Stedman employee James Martin purchased the remaining property in 1875. The Martin family in fact has a longer association with the property than the Stedmans. Martin descendants own much of the original property today.

Adding to his woes, in 1875 Mary Stedman fell down a flight of stairs and "broke every bone in her body."[96] One wonders if the accident happened in the Stedman house. We don't know. Wherever it was, his wife of forty years, the woman who had stuck with him through his many trials, was dead. Ebenezer apparently felt the time right to turn his back on the Elkhorn bottom, the scene of his triumphs and increasingly painful defeats. The decline of Ebenezer's vitality with age as well as successive setbacks had put the mills on a downward slide from which they never fully recovered, leaving others to try their hand. His mills failed and his beloved wife dead, Ebenezer moved to Texas in 1875 or 1876 to live out his remaining years with his daughter Nelly Stedman Cox. Nelly was the second wife of Cornelius C. Cox, who had moved west from Franklin County.[97] Daughter Nelly claimed that her father planted the first garden in Live Oak County. In assessing his contributions more generally, Nelly wrote that he did much "to set in motion the industrial arts of Kentucky."[98] She also recorded that in 1878 he began writing a series of letters to his daughter Sophronia "Sophie" Cox, who had remained in Kentucky. Sophie probably requested the letters, the compilation of which resulted in *Bluegrass Craftsman.*

Nelly kept her own journal, and in it she related her father's final days, noting that during his last illness he kept his senses until the end. "My dear daughter won't have a papa very much longer," Nelly recorded him saying.[99] When asked if he had any fear of the Hereafter, he said no, adding, "The Lord God Omnipotent reigneth."[100] On the evening of his death he complained of having difficulty breathing. When his breathing became more labored, the doctor administered another dose of medicine. Ebenezer Stedman died quietly on March 20, 1885, little suspecting that his family letters to Sophia Cox would make a substantial contribution to our understanding of the eventful life of an artisan/entrepreneur in antebellum Kentucky as well as a seminal history of American papermaking.

The remaining buildings of the Stedman complex, aided by neglect and the vagaries of weather, fell into disuse and ruin. Someone salvaged and reused the bricks from the massive chimney that vented the mill's steam engine to build a Sunday school room at the Buck Run Baptist Church at the Forks of Elkhorn.[101] The Martin family and its descendants retained ownership of the land on which the complex was situated, tearing down neglected houses near the mill so that today few signs remain of the population that lived and worked there. The site is reminiscent of poet Oliver Goldsmith's "The Deserted Village" minus even the village.[102]

The last building to be demolished was the Stedman family house, a large frame structure known as the Stedman "Hotel," torn down in 1982 after suffering damage from the cataclysmic 1974 tornado that devastated large portions of central and western Kentucky. The house dates from the flush times before the Civil War. It was a fine house built at the crest of the hill over the Elkhorn valley, cooler in summer because of the breeze and shade trees growing up around it. Despite these improvements, one senses that Mary's heart never completely accepted Elkhorn or left Georgetown and its amenities. Though Stedman does not mention building it in his memoir, the evidence of Mary's discomfort in their first crude house makes his construction of it probable as his finances improved. At some point, either before but probably after Stedman sold the stately house, it must have taken in paying guests, travelers, or perhaps persons who had business or employment. Two and a half stories with twelve rooms, it had a large dry cellar, an outside kitchen as well as wash, wood, spring, and smoke houses, stables, and an orchard.[103] An impressive structure, it stood high overlooking the Elkhorn Valley. It sat among a grove of maples at the center of what now is the Martin farm, above the mill complex, facing what is the appropriately named but inappropriately spelled Steadmantown Lane with access to Frankfort. Mary V. Bryson Hunsaker, who later lived in the house, left a description: "The rooms were enormous with rooms on each of the three floors. It was a Kentucky ell. You had to go into the front hall to get upstairs or go to the outside stairs on the back porch that filled in the ell. My uncle carved a staircase out of the wall where the logs were so thick. It led from one of the rooms to the next floor. The steps were steep, and there was a door at the bottom and at the top. It used to scare us children because it was pitch black."[104] Whatever her relation to the Stedmans, Mary Hunsaker seems to have known the house intimately—a place where she had lived as a child. The reference to "my uncle" carving a staircase suggests her blood ties to the family, though the precise kinship remains vague. As late as the 1970s, someone apparently lived in the house. As Judge Palmore related to me that one day during this time, he and a lawyer friend cut across the pasture toward the creek with their fishing gear when an old man who had been sitting on the porch of the old building challenged them. Asking them what they were doing, they replied they were going fishing. According to Palmore, the old man regarded them as trespassers and ordered them off the property. They went, he told me, chuckling.[105] The Stedman house represented the last intact physical vestige of the prosperous industrial complex and its colorful proprietor. Its destruction brought home to me the importance of historic buildings preserving Kentucky's past, and I wrote an op-ed piece in the *State Journal* (see Appendix C) less as a protest or lament than as an invitation to others to value their old buildings.[106]

Lewis Collins in his *History of Kentucky* refers to a relic that survived one paper mill fire elsewhere and had a rebirth at Stedman's mill on Elkhorn. Writers have identified it as a "powerful armed screw" used in the pressing of paper. Collins describes it as being of "finished English make," six inches in diameter, four and a half feet long, and weighing eight hundred pounds. Transporting it across the ocean and overland to Kentucky must have entailed a great deal of labor and expense. Like much else associated with the Stedman venture, it has disappeared. One of my friends proposed to use metal detectors to seek it out, if it lies buried in Elkhorn Bottom and should the owners be willing to grant him permission. As for the house, a Stedman descendant, John Gray, showed me a china dinner plate with the name "Stedman's" boldly emblazoned on it in crimson, a fragile but potentially durable reminder of the Stedman presence on Elkhorn Creek. In Texas, Nelly Cox took down the text of the expansive eulogy delivered at Stedman's gravesite on March 21, 1885. Though florid and a little overstated in the custom of the day, Dr. A. G. Keaney managed to catch the hallmarks of Stedman's character: "I would like to dwell on his consistency, his kindness, his fertile imagination, his marvelous faculty of winning friends, his dignity, his affability. The natural vivacity of his mind was in happy yet strange contrast to the frail body that held so genial a soul. He loved to fathom mystery and seemed surrounded by an atmosphere peculiarly his own."[107]

Eight

A. W. Macklin (1799–1863). (Courtesy of Ann Macklin Peel.)

*Wearing his high rubber boots, A. W. Macklin directed twenty-some work-
ers as they levered and fit cut stone slabs into the facing of the dam he
was completing on the South Fork of Elkhorn just above the point where
the two forks joined as one. Though aware of the burrowing cold through
his overcoat, he felt good about the near completion of a three-year project as the old log dam once seated on a wide limestone shelf was slowly
being replaced by carefully selected stones that were secured by hydraulic cement that would last for over a hundred years. The stone was taken
from cliffs on North Elkhorn near the north boundary of what everybody
called Bell's Grove. It was the hardest and most durable he had found anywhere. After it was wrested from the hillside, reinforced wagons with iron-
rimmed wheels transported the rough chunks to three separate quarries,
where it was cut precisely to fit his specifications, pieces in a giant puzzle.
The largest chunks had to be dragged to the site by oxen. Across the three
hundred feet of its facing he could see visible progress each day, though in
sum the progress seemed glacial. It would be fifteen feet high, far superior
to the one he'd built nearly twenty years earlier. He was especially proud of
the masonry, each phase of whose placement he had personally overseen,
testing the tightness of the joints, each stone tailored to withstand the persistent pressure of moving water, slabs of stone carefully set into an arch
to contain and channel the natural flow and concentrate it into a force to
feed into the two hundred-yard race and power the mills downstream. It
was built to last, and his pride in his accomplishment grew until he saw
it as the capstone of his life, his monument, as he himself proudly referred
to it. At times he cheered the men on, as a general might shout encouragement for those he commanded to advance on a fortified wall. A wiry
man with shoulders sloped a bit with age, he did not look his sixty-three
years, but his constitution, he knew, was not as ironclad as his will. At
times he pitched himself into the battle to work a stone into place, to seat
it in the precise spot it was destined to rest. Through his work jacket whose
wool had worn smooth and rent in places, he felt a foretaste of winter that*

penetrated deep into his bones. Despite the cold morning, he took pleasure in overseeing the work, satisfied in knowing that he was about to complete what he and his crew had labored toward for so long. Though he was proud of the large mill he'd built downstream which gave steady employment to four men and took in $12,000 a year, this dam, he knew, was what he would be remembered by, the stay against nature that Bennett Pemberton had failed to secure years before, the power of water streaming into the Elkhorn Valley from every branch and trickling feeder in the inner Bluegrass.

When he looked along the line of moving men, some staggering as they lifted and pounded a big stone into place with mallets or maneuvered a piece with spud bars, he thought to set an example, bending to pick up a flagstone as large as his Christmas platter but heavier. He grunted as he grasped its jagged edges with both hands, then braced himself to lift it as high as his waist to plop it with unerring accuracy a few feet away. Halfway up, he felt a stab of pain in his upper abdomen, groaning as he stepped clear and dropped the stone, the pain now searing through his system like molten metal. Some pipe in him had burst under the pressure. Those closest to him rushed over, unsure what had happened, and Macklin could not speak to tell them but clutched his stomach and lay, half-falling, in the shallow water. What they knew to do was to carry him home in one of the wagons on a pile of blankets, and that was the last they saw him except at the grand funeral at Buck Run, where the church was fuller than any of them had ever seen it, their employer lying in his best suit in unaccustomed motionlessness, somber in sleep, red felt to soften his colorless cheeks and the burnished metal coffin glinting under the banks of candles. And replaying what happened among those who hadn't been there, they decided that in fact the dam would be his monument. Many had never seen him in a tie.

ENTREPRENEUR OF THE ELKHORN

He had long had in view the building of a stone mill-dam on South Elkhorn, which should last as long as the stone of which it was built, and be an ornament to his industry and energy. In 1863, he began quarrying and preparing the stone; and, in the Fall of that year, completed the finest and most durable work of that kind to be found, at least in Kentucky.

—Biographical Encyclopedia of Kentucky, 1878

From modest origins A. W. Macklin (1799–1863) rose to become the most prominent citizen of the Forks of Elkhorn during the mid-nineteenth century. Certainly he was the wealthiest. Farmer, banker, dam builder, and manufacturer, Macklin was, like his neighbor E. H. Stedman, a self-made man who bettered himself during the boom years before the Civil War. Stedman engaged in business on a less ambitious scale, content to build his mill complex and concentrate it in one place and make that place his home, the Elkhorn Valley. Though many of Macklin's business ventures also relied on Elkhorn, he didn't limit himself to a single locale or source of profit, willing to go where he could find opportunities and markets—to Frankfort, to Beattyville, to Arkansas, and to Mississippi. A. W. Macklin had a larger appetite, a vision more grandiose. His zeal for capitalizing never fully reached saturation, and he operated on a scale that Stedman could scarcely imagine. One writer described him as starting with a wife, a mule, and $25.[1] Part of the success he achieved heeded the advice of today's investment managers: diversify, avoid placing all of one's eggs in one basket.

Elkhorn Creek, along with skill, determination, and pluck, fueled Stedman's success. An excess of flowing water and other largely natural forces also brought about his eventual failure. Papermaking formed the foundation of his prosperity, though lumber and grist helped keep the coffers full. By contrast, Macklin had his hand in farming, milling, pork packing, lumber, coal, and real estate. The two men patterned their enterprises on different models. Stedman's narrower vision focused solely on the local, drawing on local and mostly free-white labor to operate his mills, selling his paper mostly to a local market with at least one fatal exception. Yes, he owned slaves, but he limited their use largely to domestic purposes. Macklin's business model took on proportions that made it expansive and necessarily exploitive, especially of humans. Much of his wealth, he would probably acknowledge, accrued through his use of unpaid labor. He took a norm for his region and carried it to its limits. Conveniently suspending any moral questions about owning others, he, like many of his contemporaries, simply took advantage of available resources. Going along with the prevailing pro-Southern sentiments in his rural neighborhood, Stedman had no scruples about contracting with the Confederacy. Both men had sons who enlisted in its armies, though Macklin's son Alex did so without his father's consent. In simple terms, Macklin thought big, Stedman more modestly. Both proved to be exceptions to the generally accepted myth that the South derived its wealth almost exclusively from agriculture and that industry played a very minor role in its economic well-being.

Like Stedman, Macklin had a modest upbringing with few advantages. He was born on a farm on Macklin Lane (the name later changing to Jones Lane) near North Elkhorn Creek between the small farming communities of Switzer and Stamping Ground. A photograph of the cabin shows exposed logs, a small window, a puncheon door. Nothing fancy. Located near the Forks, the house had originally been lived in by a man named George Smith, and later by Reverend John Taylor, celebrated locally for founding a number of Baptist churches. A. W. could not claim blueblood. His father, Hugh Macklin, emigrated from Ireland to Virginia as a young man in 1786, later moving to Franklin County, where he acquired a farm of about a hundred acres. Hugh's precise birth date and even his Irish origins have not been fully verified but rely mostly on family tradition. Looking to get ahead, Hugh Macklin and others reputedly operated a wagon train between Zanesville, Ohio, and Kentucky. The seeds of his son's drive to make something of himself originated in this father, who possessed more than the rudiments of an education. Not only could he read and write—fairly uncommon for this time on the Kentucky frontier—but he had a "more than superficial knowledge of law and finance."[2] Active in the Forks community and Frankfort, he began lending money to others and used the courts when debtors defaulted. He also immersed himself in the community, participating in the activities of the county with a sense of civic responsibility.

A. W. (whose middle name no one could agree on: William? Watkins? Walker?) received what biographers describe as an "ordinary English education"—a euphemism for meager schooling—ending probably when he learned to read and acquired some skills at math. Family tradition has it that among his native gifts was a facility with numbers. He often performed the trick of working two mathematical problems simultaneously, one with each hand.[3] Apprenticed as a carpenter, he started his working career with a hammer, saw, and plumb bob before redirecting his future toward commerce. His carpentry skills apparently extended to furniture making, for he constructed a set of twelve faux bamboo side chairs, one of which survived in the family intact through the generations.

In 1825 he married his cousin Jane Macklin (1800–1870). Orphaned as a child in Virginia, Jane had entered the Macklin home as a ward and first cousin of her future husband. In this case, familiarity bred affection by proximity and awareness of the other's strengths and shortcomings. She grounded herself, like most of her Macklin kin, in the world of practical doings, a sensible and frugal person, sober in her outlook. One story supporting this view of her character goes that on the day of the wedding, the preacher arrived to find her spinning. She got up, married, and directly returned to her spinning wheel.[4] From the scant family accounts she comes across as a no-nonsense mother, a resourceful woman familiar with the harshness of frontier living in rural Kentucky, only half a generation younger than the Cook women. One descendant who visited the cabin in which the couple started their life together recalls playing in the attic where she saw strings of simple wooden buttons hanging from the rafters and bolts of striped denim, both used in the making of slave clothing for the family's growing number of slaves. After their marriage, the couple moved to adjacent Woodford County, where A. W. rented a farm on Glenn's Creek and taught in a country school. When he took up residence again in his home county, his neighbors elected him constable, a post he held for a number of years. Serving papers, he often found himself berated and more than once attacked, given licks with "cowhides, fists, stones and sticks."[5] Among the damages he sought (and received) was for a hat, possibly the beaver top hat found in the attic of one of his descendants with the original invoice and that his great, great grandson used to play "dress up."[6]

In late 1826 the couple purchased a 119-acre farm in the Forks of Elkhorn neighborhood. In a time when rural living encouraged large families, the couple eventually had seven children—three sons and four daughters—at least two of the sons following their father into business. In addition to raising their seven children, Jane saw to the health of the many slaves and free whites working in her husband's many businesses. Jane Macklin carried a valise full of herbs and medications so she would always be ready to treat those who needed medical help. The moral question of slavery, the labor source that largely contributed to Alexander's fortune, apparently troubled neither Jane nor her husband.[7] Among the assets in his will Macklin listed eighty-four slaves, their names, ages, and valuations, making him one of the largest slaveowners in Kentucky.[8]

For whatever reasons—to feed his growing family, a desire to better himself, a vision of himself as a captain of industry in a time when captains of industry seemed to sprout like mushrooms during a season of rain—A. W. Macklin ignited within himself a spirit of enterprise. A skillful trader, by 1836 he accumulated enough money to sell his small farm and buy a larger one of 222 acres on the South Fork of Elkhorn. In 1838 he acquired what he referred to as the family farm from John Taylor, one of the earliest preachers in the state and the author of *Baptists on the American Frontier: A History of Ten Baptist Churches,* which included the story of one located nearby on South Elkhorn Creek.[9] Joining with the equally ambitious Swigert brothers in Frankfort under the name of A. W. Macklin and Company, he manufactured hemp bagging and rope, shipping the products of his ropewalk to New Orleans. The company also diversified into meatpacking, and he built a factory on land that he owned along the Kentucky River at the mouth of a stream called Glenn's Creek. During 1853–1854 the plant slaughtered 10,042 hogs, and it continued to increase that number for a period of years.

A. W. Macklin's appetite for gain could only be satisfied with greater efficiency in his efforts to produce more. In one day during one of the boom years, his workers killed and processed 804 hogs.[10] Placing the pork in barrels, he sent it downriver to markets in the South, chiefly New Orleans. He also shipped packed pork and other products to such faraway places as New York and foreign markets. To provide barrels in which to pack the pork, he set up a cooperage, and at least one of his slaves became a master cooper.[11] He also owned an extremely successful coal yard on the Kentucky River at the foot of Broadway in downtown Frankfort. Ahead of his time, A. W. believed in owning every phase of production. When he recognized a need, he tried to accommodate it himself. In eastern Kentucky, he cut timber on land he owned to build barges on which he shipped coal he owned. When he unloaded at Frankfort, he loaded the barges with pork from his packing plant and shipped it to New Orleans to be sold along with lumber from his dismantled barges. A. W. had an eye for profit, much of it gained through efficiency of his operations. Needing more labor as his businesses expanded, he eventually owned or leased (more of the former than the latter) a small army of 120 slaves, employed across his farm, his mills, and his factories as well as engaged in dam building across Elkhorn at the Forks.[12]

In 1840 he built a factory for the manufacture of hemp bagging and rope on his land at the Forks. It operated with great success until his death, supplied with hemp he grew on land he owned nearby. In 1843 his workers constructed a dam just above the Forks to channel water to support his milling operations. In 1844 he built a large flouring mill on his Elkhorn property. It had a capacity of 150 barrels a day and was the only water-powered mill in the region that could be operated during the entire year. Located on the main stem of Elkhorn, the mills produced wheat flour, corn meal, and mill feed, then sold it at a store on Broadway in downtown Frankfort across from the Capitol Square. In addition to the gristmill, the property contained a miller's residence (with stables, garden, and outhouse), a cooper's shop, large scales, three tenement houses and gardens, a blacksmith's residence, and forty-two acres of land.[13] This large gristmill was one of the major mills in the Bluegrass region of central Kentucky.[14] Its builder was an entrepreneurial dynamo whose appetite for acquisition and development seemed insatiable.

For almost his entire life, A. W. was active in the Buck Run Baptist Church. Local legend has it that the first Baptist Sunday school in Kentucky convened in one of the Macklin mills, the children sitting on sacks

Buck Run Baptist Church, circa 1900–1910. (Courtesy of Capital City Museum, Frankfort, Kentucky.)

of meal. After his death, operation of the mill fell to his son Benoni and through several decades underwent various incarnations and technological improvements until its three and a half stories burned in 1892.

Charles Hockensmith, who grew up at the Forks and later became an archaeologist and authority on Kentucky's mills, confessed that the Macklin mills held "a special place in his heart": "As boys growing up in the Forks of Elkhorn during the 1960s, Wally McConnell [a probable descendant of early McConnells] and I spent many hours playing on the mill ruins and fishing below the mill dam. Wally's family farmed the property containing the millrace and the mill ruins. On South Elkhorn, they owned the property on the south side of the old Macklin Dam and established the Elkhorn Campground which still exists today under new ownership. The shallow but swift water below the dam was once an awesome fishing hole."[15] The area where they played adjacent to the millrace fifty or sixty years ago is now part of a camper/trailer park, though most of the mill ruins have survived in the forested area adjacent to the creek.

Macklin is said at one time to have owned almost all the land, except for the town of Frankfort, from the Kentucky River to Woodlake, the area of Franklin County to the east of the Forks. In addition to his holdings around the Forks and East Frankfort, he purchased several tracts in Beattyville in eastern Kentucky that were sources for coal and lumber he barged downriver to Frankfort to heat the growing capital city and to construct its homes and businesses. He purchased these tracts at the three forks of the Kentucky River to collect the coal and lumber for use downstream. His land holdings in Kentucky eventually amounted to over 2,000 acres. Extending his reach, he also invested in cotton land in Arkansas (5,697 acres) and Mississippi (1,000 acres).[16] Because he was not personally supervising these out-of-state farming operations, they were not successful. Despite some setbacks, A. W. had a knack for making money and the prescience to sense when his ventures were in jeopardy. When he saw the tide of the Civil War changing—probably after Shiloh in 1862—he took his Confederate money downstream to New Orleans and exchanged it for gold, thus saving his fortune.

In 1863, the year of his death, he could see the fulfillment of his dream of completing a large, cut-stone milldam on South Elkhorn just above the Forks, described as "an ornament to his energy and industry."[17] The dam was built to divert water for use in powering the Macklin mills several hundred yards downstream, near the site of the present Old Grandad Distillery. What remained of the mills burned in the 1890s. The millraces still exist but seem to be of later construction than the dam. As well, numerous fences from the complex still can be seen. The dam's masonry was considered some of the finest in Kentucky, especially the fine stone being quarried from a cliff overhanging North Elkhorn on a farm known as Bell's Grove. Some were cut two feet thick, four or five feet wide, and from six to eight feet long, large enough to fill the bed of a good-sized wagon, assuming it could take the weight. Most were dragged to the site by oxen. Unloaded probably with block and tackle, they were laid entirely by hand, so carefully placed that the dam has remained intact for over 150 years, surviving numerous floods, including one in 1932 described by a neighbor as flowing "like Niagra." Great weight as well as precision were key to the dam's longevity. Part of its durability was owing to beveling or wedging the ends of the blocks so they would fit snugly.[18] When the dam was nearly completed, the proud builder was heard to say, "This is my monument." He died shortly before its completion. The Macklin mill burned in 1892 and was never rebuilt. The races built to carry the flow to the mill are visible, though bypassed and disused. Numerous stone walls

Macklin Dam, Forks of Elkhorn. (Photograph by Gene Burch.)

along the banks of the creek and surrounding area, also built by slaves, still survive.[19] The area later became the site of the state fish hatchery as well as a recreational area for picnics and public gatherings.

In politics, A. W. Macklin described himself as an old-line Whig, and in religion a Baptist, donating $8,000 in his will to Georgetown College to educate young men for the ministry. At his death in 1863 he left an estate of several hundred thousand dollars to be divided among his seven children as well as a farm for each. First buried on his home farm near the Forks, later he was reinterred, like Harry Innes, in Frankfort Cemetery. Like Ebenezer Stedman, he harnessed waterpower on Elkhorn to run three mills—one to grind grain, one to saw lumber, one to weave woolens. Doing business with his neighbors, he must have been intimately acquainted with the Stedmans, perhaps as a rival in his lumber and grist mills but not in papermaking, one local arena of enterprise to which he did not apply his talents. A. W. Macklin apparently preferred the country around the Forks and never lived in Frankfort, but son George's townhouse on Washington Street, just down the street from Thomas Todd's in the historic district, stands unpretentiously one of the handsomest buildings in Frankfort. For a time what remains of a Macklin antebellum home (probably Benoni's) a short distance west of the Forks was rebuilt in a one-story plan after damage from the 1974 tornado. It became the residence of Judge John Palmore, who coincidentally lived in what remains of Harry Innes's home several miles down Elkhorn. Everything connects.

After A. W.'s death, his son Benoni operated the Macklin mills on Elkhorn until his own death. George ran the Elkhorn Water Mills from his Frankfort office on Broadway in downtown Frankfort. A visionary like his father, George owned the first telephone in Frankfort in 1878, two years after its invention.[20] Conservative in most respects, he also was an astute businessman who recognized the benefits of innovation.

Just as the son of his neighbor Ebenezer Stedman and many other young men in the Forks area did, A. W.'s son Alex joined the Confederacy when the war broke out, running off to Lexington in 1862 to join General Morgan's 4th Mounted Rifles, a unit later consolidated into Company C of the 9th Kentucky Cavalry.[21] He was eighteen. A photograph of him, belonging to the family, reveals a handsome and serious young man in a uniform with billowing sleeves, his slouch hat turned up in front rakishly, the coat of his uniform casually unbuttoned. Of medium height, he stood five feet, seven inches tall and had dark hair and hazel eyes. Later in the war he served under General Joseph Wheeler during the Atlanta campaign, receiving a wound at Louisville, Georgia, being shot in the left thumb. He survived his injury and the surgeon who wanted to amputate it. A family story goes that after it had healed, the thumb bore an indentation. To amuse his grandchildren, Alex would let them roll the bullet around under the skin of his thumb while they sat in his lap. When the Confederate government dissolved, he traveled for several days with others as an escort for fugitive President Jefferson Davis. He came home with a pistol he captured at Atlanta, keeping it as a trophy.

After the war and his father's death, Alex returned to the family farm and helped his mother manage it, both of them performing manual labor. Some of the slaves had gone their way when emancipation came. Though some elected to stay on, he had more work than workers. Married after the war to Annie Bedford, he fathered two children, Jane Macklin Coop and Bedford Macklin, inheriting the home farm at his mother's death.[22] When A. W. died in 1863, he had made no direct bequest to Alex in his will because property owned by those in rebellion against the Union was subject to confiscation. He received the family farm at his mother's death

Alex W. Macklin Jr., CSA. (Courtesy of Ann Macklin Peel.)

and probably operated it as his own before her passing. A longtime commander of the United Confederate Veterans as well as a generous supporter of the Confederate Veterans Home near Louisville, Alex spent the remainder of his life farming on the banks of Elkhorn, dying in 1922.[23] Doctors attributed the cause of his death to erysipelas, an "acute febrile disease," with intense diffusely spreading deep red inflammation of the skin or mucous membrane, caused by a specific streptococcus.[24] Ironically and perhaps causally, humans shared the disease with swine, to which he must have been exposed all of his life. He, as all the Macklins, must have been on as intimate terms with Elkhorn Creek as that other owner of mills, Ebenezer Stedman.

Both A. W. Macklin and Ebenezer Stedman were creatures of their respective ages. They were honest. They cared for their families and their community. They exemplified a model of the self-made man so esteemed in our culture. If Stedman's enterprise led to the decimation of woodlands in the Elkhorn Valley, Macklin's was more global in its reach. He was a resourceful capitalist in a society that had few regulations, limited science, and a laissez-faire attitude toward natural resources—coal, minerals, timber, water. Each could be converted into capital. Macklin's orbit extended to all these, many beyond Elkhorn and its waters. A captain of industry during the Gilded Age in which American industry expanded beyond most people's capacity to imagine, he and most of his contemporaries gave little thought to the environmental consequences of their capitalist aspirations. Seemingly boundless natural resources begged to be exploited. Humans invariably favored their own species over others and nature itself. During the nineteenth century, environmental science at best was in its infancy. Short-term benefits trumped long-term detriments that were not immediately detected or understood. People simply couldn't conceive of the toll of their actions on the environment. There were no environmental studies to obstruct the free flow of capital and few activists to warn them—no Roosevelts to put a check on capital or promote the saving of wild places, no John Muir, no Aldo Leopold. Henry David Thoreau seemed a hopeless romantic, a disgruntled maverick. Audubon had envisioned the effects of species extinction but held his tongue. The effects of their efforts would wait until the twentieth century to be taken seriously as environmental education slowly entered our consciousness in a country, in the Western world, that glorified hard work and the entrepreneurial spirit to the detriment of the health of the natural world.

The nature of dams themselves has undergone considerable reevaluation since the nineteenth century. To make a dollar, Macklin needed power. A resource was at hand if it could be harnessed and redirected. Dams fulfilled that function. He probably gave little thought to the effects of his actions beyond the bottom line. Since the Romans, dams have impounded vast quantities of water and altered the ecologies of regions upstream and down. What happens when that natural flow is impeded? We don't know all the possible results, but those we do recognize are seldom beneficial either to us in the long run or to aquatic life in the short term. Rivers and creeks are natural highways for more than kayaks. They are integral to the processes of geology and life on the planet. Think of dams as roadblocks. We know, for example, that in the far West they present obstacles in the path of salmon that swim upstream to spawn in upland sanctuaries. Dams fragment waterways, creating holding pools and collecting sediments where before there were none. They alter the delicate range of temperatures in which many species breed and develop. Life-forms ranging from planktons and invertebrates to mollusks and fish are vulnerably sensitive to such changes. They segregate what was once a vibrant and harmonious whole. Mollusks, for a variety of reasons, have virtually disappeared from Elkhorn. Placed under severe stress, these life-forms must either adapt, relocate, or die. They are voiceless, and we know their plight too often only by their absence, sometimes their extinction.

Unfortunately, the latter is often the case, a fact lost on mill owners and dam builders until the last hundred years or so. Something about flowing water abhors obstruction. Witness the Grand Canyon, Stedman's dam, or even the dam at the Forks, Macklin's monument. Though the structure of Macklin Dam itself remains intact, it has become a spillway along its three hundred or so feet. It slows water but no longer entraps it. What I see when I pass is a continuous band of silver curling over its stone lip. The races to which water was once redirected have long since washed away or dry docked, most of their canals swallowed by fill. The mills they existed to serve have long since all but disappeared. As Percy Bysshe Shelley's sonnet "Ozymandias" (1818) tells us, human monuments are subject to time and the humbling effects of weather and other natural forces. Permanence is an illusion. The Grand Coulee Dam is no exception. Impounding water alters eons-old cycles and rhythms of flowing water, upsetting the delicate balances between animal and plant populations as well as opening the door, so to speak, to invasive species that fill the vacuum. For better or worse, Elkhorn Creek carries a freight of sediments both natural and man-made. Erosion that stops at the dam often aggravates erosion of embankments below the dam. This effect is very visible along the lower reaches of the creek toward Peaks Mill, where natural erosion of mud banks has been abetted by alterations we scarcely understand. All the consequences of changing the natural course of streams are far too complicated and immense to comprehend fully. This is no less true for the Elkhorn than for any other waterway. Throughout ancient and modern history, the original Elkhorn Valley helped form the Mississippi Delta in the Gulf of Mexico. Kentucky, along with Kentuckians, migrated west.

Toward the end of his life, Stedman gained some perspective, looking back on the idyllic valley he'd come to in the 1830s and feeling some nostalgia for the lost game and forested hillsides. Whether Macklin felt a prick of environmental conscience, we don't know, but Macklin and Frankfort citizens could not have escaped noticing, smelling, the offal produced by his slaughterhouse at the edge of downtown, probably dumped into the

Kentucky River upstream from the core of the town's commercial and
oldest residential district. Citizens in Frankfort must also have suffered
the effects of his coal operation, wheezing with asthma and other more
serious maladies brought on by burning carbon. Smoke from burning coal
must have hung in the river valley and been a source of irritation accepted
as normal by most citizens. It was hard to violate an environmental ethic
if one grew up before such existed as part of popular understanding. Citizens raised in the preindustrial age with only horsepower and steam to
marvel at witnessed great changes in their lifetimes with new technolo-
gies and ever-rising rates of economic consumption. The theology students whose educations Macklin sponsored in his will would live to see
the values of his generation questioned, the Eden of his generation transformed in many places to F. Scott Fitzgerald's Valley of Ashes. As a result
of agricultural and urban pollution, the fishermen along Elkhorn would
witness a dramatic reduction of aquatic life, fewer and diminished smallmouth bass that everyone took for granted. Native Americans had lived
for at least twelve thousand years along the creek without substantially
changing it. They may have used weirs to ensnare fish, but they were not
engineers. The creek had long since adapted to beaver dams that somehow fit into the larger scheme of things. The pristine vistas of the creek as
a place of natural beauty and wonder that Sawyier painted must have fed
the sensibilities of those who remembered. The dam itself was finally an
emblem of our will to bend the natural world to its limits in serving our
purposes. A. W. Macklin simply followed established practices, and the
dam that is his monument should also remind us of the need to affirm an
environmental ethic and be aware of the price of violating it.

Nine

Paul Sawyier with painting equipment. (Courtesy of
Margaret Bridwell Art Library, University of Louisville,
Louisville, Kentucky.)

Pedaling his bike up the long rise out of town, Paul made it to the crest of East Main with only some deep breathing, resting near the summit by the wrought-iron gate to the Frankfort Cemetery where his people—Wingates, Sawyiers, Andersons, McKees—lay untroubled on the high bluff overlooking Frankfort and the Kentucky River. The going would have been easier if both of his tires had been fully inflated. In the rush to leave he had neglected to check, and he'd left his hand pump god knows where. As he got his wind, he looked about him. Downhill he could spy one of the turrets of the Kentucky State Arsenal. To his left a little farther out Main was the fledgling Kentucky State College for Colored Persons. About him were places he'd painted and knew he would never stop painting, including the covered bridge whose white span stretched across the Kentucky, miniature and dazzling in full sunlight. His brushes had probed the landmarks, arresting their forms on compliant paper, but today he was heading for the creek. He took to the pedals again. His low tire seemed to be holding its trapped air, no longer a major worry. Now the terrain leveled out and the mechanical circuits his feet made were easier, despite the added weight of the paint box, portable easel, his camp stool, and the cardboard portfolio that protected his brushwork—all lashed to the wire basket attached to his handlebars, though the legs of the easel took some ingenuity. As each work dried, he would carefully insert it between the covers of his precious portfolio, a shield against mishaps.

Passing a few houses where people were bustling about their business, one or two of whom he recognized and waved to, he reached Black's Pond and wheeled out Steadmantown Lane into the countryside, past the old Stedman place and along the cliff road above Elkhorn and finally to Peaks Mill Road, first stopping at the high bluff to gaze over the broad expanse of rich cropland displayed in grids as a red-shouldered hawk might view it across the creek. Though he could not see over the edge, he knew the creek was a hundred or more feet below where he stood. He could not sensibly confirm this unless he stepped closer to the precarious overhang, but he knew better.

From scores of paintings he could piece a vision of the creek's green band flowing imperturbably as it had since long before any of his people had come to this region. Elkhorn, studied almost rock by rock, pool by pool, was a fixture in his mind, and he could reel out scene after scene. Close his eyes and he could see it at any spot he summoned, named or unnamed.

When he reached Church's Grove, where the water ran only a penny toss from the road, he leaned his bike against a tree, unloaded his gear, and began eyeing formations across the creek for the likeliest site, a place to frame his hands against the water and rocks and ruffled skirt of trees along one bank to capture the best light and then reduce it to a rendering on a single sheet of high-grade paper. In his ears was the seething rush of water as it constricted in the narrowing channel along the base of Pinnacle Rock and adjoining formations where the currents were slowly excavating the rock shelves. Looking up, he saw a rag snagged about ten feet above his head in the upper limbs of a creekside tree that marked the crest of high waters. Sloping, layered, a rusty dun, the stolid rocks reminded him of the horse hoof fungus on the locust that shaded his mother's backyard, a growth affixed only to the bark of certain trees. He turned his attention to the creek. It was low enough to wade, as it generally was during August, when the whole valley seemed to dry and tighten, yellowing into fall. He took off his high-top shoes and tied the laces together so he could hang them around his neck, also removing the socks. Then he rolled his trousers up to his knees, knowing this would not prevent the water from darkening them. To cross, he shouldered his paint bag and the folded legs of his easel, picked up the canvas campstool, then stepped into the water.

It was colder, swifter than he expected, and his bare feet inched along the bottom, wary of slickness that formed from little colonies of algae or mosses. There were no gravels here, the smooth under-surface constantly swept and scoured like an erased canvas. Reaching the far shore, he stepped out on a platter of warm rock, one wet foot and then the other catapulting droplets onto the rocks and milky silt. The patterns they made on white stones put him in mind of the dappling leaves in some of his paintings that somehow resembled a flock of tiny birds. The flecks blended into the shadows at his feet. Where the current riffled the surface was broken by divots of sunlight that showed as silver crescents in the stream. For a moment he sensed that what he would paint today was no more permanent than dew, light off the shimmering leaves, or spatters of water drying on the rock. Still, he would paint. Putting on his socks and shoes, hanging his jacket on one of a cluster of scraggly water maples, he found a shady spot that offered a view downstream with some rock facings on one bank that rose dramatically out of the valley, trees on the other. He clipped a sheet of paper to the board and positioned it on the three-legged easel, vertically instead of horizontally since he meant to include the tall rock formation before him. Then he opened the stool and unwrapped his brushes and charcoal pencil. The last thing he did before assessing the light and provisionally mapping a composition was to step back to the creek to dip his water tin. Every watercolor he would paint along Elkhorn carried a residue of the creek in its dried wash—a marriage of eye, pigment, and creek water. Wherever his paintings wound up, he thought, they would carry molecules of Elkhorn, water that was the soul mate of his color.

WHISTLERIAN BLUE

Sweet silver Elkhorn, I hear thy music in my dreams.
—Unknown nineteenth-century poet

The major stylistic features are the emphasis given to linear clarity and reflective light on the surface of the water, the planar division of the landscape, and the use of light to define blurred forms in the foliage.
—Arthur F. Jones, *The Art of Paul Sawyier,* 1976

If Ebenezer Stedman represents the artisan of Elkhorn, Paul Sawyier (1865–1917) lays claim to being its artist, an American impressionist and perhaps Kentucky's most beloved painter. Like Stedman, he was technically a transplant. Born on Table Rock Farm near London in Madison County, Ohio, he was five when his parents moved back to Frankfort, where both had relatives and where his mother, Ellen Wingate Sawyier, had been raised. Living in a small-town state capital with ready access to the river and some of the most idyllic scenery in Kentucky shaped his life. His father, Dr. Nathaniel J. Sawyier, a well-to-do physician with some artistic flair as an amateur painter and sculptor, had roots in Frankfort that sank as deep. The house in which they lived on Broadway a block north of Main Street had been in the family for three generations, a gift to his grandmother from Paul's great grandfather, Reuben Anderson, one of the county's first settlers.[1] Paul and his three siblings took instruction at local schools and attended the First Baptist Church. Though in the classroom he showed few signs of "a bookish inclination," he early demonstrated a talent for drawing. To nourish this talent, his father hired a tutor to teach figure drawing to him and one of his sisters, Natalie.

After two years' additional schooling at the Dudley Institute in Frankfort, Sawyier moved to Covington to live with his cousins, the McKees, so he could attend classes across the Ohio River at the Art Academy of Cincinnati. There, at nineteen, he studied figure drawing under former Lexingtonian Thomas S. Noble (1835–1907), "one of the key figures in American art education in the second half of the nineteenth century."[2] He later studied portraiture with Frank Duveneck (1848–1919), a much-celebrated American nineteenth-century artist who returned to Cincinnati after studying at the Royal Academy of Fine Arts in Munich and establishing his own painting school there, which gained a "substantial reputation among the Americans studying in the city."[3] For a time, Sawyier shared a studio with a fellow art student named Avery Sharp and paid his way by making charcoal portraits while still living, rent free, across the river in Covington with his aunt, Sarah McKee.[4]

William Merritt Chase became his third influential teacher, an eclectic master who promoted Impressionism in America. Sawyier came under his influence when he took Noble's advice and continued his studies at the Art Students League of New York. There he learned a technique that Chase had gleaned from the work of famous American painter James Whistler (1834–1903), a trick of creating a sense of distance in his vistas by combining specific shades of blue and gray. Sawyier experimented with this combination in his own landscapes and was pleased with the results, which can be seen in many of his views of the river and Elkhorn, a corridor of shorelines fading into muzzy blues and grays that effectively create a sense of depth and distance—Whistlerian blue.[5]

If Stedman's life turned on a reliable flow of water and mechanical contrivances capable of producing material goods that were often ephemeral though in constant demand, Sawyier aimed his quest in directions less material and more ideal. During his lifetime, the demand for his productions never reached the reliable consistency of Stedman's. In the minds of many ordinary Americans, art remains an afterthought whose function is ornament, a frill in which few place much value. Instead of pursuing the American dream of material prosperity, Sawyier settled for more personal satisfactions, simply seeking to capture light and the influence it exerts on trees and rocks and water. When recognition did not immediately come, it no longer became his prime motivation—if it ever was. He painted to survive, yes, but he seems to have expended little thought in

carving out a reputation beyond modest regional appreciation. The pleasure and immediate challenge of painting Elkhorn in the late afternoon
or doing justice in rendering a familiar public fountain was sufficient. He
never seemed to look far beyond a completed watercolor unless necessity spurred him to paint another. One senses that during these moments
confronting nature and seeking how to frame it he discovered his best
self, his most-challenged and satisfied self, a reflection of the art-for-art's-
sake ideal prominent during the Aesthetic movement in England and
elsewhere at the end of the nineteenth century. Elkhorn, as well as the
Kentucky and Dix rivers, became his laboratories, the chief sources of
many of the estimated three thousand oils and watercolors that constitute
the corpus of his work. Around his mills Stedman took satisfaction in
fostering the building of what evolved as a company town. Sawyier settled
for less tangible achievements, scaled-down constructions of color and
shape that froze on paper and canvas the flux he saw in nature. He must
have seen himself as a creator of illusions whose subjects, when successfully rendered, appeared almost more real than the listing sycamores and
shimmering water that provided his main avenues of exploration.

Though possible, it's unlikely that Sawyier and Stedman ever met.
Generations apart—one at the end of his career, the other at the beginning—both derived their livelihoods from the endless permutations of
flowing water. But Sawyier certainly knew the dilapidated Stedman mills
and Stedmantown as intimately as the palisades and treescapes upstream
and down. It is tempting to imagine the aging entrepreneur stepping out
of the millhouse to greet the young painter lugging his paintbox in search
of some new inspiration along the creek. At least one of his paintings
seems to contain portions of the mill complex obscured by trees, so he
certainly knew the place, though Stedman had vacated Kentucky before
Sawyier returned from school and took up the artistic mapping of Elkhorn in earnest. Each probably knew of the other, Sawyier a little sooner
hearing than Stedman. Small towns do not honor anonymity. Though
Paul Sawyier did not live on the creek, the creek lived in him.

Paul's father, having suspended his practice of medicine to become
president of Kentucky River Mills, a local hemp factory at lock four just
outside Frankfort, summoned Paul home in 1886 to work as a salesman
for the company, one of the few commercial positions he ever held. But
selling string, twine, and rope did not agree with him, and he lasted only a

short time. Brought up in privilege, he was never to assume the responsi-bilities of most adults—a job, a spouse, children, a conventional career—what Zorba the Greek in the novel of that name described archly as "the whole catastrophe." Not cut out for the daily routine that would pay bills and support his art, Paul opted to make a go of doing full-time what he loved most—painting. He often succeeded, especially among the circle of friends who loved and supported him. If his life had a pattern, it consisted of finding individuals who appreciated and sustained him, providing food and lodging or buying his art, sometimes acquiring it by barter in return for services. One proud owner of several Sawyiers I knew in Frankfort boasted that his grandfather, a doctor, received them in barter for provid-ing Sawyier with medical care for unspecified ailments. But Sawyier was no sickly stay-at-home. He roamed creek bottoms, waded streams, scaled precipices. During the time he lived in Frankfort, he also ranged the more polite landscape, having an active social life, attending house parties and dances, rambling about the country when parlors bored him or when a fit of the muse struck, painting *plein air*. For pocket money or when times were tough, he sometimes took on students, mostly young women from prominent local families who had the talent, leisure, and funds—not nec-essarily in that order—to learn from the master. Students included Mary Belle Taylor of a well-to-do distilling family and Bertha Scott, daughter of James Scott, prominent attorney and owner of Scott's camp on the Elk-horn.[6] Not sitting at the foot of the master, they hiked and roughed it with him, skirts stuck with burrs, lugging their paint kits and easels, anxious to learn the secrets of his art.

Attending a party one night at a home near Knight's Bridge by Elkhorn Creek, he became reacquainted with the "sprightly and charming" Mary Thomas "Mayme" Bull, the love of his life.[7] Though born in the same year, attending Second Street School, and living only a few blocks apart, they showed no earlier romantic interest in each other. Both in their early twen-ties, they suddenly discovered more, soon becoming what their contempo-raries referred to as an item. Mayme became his devoted companion and patient fiancée for the rest of her life. For a number of reasons, mostly his, they did not marry. His precarious finances presented the greatest apparent obstacle to taking the plunge. Money must have been a persistent source of anxiety, affecting his relationship with Mayme and his inability, or unwill-ingness, to formalize their relationship in marriage, an arrangement that

Paul Sawyier and Mayme Bull. (Courtesy of Margaret Bridwell Art Library, University of Louisville, Louisville, Kentucky.)

would have required some compromises with his rambling after scenes to paint and altering the hand-to-mouth existence that had become his mode of living, what now we know as an alternate lifestyle.

His father's ill health presented another obstacle. What the family saw initially as premature senility crystallized into what was probably early onset Alzheimer's. Increasingly, he became dependent on the care of others, and Paul as the senior child inherited greater responsibilities. Marrying would have imposed an economic commitment on him that he never seemed quite prepared or equipped to accept. So he and Mayme fell into a comfortable pattern of socializing in the evenings and on weekends, until he took the advice of Thomas Noble and moved to New York for more training. While he remained in Frankfort, she sometimes accompanied him on jaunts, even visiting his houseboat at High Bridge when he relocated to paint river scenes. Though no one can know the depth of his feelings for Mayme, their marriage would not be feasible without a steady income. Instead, he took on the identity of a bohemian among his comfortably middle-class schoolmates, taking to the river or finding a path to Elkhorn Creek. Ultimately, the brush became his bride.

For most of his life Paul successfully negotiated two worlds—combining the bohemian life of the artist as perceived in the popular imagination and the genteel life to which he had been bred. Mild-mannered, modest, usually reticent, he presented a neat appearance that made him welcome at homes that counted in Frankfort, at High Bridge, and New York, where people generously underwrote his art by providing his basic needs. His friends commented that he could spend two weeks tramping around Elkhorn and look as tidy and well dressed as though fresh on his way to a social gathering. Not burdened with a big ego, he sometimes seemed to sign his paintings almost as an afterthought, leaving many unsigned, perhaps because he felt that letters blemished the purity of his images. Never a dilettante, he fit the mold of the gentleman's painter, though without a reliable income. He enshrined the creek in its most ideal form, leaving its surroundings untroubled.

Trying to visualize Sawyier in Elkhorn Bottom, I first wondered about his modes of conveyance. One likely answer is that he got around by shank's mare: he walked. Riding his bike arose as a second possibility, though a bicycle, given the equipment he needed to carry, would have been at times burdensome and impractical. One of his friends at Camp Nelson confirmed that in fact he owned a bike and often used it.[8] Elkhorn Creek lies at least four and a half miles from Frankfort, depending more or less on which section of the creek he wished to visit. Occasionally, he may have hitched a ride aboard wagons or carriages, but probably no public conveyance extended far beyond Frankfort—no taxies, no buses except for railroads in their unswerving courses. Most of his life—the time in Kentucky until 1908—passed too soon for automobiles to be common. Often his friends would also provide him with food and a place to stay. Other times he camped. Almost certainly he did not come by skiff or canoe since at some point he would have to go upstream, and paddling upstream on Elkhorn, even when it's calm, becomes physically challenging, especially when creek levels drop. As for eating, I can easily imagine him packing sandwiches and maybe some fruit, at times cooking the fish he caught over a campfire. Though he knew not to drink the polluted water, he probably would have also known where to find relatively unspoiled springs and freshets. Because he didn't keep a journal and wrote few letters that survive, his life seems overinvested with many such small mysteries.

A persistent undercurrent of public opinion has held that Paul Sawyier suffered from a drinking problem, the perceived malady of artists. Certainly he drank alcohol, and at times probably overdrank, but reports of his toping seem more the result of public discomfort with the lifestyle of the artist than alcoholism—the then rigid insistence in small towns of adhering to small-town mores. For whatever reasons—feelings of moral superiority or veiled envy—Victorians often viewed artists as dissolutes. Friend and patron John Wilson Townsend, who visited Sawyier at High Bridge, acknowledged Sawyier's "admiration for the bouquet of that famous Boone's Knoll whiskey."[9] Another patron, prominent architect Leo Oberwarth (1872–1939), a native of New York state who settled in Frankfort in 1894 and "became the city's major architect," recalled that Sawyier liked to visit a local saloon, Jimmy Gibbons', sitting in a back room with friends drinking, smoking, and telling yarns.[10] Although drinking may have offered him some relief from the strains of caring for his increasingly debilitized family and his perennial concerns about money, solid evidence that it was either chronic or uncontrollable in the middle years of his career is scant.

In the cozy smallness of Frankfort, Paul Sawyier had a circle of support as well as a few other artists to offer stimulation and critiques. At no time during these formative years did he work entirely in a vacuum. In addition to teachers Frank Duveneck and William Merritt Chase, informal associations with other area artists inevitably formed, including Will T. Hunleigh (1848–1916) of nearby Millville and poet, novelist, and painter Robert Burns Wilson (1850–1916), who lived in Frankfort for a time. Both painted their own impressions of Elkhorn. And Sawyier's association with them benefited his art, as probably his benefited theirs. Sawyier's early creek scenes share a "luminous quality" with Hunleigh's as well as Hunleigh's soft-focus treatment of certain landscape subjects. Even when he ventured to actual sites, Sawyier sometimes used photographs to supplement his sketches in the field. They helped to fix, to frame, and to proportion his images. For a while he had an association with Frankfort photographer H. G. Mattern. Leo Oberwarth said that during periods when he wasn't painting, Sawyier took rambles over the hills and creeks with his camera looking for new scenes he thought paintable.[11] According

to Oberwarth, he took many small Kodaks, the prints measuring about
2 by 3⅓ inches.[12] While living in New York, Sawyier even suggested to
Frankfort patron J. J. King that he send photographs of scenes he would
like painted.[13] Whatever the source, Sawyier clearly did not always paint
directly from nature. Photographs that match his painted scenes in detail
and composition continue to turn up, many from his own scrapbook.

Despite periods of inactivity, Sawyier pursued his art single-mindedly,
capitalizing on his own and the public's sense of nostalgia for former
times as Frankfort passed from a quaint capital—second smallest in the
nation after Vermont's—to a full-fledged city with its share of crowds,
concrete, and motor vehicles. Popular scenes he often painted several
times when he knew he had a desirable subject. Examples of playing on
nostalgia turn up in two copperplate etchings he did of the old covered
bridge that connected downtown Frankfort with South Frankfort, the
city's extended residential area. He made multiple editions of the two
scenes, whose sales increased when the old wooden structure had to be
dismantled in 1893. They sold for $6 or $7 each, and Sawyier received 50
percent of the sales. He also exploited the old public fountain on Wapping
Street, a Frankfort landmark, as were such familiar sites as Indian Rock
and views of familiar residences along the creek, including at least one or
two with glimpses of the Stedman mills, the enormous smokestack and a
patch of roofline nearly obscured by foliage. Forced to title his watercolors
for exhibitions, he adopted stock titles and repeated them—*Scene of Elkhorn,* or simply *Elkhorn,* for example. Taken as a whole, the scenes in his
work seem a throwback to a timeless, less stressful era when life seemed
simpler, the future full of promise. His life spanned the transformation of
rural America to an industrial powerhouse. People found comfort as they
reeled from the rapidity of change. He became Kentucky's prince of the
pastoral, capturing the natural beauty being displaced in many areas by
a growing sophistication that heralded Frankfort's and Kentucky's forced
entry into the twentieth century.

He struggled to keep afloat in the eddies of economic change. A proud
man, he was determined to live or die by his brush. Like the creek, his
money flow must have been erratic, with periods of drought and occasional plenty. He devised several strategies to market his paintings. Early
in his career he made an arrangement with a Frankfort drug store, which
also stocked art supplies, to sell his work. For some time he raffled his

work through a local hardware. When the limited market in Frankfort became saturated, he arranged for a fashionable furniture store in Lexington, C. F. Brower, to market his work. It has been estimated that over a period of years Brower sold five hundred or so paintings. Throughout his career, collectors dogged Sawyier's trail, not distant Fricks and Morgans but local businessmen and admirers who perceived value in his work and felt a sense of local pride in possessing images of places they knew and loved.

John J. "J. J." King, one of Sawyier's most steadfast patrons, owned the Frankfort Hotel on Main Street, proudly displaying many of the paintings he acquired from Sawyier that formed the core of his collection. King also had a home in the country at Mount Pleasant near Stedmantown, he too having a special affinity for the Elkhorn Valley. A decorative panel of trees, reputed to have been part of the demolished hotel's décor, recently turned up for sale, selling for more than Sawyier earned in a year of painting. Painted on wood, it was roughly triangular to fit into decorative woodwork of the hotel, and I could kick myself for not trying to buy it when I had the chance. I would have displayed it with a small etching of his that I own—a view of Frankfort from the high ground where Kentucky State University is now located. The etching is an unusual early work, probably done while he was studying in Cincinnati.

Not until the summer of 1913 did Sawyier—in his late forties now—strike out for new territory again, this time to New York, where he hoped to find new subjects, new buyers, new inspiration, and perhaps greater recognition. His moving east may have been a resolution to aim for fulfillment, a way to confirm talent he believed he possessed. He was able to leave the placid and protective environment of Frankfort. In New York, he might improve his art and make his mark as more than a minor American painter. C. F. Brower had ended its contract with him, as the market was saturated into stagnancy with his work. Sawyier's production of paintings exceeded the demand and had reached local limits. His sister, Lillian, took him into her home in Brooklyn, where, following the patterns he'd established on Elkhorn and at High Bridge, he searched for and found new subjects, most of them urban, though he made trips to Long Island for *plein air* studies. As in Kentucky, he occasionally took students when he needed the income. He spent nearly two years in the area before taking advantage of a patron's offer to live in the Catskills.

The death of Mayme Bull in October of 1914 briefly brought him back to his hometown. The trip must have been bittersweet, another facet of his life that went unfulfilled. After her death, he was to live for three more years, being diagnosed with heart disease. During this time drinking became a problem, especially when raising a glass was less for social purposes than an escape from a society that, he seems to have felt, did not appreciate his work. Occasionally he went on drinking sprees to lessen his despondency, and during these bouts he did not paint.[14] Loneliness, lack of recognition, the loss of Mayme, a separation from Kentucky and his most intimate friends in an impersonal urban environment—all these things probably contributed to a state of mind that led to solitary drinking. Yet he produced much of his finest mature work—most of it in oils— while living in the home of Phillip Schaefer in Fleischmanns, New York.

On November 5, 1917, feeling pains in his chest after a field trip to paint, he was placed in his bed and died of cardiac arrest, departing just as his art was taking on new vitality and innovation. In 1923, family and friends reinterred his body in Frankfort, buried in the family plot near the grave of Daniel Boone, that other explorer of creeks and rivers. On a bluff high above the Kentucky that winds lazily through Frankfort and splits it in two, the view from his gravestone overlooks much of what animated him—water, plumes of trees, the quaint cityscape he studied almost as intently as the river and wilds of Elkhorn, the place with which admirers most identify him.

Among his contemporaries, he represents a late American romantic, polite, at times gregarious, but ultimately a solitary intent only on his art, leaving the rest of us eyeing the waterline and flushed trees on the walls of our comfortable dens to imagine him as he treks the terrain of Elkhorn or tows his skiff on the river toward another expanse that challenges his brush.

Paul Sawyier has a celebrity now that he never experienced during his lifetime, though he had a few shows and an abundance of local praise. With acute vision only for what stood before him, he could not have foreseen the later demand for copies of his work, hung in hundreds of houses and offices throughout Frankfort and beyond. Generally, he kept himself inconspicuous, and he did not have an ego that spurred him to do more than continue painting. Immediate fame he could defer even if a part of him must have longed for it as vindication. His sister Lillian, with whom he lived in Brooklyn, reported that he seldom joined her family in the evenings because he had lived alone too long and had become an old "hermit crab."[15] So it surprised no one that he did not pounce on chances for celebrity. President William Howard Taft, a friend of his family in Ohio, even suggested an exhibition at the Corcoran Gallery in Washington, D.C., a show that might have catapulted Sawyier into the national spotlight. Some of his paintings even appeared at the St. Louis World's Fair, though not in the prestigious American pavilion where his contemporaries exhibited their work. In 1917, the New York Federation of the Arts selected him for the list of noteworthy artists that appeared with accompanying brief biographical sketches in the *American Art Annual.*

Toward the end of Sawyier's life, his Frankfort patron J. J. King commissioned him to paint eight or ten original scenes in or around the state capital, paying him $300 in advance. Sawyier sent him from the Catskills ten watercolors of scenes in Frankfort and the vicinity only a few months before his death.[16] He must have felt his status as an artist elevated by the order. When he died, King owned upward of one hundred Paul Sawyier paintings. Most of his collection was passed down intact, finally landing at the Kentucky Historical Society. Ironically, those who sought to preserve the history and accomplishments of Kentuckians razed his boyhood home on East Broadway to make way for the Thomas D. Clark Center for Kentucky History, a monstrous building that occupies most of a block in downtown Frankfort and houses the largest collection of Sawyier's work, most of it seldom exposed to the public. A considerable part of the center serves as a warehouse for Kentucky's past, including over a hundred of his paintings hanging from peg boards on moveable partitions separated from the public and not available for general or easy viewing.

Collectors of Kentucky art hotly pursue his paintings still in private hands, trophy paintings. One I met recently from Louisville owns upward of a hundred. And they turn up with surprising frequency, often but not always from outside Kentucky. One collector friend went to an auction in Lexington of the estate of an ancient lady who lived, coincidentally, on Paul Sawyier Drive, a comfortable residential street in South Frankfort running along the Kentucky River near the site of the former Hermitage Distillery, a local landmark, now vanished, that Sawyier also painted. She had told another friend that she loved Sawyier's work and that she owned some originals. When she died, he imagined that the family would at least claim the originals. They didn't. Attending the auction at the most reputable auction house in Lexington, another collector friend saw Sawyier prints selling for $35 each. Looking closely at one, he suspected it might be an original that was worth thousands. Like the others, it lay behind glass and he couldn't be sure whether the brushwork was printed or real. So he took a chance and bought it—a typical creek scene—coming home and deconstructing it at the gallery of a local artist, who assured him that he had happened on an original watercolor and that its matting resembled what Sawyier consistently used. Instead of crowing about it, the proud new owner hung the original on his wall and congratulated himself on his instincts and good fortune. Only later did my other collector friend learn that the painting had come from Paul Sawyier Drive. He cursed himself for not attending the auction.

Though Sawyier preferred landscapes to portraits, he occasionally painted public figures, such as Governor Charles Scott (1739–1813) and Bishop Henry Bidleman Bascom (1796–1850), in these cases posthumously. The latter painting was commissioned by Transylvania University. Nearly a hundred years after his death, Sawyier still holds an unchallenged reputation as the best exemplar of American Impressionism in Kentucky. Currently, his stock locally has never been higher. Thousands of reproductions—pale and often downsized versions of the originals—testify to his durability on the walls of residences and offices throughout the capital city and less densely about the Bluegrass. Periodically, a Lexington antique dealer hosts a Sawyier show, accepting Sawyier paintings from near and far on consignment, many of them from the painter's final period in New York at Fleischmanns. Recently, former Governor Steve Beshear and First Lady Linda Beshear hosted an exhibition at the governor's mansion devoted to Sawyier's oils, all of them borrowed from public and private owners. Only a few depicted local scenes, since watercolors were his preferred medium until the move to New York in 1913, when oils predominated. Never breaching the citadel of America's recognized major painters, Sawyier found a few ardent admirers and collectors in the East, but many more on his native ground.

The recently built library in Frankfort's historic district perpetuates his name as the Paul Sawyier Public Library. Those of its walls not covered with shelving hold reproductions of his work, many of them reduced facsimiles of historic structures and views of Old Frankfort in the surrounding neighborhood, which is still called "The Corner in Celebrities" for the number of prominent public officials who lived there. Two of the library's images are original paintings, one a charming portrait titled *Miss Finnell*, a pastel. According to information at the library, the subject is Virginia Snead (a married name?) at age eleven. Somehow she had broken her leg, and Sawyier found her despondent. Knowing her as a neighbor, he presented the portrait to lift her spirits. The story goes that Sawyier made up the dress she wears. Virginia loved the outfit so much that her aunt and caretaker, Stites Duvall, had one especially made for her. In the portrait Sawyier had the dress tastefully covering up her crutches. *Church's Grove*, the other original owned by the library, depicts one of Elkhorn's most iconic settings. The funds to buy the paintings came from money raised by sales of recycled reading material at the Friends of the Library bookstore. I'm proud, as are many other patrons, that as a frequent customer I contributed considerably to its purchase.

Sawyier's life also survives in literature. At least one novel has been published, Nettie Henry Glenn's *"Love to All, Your Paul,"* as well as a recent play by Frankfort writer Don Coffey, who also produced a time line biography of the artist.[17] Coffey also wrote the play *Two Loves and a River*, which was performed during the summers of 2014 and 2015, centering on Sawyier's long on-again, off-again love affair with Mayme Bull. Appropriately, the players performed at an amphitheater in a park located on the banks of the Kentucky River. In 2015 someone writing under the pseudonym Russell Cavendish wrote a one-act play titled *The Two Villages*, and someone is currently composing a musical based on Glenn's *Love to All, Your Paul*.

Sawyier's imagination fed others. His images of Elkhorn continue to exert a pull for artists. Some that come immediately to mind are Betty Beshoar, Karen Carey, Sallie Clay Lanham, Mary Neely, Marianna McDonald, and Dan McGrath, two of whom live at or near the creek. And there are many others I don't know. All of those named, at least some of the time, are *plein air* painters, though most, like Sawyier, often cement the scene in photographs and complete them in their studios. Others, like James Archambeault (who lives upstream on North Elkhorn) and Gene Burch, capture Elkhorn in photographs that are art in their own right. Ellen Glasgow, the best-known painter of landscapes in the area, often chooses the Kentucky River over Elkhorn, though she has done a number of smaller paintings of scenes along the creek. All paint at least partially in the shadow of Sawyier, inspired by his work but undeterred from pursuing their own vision. In fall 2017, the Plein Air Artists of Central Kentucky and the Plein Air Artists of the Bluegrass combined to present the Paul Sawyier Commemorative Art Show and Sale. Most scenes these artists depicted revisited landscapes that Sawyier painted.

What is it that draws artists to the Elkhorn? The simple answer is what many nineteenth-century artists valued in the picturesque, beautiful places that preserved their wild character and often a grandeur lacking in their surroundings. For those who balk at the notion of grandeur on Elkhorn, simply visit its palisades stacked in lofty solitude. They strike me and others with awe each time we see them. Chatter among the kayakers stops, especially as we look up from their foot to see the distant summit overhead.

Serenity summarizes the prevalent mood of Paul Sawyier's subjects. Nothing seems to be in motion, not even waters of the creek itself. Though the creek has its own moods of turbulence and violence, Sawyier's preferred mode, like the portraitist's, is stasis. If the tone of Sawyier's paintings is often physical tranquility, it may have been an anodyne and a cover for an inwardly turbulent life. His art was not so much an escape as a refuge, an engagement with life at a remove through pigments and imagination. His scenes usually seem to predate the Cooks and Inneses, the Stedmans, the Macklins, and their like who transform wildness, consume it, denude it. An occasional boat sets the scale of the larger riverscapes on the Kentucky, but his creek paintings appear almost entirely depopulated. Few people inhabit them, not only because he found the human form more challenging to paint but also because he seems to have wished to keep his nature pure and undefiled, as if imagining Eden before the fall. Those human figures that populate them are stationary, frozen in portrait poses rather than depictions of action—singularly free of complication. The trees, the water, light and shadows, all hold a timeless fixity as if Sawyier attempted to slow down the creek, the world, to fix it in his brush and memory, to map it in rectilinear portions.

Landscapes constitute Sawyier's genre of choice, especially his renderings of Elkhorn, though the occasional angler makes a modest appearance. But he painted at least one portrait in a creek setting, a figure that encapsulates much of his own temperament as well as the spirit of the times. The painting presents a full-length view of a young man in a straw hat, holding a bait bucket in one hand, a simple cane pole in the other, an illustration plausibly out of *The Adventures of Huckleberry Finn*. Here, Sawyier indulges himself in a celebration of pastoral innocence, a soft-edged evocation of a kinder, gentler time. Confident-looking, unencumbered, standing against a backdrop of trees in a sunlit meadow, a boy brandishing a fishing pole embodies America's pastoral ideal, a carefree youth about to embark on a day of fishing immersed in nature. The painting arrests the eye for its brightness, its nostalgic view of a simpler era, its promise of a future of idyllic afternoons spent in a natural setting away from burdensome responsibilities. An exhibit at the University of Kentucky Art Museum featured the painting in a show of masterworks by Kentucky painters in 2008. Somehow, Sawyier's full-figure depiction of the expectant angler is Sawyier himself, equipped for the journey but opting to live close to nature, apart from the duties of family and a regimented vocation, a variation of the bumper sticker: "A bad day of fishing is better than the best day at work." In this fantasy, he becomes Huck shaking off the dingy world of obligation and decaying institutions, lighting out for the ungoverned territory.

Paul Sawyier remains an enigma to most of us—a man who refused to join the parade. Unmarried, by turns solitary and sociable, he encapsulates small-town values, a painter whose color illuminates as it depicts the natural world with uncommon skill, using a brush that is feather light, a palette that is subtle and right. He is our sometime hermit, our Thoreau whose study is not so much the workings of nature as its sun-drenched surfaces. On his tombstone in the Frankfort Cemetery, near the grave of Boone and overlooking the river and the town he loved, is the epitaph that captures this balance between art and nature: "He loved and painted Nature." He is not so much a naturalist as a chronicler of nature in its mostly bright moods, sunny days when the creek and access to it were most favorable, but decidedly he was not a gilder. His illusions are translating pigment into recognizable portions of the world—a shoreline, the reflections of trees in water, the gist of motion in Elkhorn's current. In his steadfastness, his mastery of illusion, he represents the perennial bachelor wedded to his art, the elusive artist whose paintings embody our love of place, but he never invests himself fully, willing toward the end of his life to forsake Frankfort and its beloved waterways for new vistas, the Catskills and urban harbors, leaving only the afterglow of his studies and a sense that the painter lurks forever just beyond the shade of sycamores and flecks of color that seem suspended in the air.

For me, that Sawyier etching on my wall, a small view of Frankfort from a bluff on what is now the Kentucky State University campus where I spent much of my teaching career, keeps the presence of him close at hand. Unlike Stedman and Macklin, he took nothing from the creek. He simply tried to arrest and preserve it as it was. Sawyier remains a reminder of our gentler past, the less frenetic and complicated times of our great-grand-parents, a fading gentility—at least as nostalgia paints it—before the transformation of the Bluegrass with its acres of subdivisions and asphalt parking spaces, malls that gobble horse farms, and multilane interstates that slice the countryside into irreparable shards. Paul Sawyier was our most committed local topophiliac, a lover of place whose devotion transcended infatuation and entered a state of profound spiritual attachment. If the poplar relates to Harry Innes and the oak to Ebenezer Stedman, the sycamore is Sawyier's totem. If the flora of the Bluegrass had to be reconstructed from his local paintings, the sycamore would dominate.

In Praise of Sycamores

Mention that tree around here
and you summon up Paul Sawyier,
our local impressionist
whose creekscapes blaze with sycamores,
gaudy lemons and ochers
that burn in some eternal summer,
their broad leaves shimmering
above the placid nooks
of some angler's dream.

Cross-grained, unsplittable,
their wood makes butcher's blocks
and not much else
beyond nourishment for the eye—
a blue heaven for the artist.
Lugging only his paint kit, bedroll,
and a tin of night crawlers,

Sawyier vanished for days up Elkhorn Creek
to commit his gentle arsons,
constellations of briars starring
the worsteds above his scruffy boots.

—Richard Taylor, *In the Country of Morning Calm,* 1998.

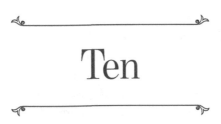

Ten

Boating on the Elkhorn at Switzer Bridge, circa 1900. (Courtesy of Capital City Museum, Frankfort, Kentucky.)

Though he coveted the wide, rich, curving bottom across the creek that was Church land, William Knight held a certain pride in the rugged uplands he'd acquired acre by acre over decades, beginning in the 1830s when he was scarcely twenty and already on his own, six hundred acres. Slowly he had added to the original cabin that squatted on the plateau above Elkhorn, shaded by a huge elm that he hadn't the heart to fell when he timbered the hillside that soon would be reduced to pasture. Whenever things let up a little, he and his two slaves, Clovis and Sam, would whet the axes and work up the hill, two mules hauling walnut, cherry, and maple saw logs down to the road, where they could be hauled to the mill farther north in the county and slabbed into lumber, most everything else sawed up for firewood to be stacked inside the stock barn. Over thirty years, he and whatever help he had or hired chipped away at the woodland, burning roots and stumps until the cleared ground could support a growing herd of milch cows. He was proud of his husbandry, proud of eating away at the dark trees that dominated the landscape. Now he was nearing the vegetal crown of the back hill that reminded him of a monk's tonsure, a dome part covered, part bald, proud of the unobstructed view of the cleared ground that wound along the valley and from which he could survey platted fields of corn and wheat and tobacco, the creek threading invisibly along a trough in the treeline by the banks he knew better than to cut.

Today, August 11, 1863, while others fretted about the war, he sat down to a pink ham and some greens with cold biscuits slathered with sugar molasses and ate his fill, food cooked by Sam's wife, Tillie, who shared the second cabin with her man. He ate without company, consuming his daily bread and sleeping in his own house, which like the farm had grown through several additions and improvements. Self-sufficient, he thought himself, alone but not lonely. Though the sky showed blue-gray in the west, he whimmed to climb to the crest of the hill and rest in the remaining shade where he could look out over the valley, much of it his valley. His breath grew short as he climbed. Raising a sweat, he waded through the field grass that would take another cutting before the first frost. At the top, spreading out his old farm coat, he lay back to rest his eyes and dozed off with the valley in his mind's eye, God's window, as he once heard a preacher describe Creation. He woke to a distant rumble as though the clouds had a case of indigestion. The sky had darkened to the tint and tension of a bruise as the first drops began to speck his shirt and then his forehead, a droplet running down the little valley by his nose. He rose and threw on his coat. A burly man with a spreading girth, he trundled toward the house, picking up his pace as lightning split above Peaks Mill two miles away, the rain now a torrent. His trousers were soaking from the knees down, and he met more resistance in the sodden grass. He thought of his pasture greening again, and the creek rising as the rivulets worked their way down the valley, rills joining rills. The roll of thunder brought him back to the war he knew was raging one or two states away and simmering in Kentucky before again coming to a boil. He knew that guerrillas and deserters roamed the back roads and terrorized whomever they chose. He moved through the open field, feeling more vulnerable, more exposed, the sky above him eclipsed in shadow, feeling each tremor as electricity rent the valley with its flashing sword and spilled its anger over the earth. He saw a swatch of gray roof no larger than his knuckle behind the swaying elm and ran for all he was worth.

REMNANTS, GHOSTS, AND CIPHERS

[A liberal arts education that involves a familiarity with nature] would teach students that there are some things that cannot be known or said about a mountain, or a forest, or a river—things too subtle or too powerful to be caught in the net of science, language, and intellect. It would introduce students to the mysterious and unknowable before the mere unknowns of a particular discipline.
—**David Orr,** *Earth in Mind,* 1996

Men go fishing all of their lives without knowing what it is they are after.
—**Unknown,** often attributed to Henry David Thoreau

The Forks is at the head of main Elkhorn. It is, so to speak, the zero milestone of a valley of haunting beauty, which, through the centuries, has sheltered Indians, enriched waterpower millers, inspired poets and artists, and exhilarated devotees of gun and rod.
—**Allan M. Trout,** "Forks of Elkhorn," *Louisville Courier-Journal,* September 27, 1964

Fifty years ago, the late Kentucky columnist Allan M. Trout wrote an article on the Forks of Elkhorn in his Hometown Kentucky series, painting a portrait of the Forks as a small, picturesque community where the waters converge to form the Elkhorn's main stem. The Forks, then and now, retains its identity as a small community of mostly residential housing, a restaurant or two, and Buck Run Baptist Church, the successor of Forks of Elkhorn Baptist. Currently, it contains a restaurant, an auto repair garage, a barbershop, a trailer camp, a semi-permanent-residence campground, Old Grandad Distillery, a state facility for fishery and water management, and, midway through, a lonely stone chimney standing in what is now an asphalt lot. The churches on both sides of the road have been abandoned in favor of a megachurch four or five miles away. Foot traffic is all but nonexistent. The Forks has no sidewalks, and few drivers heed the speed limit—in a hurry to get somewhere else. Then as now, it consists mostly of residences along U.S. 460 set back from the road along an avenue of old trees. Not much has changed in the sleepy hamlet. Churchgoers no longer visit it twice or so a week, the greatest number of outsiders coming to launch their boats. Now the abandoned churches are for sale. When water levels rise, kayakers can be seen putting in by the bridge adjacent to Stillwater Campground. The Forks remains a staid commuter community where two waterways converge to form a larger flowing into the Kentucky. Vehicular traffic flows one way, the water another. The worlds of industry, art, and nature followed not the road that engineers prescribed with instruments but the route selected by natural processes.

The most infamous visitor at the Forks was General Antonio de Padua Maria Severino de Santa Anna Perzez de Lebrary, then a prisoner headed east. General Santa Anna (1794–1876), one of the most pivotal figures in Mexican history during the nineteenth century, enlisted in the Mexican Army in his mid teens, rose rapidly to the rank of general, and was elected president of Mexico in 1833. When Texans revolted against the repressive policies of the Mexican government during the Texas War of Independence, he personally led an army to the Alamo and annihilated its defenders, including such prominent figures as Jim Bowie, William Travis, and Davy Crockett. The dead included seventeen Kentuckians. Americans took Santa Anna himself prisoner in 1836 after General Sam Houston defeated his army at San Jacinto, the battle that led the way to Texas's independence. After his capture a party escorted him back to the United States in October of 1836 and conducted him to Washington, D.C., for an audience with President Andrew Jackson. On the way, the party avoided big towns so as to attract little notice, stopping for the night at Stephens Tavern at Green Hill outside Frankfort on the Georgetown and Versailles pike, about a half mile west of the Forks.[1] Santa Anna's trip through Kentucky spawned an apocryphal story that has become the stuff of local legend. According to the story, word reached Frankfort that Santa Anna had arrived at a local tavern, and a party of furious citizens went out to confront him. Three men entered the tavern to bring him out for hanging but soon returned astonished. Supposedly, one of them recognized the general immediately as a cousin, and the other two recognized him as

Nathaniel "Bull" Sanders, a childhood playmate at Forks of Elkhorn. As the story goes, Santa Anna recognized them and asked for mercy.[2]

Though someone could write a book of both accomplished and unsavory individuals connected to Elkhorn and the vicinity of the Forks, its image through most of its history has been positive, depicted by scores of visitors and residents as a special place. One finds a good example in Tom Wallace, who visited the area during the 1890s. Wallace, a former editor of the *Louisville Times*, toured the Bluegrass straddling his bicycle. The Forks and the creek that gave it a name charmed him: "But the greatest attraction to me, a tourist, was Forks of Elkhorn. I delighted in the village and its approaches. From the time of my first visit, I never wearied of telling people, often people who might visit Kentucky, not to miss that scene of rare picturesqueness. Elkhorn, unless power dams are built in its gorges, will always be as Robert Burns Wilson described it—'song making.'"[3]

Kentucky is not old enough, civilized enough, to have plentiful ruins. Much of it has not graduated in appearance from frontier roughly as the first comers saw it. Yes, deserted houses and barns aplenty in various stages of dilapidation, broken symmetries of caved-in roofs and silver clapboards with black apertures where windows admitted light and once looked out upon the world through wavery window glass. If the house has vanished as a result of fire or slower processes of decay in nature, often the outbuildings survive, a shed, a sagging crib, a privy. Even derelict tobacco barns eventually relinquish their stiff habit of standing. Roofs relax and collapse, sinking back into the landscape, their weathered siding sometimes salvaged for suburban dens. Left behind are wells with rotten covers into which cattle or the unsuspecting hiker may step. Lingering non-native shrubs and ornamental trees tell their own domestic stories. Smaller artifacts on the surface sink under accumulations of unraked leaves. Fences dwindle into twinings of rust. Discarded metal parts rush in gullies and trash heaps, a bottomless bucket in the fencerow. Little is left, less over time.

Three hundred years in a sparse rural setting hardly impresses the landscape with an indelible human footprint, especially in a state neither prosperous nor experiencing rapid growth whose greatest promise came before the Civil War. Not only our relative youth but also climate conditions account for this dearth of things that summon up the past. As any archaeologist will tell you, wet climates have little regard for artifacts as well as structures made of biodegradable materials, such as wood, cloth, paper, and leather. Just about anything organic. In proper democratic fashion, all decompose and revert to soil. No exemptions exist for human and animal remains. This explains, in part, why so much of Kentucky's past remains a cipher compared with arid regions of the country, where the processes of rot and disintegration creep instead of race. Some of the clearest signs of human presence persist in trees and plants that survive their planters. How many times have I trekked through dun-colored woods in early spring and come across a flash of color: clumps of daffodils that have outlasted houses and their vanished inhabitants.

Yet the deserted meanders of Elkhorn Creek contain abandoned structures that served as home to nameless farmers and outliers who pinned their preferences on remoteness with only meager accessibility to markets. Stone endures, as does wood when properly protected from the elements. On or near the Hutcherson farm, where the lip of a large mechanized shovel unearthed a mammoth, stands in my memory a cabin surrounded by flat bottomland spreading to the creek. Isolated, a single-pen log cabin, it rose as a vertical reminder of the past, then as now surrounded by acres of flat, tillable ground. No outbuildings, not a single tree. Files of the Kentucky Heritage Council simply refer to it as the J. Fuller cabin. No Christian name, though I elsewhere learned that it was James. The cabin may have dated to the time of the Innes settlement but more likely went up during the first quarter of the nineteenth century. A familiar landmark to those in the neighborhood whose eyes wander off the road, the owners demolished it in the 1980s or early 1990s. While the mammoth remains not crushed by a bulldozer in 1945 rest in specimen drawers, documented and stashed away, somewhere at the University of Kentucky, the only remnants of the Fuller cabin were saved by the farm's current owner, Bobby Hutcherson, who told me he made a table from some of the wood he salvaged from it when it came down. Rural demolition around us often consists of setting fire to what seems no longer useful when the wind dies down or with even less effort simply neglecting to keep a roof impervious to rain.

Just down the creek from Hutcherson's, one finds what remains of the Innes house, incorporated into the larger brick neocolonial mansion after much of the original structure burned in 1961, now owned by the granddaughter of Judge John Palmore. It cannot be seen from the creek because of a high embankment. Instead, an oddity takes its place: four tall Ionic columns standing on a little promontory that overlooks the creek just upstream from what kayakers know as Barking Dog Rapids. To maintain stability, crosspieces join the columns just above their scrolled capitals, a stay against high winds in that exposed space. They form an inescapable landmark. How they came to be there sparks much local speculation since the columns resemble something that might be encountered off the coast of Chios in the Aegean rather than Elkhorn Creek. Standing on their concrete pad that extends over the water where huge carp can be spotted at low pool, they have become a local conversation piece, a remnant of another variety—imported. How many anglers and kayakers passing down the creek have been flummoxed by finding a partial Parthenon in those borderline wilds?

The columns in question had legs. Initially, builders ordered them for the so-called "new" state capitol, but for some undisclosed reason, perhaps mismeasurement, they were never installed. A local businessman, Charles E. Hoge, bought them around 1908 and had architect Leo Oberwarth (Paul Sawyier's friend) redesign "Ingleside," Hoge's antebellum mansion, to "colonialize" its facade. The columns remained there through several subsequent owners until one of them sold the property to a developer who razed the house to make way for what is now Tierra Linda subdivision. Losing it represents loss of another irreplaceable structure in the county, punching another hole in its identity and history. When the old house came down, J. B. Marston purchased these white elephants as salvage and relocated them on Elkhorn Creek, first planning to use them on the house he built around what remained of the Innes residence. He reconsidered and placed them on the banks of the creek where they stand today behind the home. According to Willard Rouse Jillson in his *Literary Haunts and Personalities of Frankfort,* Ingleside provided the model for the "old-fashioned brick house" described in John Fox's popular Civil War novel, *The Little Shepherd of Kingdom Come.* It served as the fictional home to which Major Calvin Buford, returning from Lexington, brought his chief character, little Chad. Apparently, Fox researched part of the novel on a visit to Frankfort. The novel became a national bestseller, selling over a million copies when it was first published in 1903.[4]

As for the possible alternate site of Innes Station—the structure near where the raiding party captured two of Innes's slaves, the owner demolished it sometime between 1960 and 1975. The only evidence that it ever existed are shards of dishware and pottery as well as a few pieces of flint that plows turn up when the field comes under cultivation. A short distance away a fine spring issues from a hillside with a springhouse of beautifully hewn stone, built later, probably, but on the site of the original. The spring would have enhanced selection of the site as a place to build a structure to serve both as a residence and place of defense.

At the Stedman mill site, the only signs of human presence are portions of a stone wall built of enormous chunks of limestone and some trenches, now gullies, filling in with silt and leaf fall. Nothing remains of the twenty or so houses, nor the mill houses or dependencies that once stood in Elkhorn Bottom. Nor did the Stedman "Hotel" above the mill near Mount Pleasant fare any better. What the tornado of 1974 didn't take from the roof, the methodical salvaging demolition completed in 1982 did. One or two outbuildings may remain at the site, orphans of the storm. Period photographs that document the Stedman "Hotel" are few, as are ones accurately depicting the mill site, with the exception of those taken by amateur photographer J. W. Jeffers over a hundred years ago. One of Cox's descendants, Mary Nash Cox, owns an anonymous watercolor of the mill complex and another of the house as it looked from a bluff above Elkhorn. Reproductions of it appear in the revised edition of *Bluegrass Craftsman.*[5]

Downstream a little piece is the oldest surviving house in the area, the Henry and Zack Church house, a two-story, double-pen cabin, located just north of Peaks Mill Road one mile east of Holt Lane at Church's Grove. Designed as a central passage log house built on property originally owned by Robert Church Sr., it occupies part of an original land grant from 1782—one of the earliest in the area.[6] Gravely wounded in the Revolution, Church recovered and came to Kentucky in 1785, taking up 2,497 acres of land granted him for his war service. He discovered that his land occupied much of a fertile, thickly forested valley. Ash, sugar maples, beech, locusts, walnuts, and several species of oak mantled the portion through which the creek ran, many draping thick grapevines from their canopies, the landscape broken by canebrakes in a part of the county most sought after as farmland.

The 1882 *Atlas of Franklin County* identified the owners of the house as Henry and Zack Church, Robert's descendants.[7] More recently, another descendant was Zack Saufley, a retired major general and bank president who owned much of the fertile bottomland along Elkhorn, as well as uplands on the Holt farm and the Church house. For many years, he lived in the renovated and enlarged log house before building a larger, one-story home overlooking the Elkhorn Valley farther out Peaks Mill Road near Knight's Bridge. The clapboarded log house in which he and other Church descendants lived sits on a slight rise north of Peaks Mill Road and overlooks Main Elkhorn. Church's Grove, the subject of one of two original paintings in the Paul Sawyier Library, served as a well-known picnic ground as well as being a spot where weekend fishermen gathered to whip their lines into the wrinkling water.[8] One of the landmarks along the creek, it sits mostly north of the Peaks Mill Road and runs parallel to the creek for a mile or so. Fishermen know the spot as "Church's Hole," "a great, deep pool" described by one informant as "a good big bunch of water."[9] Old photographs of church and political picnics must survive in the attics and picture albums of Frankfortians, white-shirted men and full-skirted women seated at makeshift tables against a backdrop of rock formations and hazy trees, the tables laden with bounty drawn from local gardens and henhouses.

In the 1840s Captain William Church lived a little farther down the creek and set up a small corn mill and a distillery. His granddaughter, Mrs. H. C. Colston, told of a house party her mother held in January of 1845, one that lasted for ten days. The creek froze over, and the revelers enjoyed skating on the creek until a snow came. One of the party left his horse and buggy close to a hill, placing a rug or blanket over its shoulders. Next morning, he found the ravine filled with drifted snow. Only two funnel-shaped holes could be seen where the horse was breathing. In trying to find the road, they blundered over rocks and logs, "one thrill after another."[10]

The vertical rock formation across the creek from Church's Grove represents another of the unknown and perhaps unknowable items of folklore relating to this section of the creek. It lies half in Elkhorn and half on the bank and hasn't moved since its plunge from the rock facings above perhaps millennia ago. Most identify it as Indian or Pinnacle Rock for its questionable associations with the Cook Massacre and the Sawyier painting of that name. But others know it as Lover's Leap or Wooden Indian, according to the late local historian Clem O'Connor, who wrote a self-published pamphlet named "An Automobile Ride through History" in the early 1970s. Lover's Leap has a long history as a generic name for ubiquitous spots where lovers allegedly jumped hand-in-hand into eternity to escape the perils of obstinate parents, persistent rivals, or would-be assailants. The scenario faintly echoes the myth of the origins of Elkhorn's name in the kind of garbling that occurs in passing orally through generations of listeners. Lover's leap sites abound in Kentucky and beyond. Wooden Indian is more enigmatic, though it may be another fumbling reference to the Indian whose remains lodged on a rock a bit farther downstream.[11] The folk imagination is as deep and fertile as Elkhorn's floodplain. The name may also have been derived from the probably apocryphal and confused account of the woman who shot the same Indian killed at the Cook Massacre, though in this case he is positioned atop the high bluff. What he was doing up there is anybody's guess. The person who fired the shot must have been an extraordinary marksman because the distance between the upper window of the Church cabin and the bluff is over two hundred yards over uneven terrain through intervening foliage. Such a shot, though not impossible, taxes credibility.

At least two of the cabins from the Cook settlement still stand with fairly sound roofs. Though vacant and windowless, they are slowly succumbing to insects, the revolution of seasons, and occasional violent weather. No one can positively identify the structure from which the desperate Cook wives shot the Indian consigned to the water and accounting for the name Indian Rock. Most of the buildings in the settlement have long since disappeared, but the Cook cabin may be one of those remaining. Traditions persist, especially when local historians want to believe they are looking at the site of the attack, the actual cabin.

Not far from Indian Rock, James Andrew Scott over a hundred years ago set up a campground. A prominent Frankfort attorney, Scott represented the county in the General Assembly (1885–1886), also serving as a master commissioner of the Franklin Circuit Court.[12] He and his family lived in South Frankfort at the southwest corner of Shelby and Fourth Street.[13] A close friend of William Goebel, the Kentucky governor assassinated in the shadow of the capitol grounds on January 30, 1900, before taking office, Scott played an active role in the criminal trials that followed.[14] Some of the mystery related to Scott's camp became a little clearer when I chanced upon an undated newspaper clipping from the *Louisville Courier Journal* about Judge Innes (probably in the 1890s) in the Innes family files at the Kentucky Historical Society. Though I had encountered brief references to Scott's camp, the article provided more specific information. According to the piece, Scott owned nine acres and established an "ideal camp," where he and his family lived during the summer months, starting in June. Set up to entertain guests as comfortably as those who seek the seashore and mountains, Scott entertained friends from all over the state, many of them attracted by the fishing: "The camp consists of nine acres. The equipment is complete for almost every comfort and convenience, with a covered pavilion for a dining room, a splendid kitchen, and material to raise as many tents as are necessary."[15] A large sign of painted wood on Peaks Mill Road pointed across the creek, directing visitors to "Indian Rock, Mr. Scott's Camp." The correspondent described the area as being situated on a level spot with a high cliff rising on the south, and a "splendid" ravine breaking through in the southwest joined by a second leading to the south. Both ravines have fine cataracts. The falling water gives a beautiful effect and cools the atmosphere. The larger of the ravines has a double cataract, the first falling from twenty feet. The sun does not shine into the ravine except at noonday.

The writer to the *Courier Journal* also described a huge sycamore growing on the bank that provided the angler with shade if he chose to anchor his boat and fish for the bass "for which Elkhorn has long been noted." By the stream at the roots of a sycamore was a "never-failing" spring that provided the camp with "fine water." From all reports, Scott dispensed genuine Kentucky hospitality "with a lavish hand."

Near the site of the former campground, one approaches an even wider field, another abandoned meander, cultivated then and now though difficult to reach since isolated by the creek on three sides. Farmers must have forded the creek at Church's Grove. Some distance from any road, the creek binds Scott's camp in isolation, accessible only by fording or perhaps by a tractor path from a farm a mile or so up the wooded ridge. Back at the creekside a cabin once stood, marked only by a stone chimney, and one can roughly make out the shadow of the house. A root cellar has been dug into the base of the cliff where leaf fall and mulch has accumulated and nearly buried it. More recently constructed, its walls seem to be made of a conglomerate, probably concrete. It, too, lacks a roof.

After making several visits to the house site, the answer to the enigma of access to the isolated bottomland finally emerged for me, confirmed later by the same curious friends who investigated the uplands. What once had been a wagon road wound around one of the ascents like a thick vine around a host tree. On the cliffside much of the trail lay buried in accumulated debris and leaf fall, but one can easily imagine a narrow way rising up to the high bluffs above where the land leveled into a highland pasture. Too steep now for motorized vehicles, only mules or a team of horses could have pulled produce or people out of the bottom. Even then, the path involved risk since the creek side of the road fell off precipitously without protection of any kind. One misstep and driver and wagon put themselves in real jeopardy. Inaccessibility may have been another reason that whoever lived there abandoned the site, especially as cars and farmtrucks replaced horses and mule-drawn wagons.

Not far from the remaining chimney of the cabin lies a concrete Indian, half-buried in the spongy mulch, a curiosity to those who stumble across it. A staff writer for the *Frankfort State Journal* wrote a story on this statue. He speculated that it commemorates the last Native American killed in Kentucky. Not by a long shot. Doubtless other Indians gave up their lives in Kentucky after 1792. However, the one killed here during the Cook Massacre may have been the last slain in Franklin County. No one knows who sculpted the Indian and placed it wherever it was placed, though the concrete tells us that it dates not much older than a hundred years, and probably less. Imagine the topography by this section of creek as a horse's hoof, its forepart a steep ascent of timbered uplands and cliffs that rise two hundred feet above creek level and at whose foot the flat land spills level for forty or fifty yards to the creek. Between the cliffs is a cleft in the hoof through which runs one of the many feeder streams that swell Elkhorn after rainfalls. Such part-time creeks are cobbled with platter-sized rocks, fragments of the fractured limestone shelves eaten by eons of erosion. This one typically runs wet and dry during the late summer and winter months, always responsive to rain. One of them may have held the concrete Indian at its summit. It may have fallen from its pedestal or, more likely, vandals tumbled it off the cliff, as local rumors hold. Blocky and crudely fashioned, it has rebar protruding from one of its legs, probably dating it to the Depression era or World War II. The writer of the article offers one local legend of a Native American who returned to live near the site. Another version credits Boy Scouts for crafting it and placing it there as a salute to Elkhorn's past. The first Scout troop in Frankfort was founded in 1909, so if Scouts made it, they made it after that date. The level land with its stone chimney, root cellar, and prostrate concrete Indian apparently comprise all that remains of Scott's camp. It, therefore, also makes sense that Scott himself may have had the effigy made to serve as an ornament, a connection to history, but most purposefully as an advertisement. Who in fact made it and placed it there remains a mystery, one that prompts as many unanswered and unanswerable questions as the full particulars of what happened at the Cook cabins on April 28, 1792.

An even greater mystery is a roofless stone building that lies farther up the creek toward Church's Grove, closer to the wide, fertile floodplain where crops have seemingly been planted for a long time. Window openings with rotting oak lintels and a single doorway break up the stone walls. During my first visit to the site, I supposed it may have functioned as a barn to store hay or farm implements. The stonework seemed cruder than what I'd seen in similar buildings. Had it been shelter for cattle pastured on the open ground? The doorway was too narrow. Then I noticed the fireplace, a sign that told me people had lived there or at least used the building as temporary shelter. Instead of the customary stone chimney centered at one end of the one-room, thirty-foot-long structure, someone had built a hearth into the corner of the building. Smaller than an ordinary fireplace, it too was crudely built. Maybe the building served as overnight lodging for hunters or campers. No signs of outbuildings appeared, no surviving road, surrounded as it was by trees, some growing in such a way that they would crowd and eventually fracture the wall, one or two growing out of the now-earthen floor. Aside from the small fireplace and window openings, no detail or personal touch contributed to giving it an identity. It stood simply as a rectilinear box of stone with one door and several windows, a place unlisted by the Kentucky Heritage Council and whoever compiled the inventory of old structures in the county. What remains in this area where at least two families lived within calling distance of each other, a hundred or a hundred and fifty yards away? Or maybe one family with a separate stone shelter for a tenant or perhaps a slave. The pieces of this puzzle remain disconnected in search of a whole, a fuller explanation: a stone building, a root cellar built into the base of the escarpment, a supine concrete Indian, a still-intact stone chimney as well as various bits of rusted-out metal, broken glass, and a few shards of pottery.

As one floats down Elkhorn, the Knight-Taylor-Hockensmith place can be seen on a bluff to one's right, the last house before Knight's Bridge. Broad fields surround it in the valley, much of it pastureland and upland woods rising to the east. The original structure dates from about 1851, built by an enterprising farmer, William Knight (1810–1863), who began acquiring land in the area.[16] Before 1850, the farm, mostly located on the east side of Peaks Mill Road, consisted of about six hundred acres. The original log house faced Elkhorn Creek, though later additions changed its orientation to front the road. Starting with the log structure, the house grew with additions over the century. Its changes reflect evolving changes in tastes and styles of architecture, from Federal to Italianate to Gothic Revival, forming a scrapbook of building fads. In addition to the main house, William Knight owned two earlier log structures, also facing the creek, possibly built in the 1840s. Knight remained a bachelor through-out his fifty-three years, originally living in one of the cabins, his slaves in the other. Whatever the arrangement, Knight did not long enjoy the fruits of his labor because on August 11, 1863, lightning fatally struck him down, according to the headstone in the cemetery on the property. Four years after his death, the Franklin County Court divided the property into parcels and sold several, including the houses, to Robert C. Taylor. Taylor in turn sold the property to Jesse Hockensmith (1835–1913) in 1883. Hockensmith, a member of one of the county's largest rural families, had served in Morgan's cavalry, another of the fraternity of local boys who had joined the Confederacy.

William Knight's death in 1863 at one end of our eight-mile run of creek bookends with A. W. Macklin's at the Forks at the other end during the same year. They doubtless knew each other because they lived and interacted in the same tight community. Their accidental deaths add to the succession of human passings that comprise any history of a rural neighborhood and stand in contrast to the seeming agelessness of the creek itself, though the multitude of anonymous lives it contains defies any accurate calculation, as Darwin's principles play out in uncountable dramas among hundreds of plant and animal species. The bankside syc-amore, listing toward midstream to capture more light, falls victim to eroding banks or unusually turbulent water. Big fish eat little fish. Herons, poised in the shallows, eat whatever they can spear. Buzzards clean up the mess. The creek is simultaneously a vital life source and a mortuary—as, of course, is the planet itself. The roll call of the dead extends at least as far back as the Pleistocene mammoth trapped in a postglacial marsh that became the Hutcherson farm. And Old Man Birchfield, Jack Birchfield's unnamed father—one foot in the frontier past, one in the half-civilized outlands of Frankfort—was hired by his neighbor Harry Innes to put wild game on the judge's table.[17] One can imagine him toting a dead buck over the pommel of his saddle, his game bag containing a few squirrels, a rabbit or two, maybe some game birds if he owned a shotgun.

Between the Forks of Elkhorn and Knight's Bridge, especially in the vicinity of Church's Grove, evidence points to several other abandoned homesteads. Gradually melting into the landscape, they do not announce themselves, but each offers clues to the fuller life that subsisted there. A quarter mile downstream from Church's Grove along the creek you will pass remains of a stone retaining wall, rocks dry laid along the bank to curtail erosion and that now provide a place for kayaks and small boats to tie up, a good place to stop in the shade for a beer. Beyond it lies a plat of level land now overgrown with woods that must have once been cut back to form a clearing around a dwelling house. The trees seem uniform in size and about the same age, suggesting a common sprouting once the house had been deserted. Despite its remoteness, the site seems well chosen because the amount of flat land at the base of the high cliffs spreads wider, more generously than the comparatively narrow strip along the creek on its high side.

Among the abandoned structures on Elkhorn are bridges—or the ghosts of bridges. According to the *Kentucky Encyclopedia,* at one time there were over four hundred covered bridges in Kentucky. Constructed by highly skilled artisans in wood, the number of these bridges, like the number of those skilled enough to work on them, has dwindled. Covered bridges, the earliest in Kentucky dating from the 1790s, went up in an era of less ponderous vehicles and were roofed to protect their flooring and trusswork from the weather. As might be imagined, many fell victim to fires, accidental or deliberate, a disproportionate number during the Civil War. Builders learned that when the roof went, the bridge went. By 1990, only thirteen remained standing in the state, most no longer open to traffic for safety reasons.[18] To see the one surviving covered bridge of the thirty-three that once serviced Franklin County, one must go to the nearby crossroads village of Switzer, where the Switzer Covered

Bridge still extends grayly over the North Fork of Elkhorn four or five miles upstream from the Forks.[19] George Hockensmith constructed the bridge in 1855, and George Bower restored it in 1906. The bridge is 12 feet high, and its 11½-foot-wide bed runs 120 feet.[20] In 1997, unusually high floodwaters nearly destroyed it, though it has been painstakingly restored and stands adjacent to the functional but unadorned concrete bridge that has replaced it. Locals gave it a nickname as "the kissing bridge." An early photograph depicts workers and dignitaries standing by the portal of the bridge, including the Jones brothers who owned the mill at Switzer. Proudly they gaze into the camera. In the foreground stand stacks of cedar shakes used to shingle the roof.[21] Slated for demolition by the state, local residents-turned-activists saved it, preserving the original structure and relocating the adjacent concrete bridge fifty yards or so downstream. Safety concerns closed the bridge to traffic in 1954. A photograph captured the last vehicle to cross it, a vintage sedan resting at its portal, only the forearm of its driver, Floyd Pervis, being visible.[22] In 1998, the General Assembly of Kentucky designated the Switzer bridge the "Official Covered Bridge of Kentucky." Elkhorn's ubiquitous chronicler, Paul Sawyier, painted it and many of the other bridges that survived into the first two decades of the twentieth century. Finally, the public fascination with covered bridges represents a sentimental clinging to the past, a yearning for permanence in the face of dizzying change. Switzer Covered Bridge, its walls defaced with graffiti, has an allure that draws both strangers and locals to slow down or park their speeding vehicles for a gander. They stop, get out, pose for pictures at the black mouth of its sawtooth entryway. Stepping inside its dark corridor, they puzzle over the ciphers scrawled on its siding to discover who loves and who hates whom, as well as what new obscenities might scoff at public morality.

Stone abutments still visible in the eight miles between the Forks and Peaks Mill Road testify to the demise of two covered bridges. Early in the nineteenth century, skilled bridge builders erected the first span over the creek, then replaced it in 1867 as an improvement on the one Ebenezer and his bride crossed at the Forks in their move to the Elkhorn Valley. Described as a McCallum's Inflexible Arch Truss, it stretched as a double-span bridge 120 feet long. Leslie Costigan, whose family farm bordered the bridge site, said that boys used to hide in it to scare local girls as they crossed on their way to school.[23] A. W.'s great-grandson Alex (b.

1899), growing up in the early years of the twentieth century, had his own memories of the bridge, describing it as a "landmark for generations": "It was an adequate, one-lane affair, but the enormous wagonloads of hay that only Bedford Martin and Howard Black could load sometimes became jammed in the bridge, on the way to the livery stables in Frankfort. On those occasions traffic was at a standstill for hours. Milk cows were allowed to graze on the roadways and sometimes when one's buggy horse abruptly stopped in the pitch-black darkness of the bridge, it was necessary to drive one or more cows out to make room for passage."[24] He also referred to the local joke that on Saturday nights locals claimed that two buggies passed on the bridge by the expedient of one going over the top of the other. With no record, he added, of anyone being injured. Alex also noted the number of water snakes that sunned on the abutments and piers during the summer. The boys held contests to see who could snag the biggest one with a fishing line and land it on the bridge or road.[25] He also remembered trapping along the creek, catching muskrats, whose pelts brought from fifteen to twenty cents apiece.[26] Among his warmest memories was galloping to the hills above Elkhorn to see the leavings of the hemp harvest on A. W.'s and other local farms as it burned in the fields. A Georgetown College graduate, Alex had a poet's eye for beauty: "Long after the mill and rope walk were idle, I loved to go out at night in the fall of the year to count the many, many little fires where hemp 'herds' were burning like so many jewels dotting the horizon all around." He recalled that he would ride his pony to the top of a hill "just for a view of Elkhorn Creek and the valley below where great-grandfather had built a dam to power his grain mill."[27]

With the advent of the internal combustion engine, the weight and volume of traffic on the wooden structure at the Forks increased, creating problems for those in charge of road maintenance. As might be expected, officials found reasons to postpone expending large sums of money. To increase the bridge's load capacity, the state highway department removed the siding in 1926. This miscalculation exposed it to the weather, speeding its deterioration and eventual replacement in 1936.[28] Added expense may have been a factor in not reinforcing the bridge to accommodate heavier loads. Vestiges of the drystone road giving access to the covered bridge are visible in winter when the surrounding foliage is sparse.

Knight's Bridge on Peaks Mill Road crosses Elkhorn nearly two miles downstream from Pinnacle Rock. The first bridge at this site dates from 1820. We know that the builders used tolls to recover its cost, mostly from travelers and local farmers going to market in Frankfort. The original wooden span of Knight's Bridge stood 150 yards or so downstream from the Knight-Taylor-Hockensmith House, where William Knight himself lived and suffered his untimely death. Opened in 1863, the bridge extended for 200 feet with two spans, a McCallum's Inflexible Arch Truss in design built by John Gault. The earlier wooden covered bridge has long since disappeared. I see the drystone abutment across the stream each time we drag out our kayaks by the lot generously provided by the American Whitewater Association. Built into the banks, the matrix of stones probably mystifies most who pass it and take casual notice. Other portions of the concrete remnants must have tumbled miles downstream, propelled by the force of water of spring freshets and seasonal floods. In 1935, engineers replaced this bridge with a steel pony truss bridge, and a more recent concrete one now spans Elkhorn's main stem.

During Kentucky's Black Patch War in the early 1900s, tobacco farmers united to punish their brethren who refused to join an association pledged to withhold tobacco from the market. Their goal was to force tobacco companies to raise the unconscionably low prices paid to farmers for the product of their long, back-breaking labor. Though the conflict, including barn burnings and the trampling of seedbeds, centered in western Kentucky's dark-fired tobacco country, the threat of Night Riders spread to wherever growers resisted. My own grandfather, a tobacco farmer in north-central Kentucky's Oldham County, put in a request for the state to provide him with Winchester rifles from the state arsenal to defend his crop. These vigilantes destroyed property and physically punished those who refused to join the association. One such farmer, nameless in the account, lived by Knight's Bridge along Elkhorn and somehow got word that Night Riders planned to raid his farm on a certain night. As he and his son lay in wait to confront them, the clip clop of hooves on the wooden bridge announced the approach of the raiders. As the party neared, the farmers fired their shotguns into the heavens, scattering the would-be enforcers.[29] In less violent times the bridge had a reputation as a trysting place for lovers.

Just upstream from Stedmantown stood a stouter bridge and trestle where the Frankfort and Cincinnati Railroad crossed Elkhorn Creek. Unfortunately, rail service did not become available until after the Stedman mills had ceased functioning and Ebenezer himself had headed for Texas toward retirement and death. Locals referred to the line as the "Whiskey Route" because it served so many distilleries.[30] As with other rail lines, it had its share of jokes and folklore: "One visiting journalist speculated that thirsty natives have been waiting for years for the train to derail and send barrels of whisky tumbling down the hillside into Elkhorn Creek."[31] Originally, the line had been projected to run from Frankfort to Paris through Georgetown. Though chartered in 1871, laying of the track did not begin until 1888—and the line from Georgetown to Paris was never completed. Until the incorporators dismantled it, anglers liked to fish from its single-track expanse over the water, making it a source of potential liability. I warily crossed it a few times before rail traffic entirely stopped, always pausing to listen in expectation of a fast-moving freight as I approached the center point. Demolition came sometime during the 1970s or early 1980s.

One can find more recent abutments near Church's Grove, all that remains of an uncompleted modern concrete bridge erected to unite separated portions of the Saufley farm divided by the creek. Zack Saufley's son, Church, and others attempted to join the two halves of the farm rather than rely on low water for fording. A rush of high water washed out the piers before they could complete it, reminding me of James Joyce's *Ulysses*, in which he defined a pier as a "failed bridge."

The history of Elkhorn is in part a history of its bridges. Bridges connect. They connect point to point in physical space. They also join memory and consciousness in time. The history of bridges touches the history of every person who ever walked or trundled over a span above a stream or chasm. They testify to our resourcefulness in adapting nature to human purpose. As the abutments to dismantled bridges on Elkhorn attest, bridges function as temporal conveniences in the longer history of landscape, a practical means to tease and thwart the eternal flow of water in its customary bed. They also reflect the evolution of technology, from a felled tree to elaborate trussworks to steel construction and, finally, steel-reinforced concrete. Bridges also connect the living and the dead, the hands of unnamed workers, skilled and unskilled, who built them to benefit the tens of thousands of unnamed users who adopted them as servants to convenience. Though they defy gravity, eventually they succumb to it, either through desuetude or replacement. Each represents a testament to human ingenuity and our determination to bend topography to our will. As the tourism associated with covered bridges confirms, they hold a mystique, and our ancestors must have marveled at the earliest spans that made their lives a little less arduous, a little less perilous. Free of their phantom spans and raison d'être, the abutments of the two covered bridges that spanned the main stream of Elkhorn, upstream and down from Church's Grove, will eventually yield to the future along with the vanished dams and swinging bridges that punily challenged flowing water. The war against bridges comes from two directions: its great enemies are wind, rain, and human fickleness from above, "troubled" water, gravity, and erosion below. Elkhorn forms one long cemetery of vanished bridges.

Too often, the world of women who lived along the creek appears in halftones or shadow. Although she spent many more years living on the creek than did her husband, the life of Ann Shiel Innes remains an amorphous gray world. We know little beyond the way Jouett painted her. Mary Steffee Stedman also had a story to tell, as did her household slave Isabella, as did nurse and homemaker Jane Macklin. And how would Bertha Scott have described summers at her father's camp on Elkhorn or the procedures she witnessed Sawyier using in painting a creekscape? Elkhorn speaks almost wholly in a masculine voice, lacking the testimony of perceptive women. Like vanished bridges, they have become ghosts of the landscape.

Yet, if Elkhorn has an environmental hero, a symbol of the dozens of wildlife and freshwater biologists that give the creek regular health checkups, measuring the effects of pollution and its disappearing species, it would be a woman—Emma Lucy Braun (1889–1971). To many naturalists, Braun stands as an American icon, the gutsy daughter of educators in Cincinnati, Ohio. A student of botany and geology, she and her sister Annette, an entomologist, became the first and second women to earn Ph.D.s at the University of Cincinnati. In disciplines dominated by men, they made extensive field studies together, focusing on the Appalachian Mountains, with a specialty in Eastern forests. An ecologist as well as a naturalist, Lucy Braun fought to protect wildlands and set up nature reserves. The author of four books, she is best remembered for her

Emma Lucy Braun (1889–1971). (Courtesy of the Archives and
Rare Books Library, University of Cincinnati, Cincinnati, Ohio.)

classic *Deciduous Forests of Eastern North America* (1950).[32] This book
inventories the plant life of the mountains and the evolution of the forest
community from the most recent ice age to the middle of the twentieth century. The recipient of many awards, she was elected president by
her peers of the Ecological Society of America and the Ohio Academy
of Science, both firsts for a woman. A collector of pressed flowers since
childhood, Lucy Braun kept an extensive herbarium that is now in the
National Museum in Washington, D.C. For a time, she also edited a mag-
azine called *Wild Flower.*

Each year Pine Mountain Settlement School in eastern Kentucky
sponsors a Lucy Braun Weekend, including a walk along Bad Branch and
to the summit of Pine Mountain, roughly following the path she followed.
My bone-sore feet testify that she must have been a seasoned hiker. As for
whether she scaled the steep slopes by Elkhorn, the answer remains open;

doubtless in her prime she was more than equal to the task. Her boots, one suspects, took her wherever she sensed she needed to go, especially places most of our species didn't. The chief botanical phantom inhabiting the region around Elkhorn is named after her: Braun's rockcress (*Arabis perstellata*). Braun's rockcress is an elusive member of the mustard family that grows only in three counties of Kentucky, including Franklin. Who named the plant in her honor and whether she climbed the steep slopes by Elkhorn to see it I could not ascertain, though her field notes, I'm told, indicate she was familiar with Elkhorn. A plant native to Kentucky, it is found only in the Kentucky River drainage north of Frankfort on steeply sloped, dry to mesic forests on thin calcareous soils (those derived from limestone). It characteristically grows near streams and rivers. Its stellate, or star-shaped, hairs on the leaf surface distinguish it from other species. This perennial herb stands usually about one foot high and has narrow, wavy-edged leaves alternatively appearing on the stem. The four-petaled flowers range in color from white to lavender. It sends out a long tap-root that gives it a purchase among the rocks and thin soil of the slopes above Elkhorn. Because of its location in places inaccessible to humans, few have seen it. It owes its rarity in part to land uses that have reduced its habitat. Roads and grazing farm animals have had an effect, as have timbering and other disturbances of the soil that invite weeds and invasive species, such as garlic mustard, which forms a thick ground cover and muscles out fragile natives or contributes to the erosion of the thin soils on which they rely.[33] Braun's rockcress is listed federally as an endangered species. Ninety percent of the rockcress that exists worldwide grows in a tiny corner of Kentucky, mostly in the humid corridor along the Kentucky River, a natural hothouse.[34] Its namesake likewise represents a natural rarity among her own species. Think of it as Elkhorn's essence, a plant still relatively unaffected by the degradation around it.

According to naturalist Deb White, Braun identified several other rare species in the area that later botanists have not been able to find again. Rare plants along Elkhorn's waters include Canada anemone, globe or Short's bladderpod, and Svenson's wild rye. According to White, an environmental biologist, Franklin County has most of the important populations for some of these plants. Many grow along the cliffs by Steadmantown Lane, the area of the Cook Massacre and the Stedman mills.[35] Many escaped the ravenous appetites of Stedman's axmen and clear-cutting lumbermen in the area because of their inaccessibility, though the degraded and disturbed environment around them must have threatened their existence. Blessedly, the slopes are also too steep for grazing cattle and wildflower pickers. Whether deer consume it I don't know, though they can likely find suitable forage in more accessible places.

While Braun came to the region looking for rare plant species, throughout the history of Elkhorn, people more commonly have come here to fish. In some handwritten notes with entries dated, mined perhaps from one of the Frankfort newspapers, I found this early reference to fishing at Stedman dam, which reveals just how abundant with fish the Elkhorn used to be: "August 10, 1878—Nine members of the Mud Cat Club, under Commodore Joel Scott, met at the head of Steadman [sic] dam Thursday night and though the waters of Elkhorn were not in extra good condition, succeeded in taking about fifty pounds. The largest weighing eighteen pounds. There will be no other meeting of the club until after a good rain."[36] Even when conditions are "extra good," fishermen today could never report a catch that large.

Except in the coldest weather, I have almost always encountered fishermen on Elkhorn, sometimes in pairs, sometimes solitary in boats or as often in waders, sometimes sitting on the bank in portable lawn chairs. They will return a greeting or an enquiry about whether *they're* biting, but they seem a laconic lot mostly dedicated to silence, the silence of empty churches and library reading rooms. The talking comes over the cook fire or when they return to the din of the workplace, where someone asks them what they did over the weekend. The silences of Elkhorn foster contemplation and contentment. The silence, of course, is illusory, never complete. The water riffles, birds call, leaves mingle, insects fidget, brush rustles in a breeze. But generally Elkhorn insulates from droning engines except for the hum of an occasional tractor mowing or cultivating in an adjoining field, no outboards, no sirens, none of the yammering so characteristic of our species. Here, we are other. Rather than definitively silent, Elkhorn holds an abiding stillness. A limb or tree falling a quarter of a mile away becomes a sonic event, one that underscores this nonhuman silence.

Bob Smith—a fishing enthusiast and late uncle of my friend Pat Kennedy—named and mapped the fishing holes along Elkhorn Creek from the mouth of Elkhorn at the Kentucky River to the Forks as well as some

ELKHORN CREEK IN FRANKLIN COUNTY

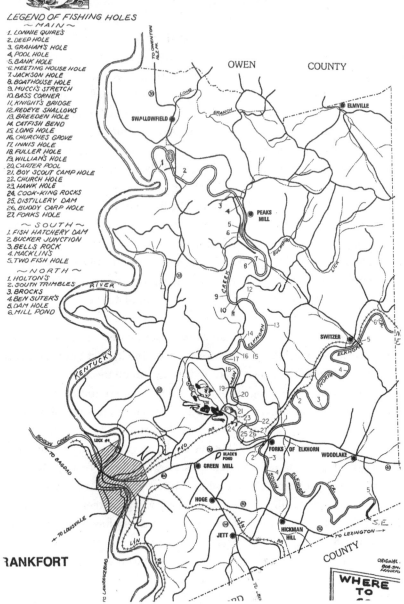

LEGEND OF FISHING HOLES
~ MAIN ~
1. LONNIE QUIRE'S
2. DEEP HOLE
3. GRAHAM'S HOLE
4. POOL HOLE
5. BANK HOLE
6. MEETING HOUSE HOLE
7. JACKSON HOLE
8. BOATHOUSE HOLE
9. MUCCI'S STRETCH
10. BASS CORNER
11. KNIGHT'S BRIDGE
12. REDEYE SHALLOWS
13. BREEDEN HOLE
14. CATFISH BEND
15. LONG HOLE
16. CHURCHES GROVE
17. INNIS HOLE
18. FULLER HOLE
19. WILLIAM'S HOLE
20. CARTER POOL
21. BOY SCOUT CAMP HOLE
22. CHURCH HOLE
23. HAWK HOLE
24. COOK-KING ROCKS
25. DISTILLERY DAM
26. BUDDY CARP HOLE
27. FORKS HOLE

~ SOUTH ~
1. FISH HATCHERY DAM
2. BUCKER JUNCTION
3. BELLS ROCK
4. MACKLIN'S
5. TWO FISH HOLE

~ NORTH ~
1. HOLTON'S
2. SOUTH TRIMBLES
3. BROCKS
4. BEN SUTER'S
5. DAM HOLE
6. MILL POND

OWEN   COUNTY

ELMVILLE

SWALLOWFIELD

PEAKS MILL

SWITZER

FRANKFORT

LOCK #4

BLACK'S POND
GREEN MILL

FORKS OF ELKHORN
WOODLAKE

HOGE

JETT

HICKMAN HILL

COUNTY

WHERE TO

Bob Smith's fishing map of Elkhorn Creek. (Courtesy of Patrick Kennedy.)

of the pools along the North and South Forks. All told, he marked and
identified and named thirty-eight holes. A hole or a pool, as I understand
it, is a spot between riffles where the creek widens and deepens to form
an ideal habitat for game fish. Between the Forks and Knight's Bridge, Bob
Smith identified sixteen such holes, and their names mostly designate
adjacent property owners or features identifying the site. Following is a
list from the Forks of Elkhorn downstream: The Forks, Buddy Carp Hole,
Distillery Dam (Old Grandad), Cook-King Rocks (site of the massacre),
Hawk Hole, Church Hole (Church family), Boy Scout Camp Hole, Carter Pool, William's Hole, Fuller Hole (the site of James Fuller's vanished
cabin), Innes Hole, Church's Grove (property of the Church family), Long
Hole, Catfish Bend, Breeden Hole, Redeye Shallows, and Knight's Bridge.

Understanding the lore of Elkhorn hinges somewhat on familiarity
with the local. Fishermen and kayakers, like Bob Smith, have given names
to fishing holes and other distinctive topographical features that appear
on few maps. Until they map such spots in memory, I can visualize serious anglers having the map pinned to a garage wall or folded in a tackle
box. Many fishermen, both local and distant, have probably never seen
this map or heard the names, though they accumulate their own knowledge through roaming the creek in search of preferred fishing spots. They
probably also create their own names for places based on their experiences: Bonanza, Washout, Bait Bucket, Scared Buck, Lost Shoe. Several
guidebooks impose their own read on things, sometimes helpful, sometimes not. Locals have designations for things that compilers of guidebooks never imagined, naming places at least partly on their individual
experiences. Anglers choose their sites by the fish they have caught there
on a lucky day or the fish they believe they can catch when conditions
seem right, depending on weather, season, water level, or the disposition of the mysterious forces, natural and supernatural, that govern water.
Like much else concerning Elkhorn, no glossary or gazetteer exists, so the
stories behind the name may be known only to a very few, a number that
must be diminishing with the passing of years.

Just below the Innes place, the creek bends sharply and passes by scal-
loped shelves of sedimentary limestone resembling a stack of pancakes
before the creek breaks up in a series of chutes and riffles. When the creek
runs full, this is a tricky spot, a constricted throat of white water where
the stream furrows into frothy turbulence that can overturn a kayak in

its churning, rock-obstructed currents, a place where my son, overconfident, lost his prescription sunglasses and where I have overturned or foundered many times. One of my former university colleagues lives on the plateau at this bend in the creek. For years, his pet dog would come out to bark at the kayakers who played the currents as they passed below his yard. Invariably, the dog would appear barking as they approached, so this portion of the creek, according to inveterate kayaker Mike Larimore—a creek dweller and former head of the Kentucky Fish Hatchery on Elkhorn below Peaks Mill along Indian Gap Road—became known as Barking Dog Rapids. Slightly upstream in what would have been Judge Innes's backyard stand the four salvaged stone pillars moved to the site by J. B. Marston, to bring a semblance of Greek ruins to the creek. A landmark on the creek, kayakers must have also given them a name. Little Parthenon? Elkhorn people must have named other spots along the creek from a geological feature or a piece of local history, such as Pinnacle and Indian Rocks, Church's Grove, or simply the names of those who currently live along the creek—Lanhams', Wilsons' (whose landmark is a leaning sycamore hollow at its base), or Burch's (named for Gene Burch, who owns a lot in a subdivision above the creek, purchased as an ideal entry point for a put-in at the head of a series of rapids.) Few of these names circulate beyond a circle of friends. Others just give these spots other names though their purpose and logic often overlap.

If one had to choose a single object with more universal associations relating to Elkhorn, it would be the Milam fishing reel. About the time that Ebenezer Stedman set up his papermaking operation on Elkhorn, two local watch and jewelry makers—Jonathan and Ben Meek—began to manufacture fishing reels for friends and family. As word of the excellence of these reels got around, the brothers began to receive orders for custom-made reels. As demand increased, they converted their business exclusively to making reels, adding B. C. Milam, who eventually took over the firm, producing Milam reels that won prizes in such venues as the Chicago World's Columbian Exposition of 1893 (where Paul Sawyier also exhibited) and the International Exposition at Paris in 1900. Elkhorn must have been a testing place for these reels, and serious fishermen who could afford to insist on the best invariably fished its waters equipped by Milam and Company.[37] Today, collectors avidly seek out Milam reels, more likely to be found under glass or in safe deposit boxes than alongside one of

Elkhorn's pools. The Capital City Museum scheduled an exhibit of the famed reels, and collectors had an opportunity to see a major collection of them in one place.

A descendant of Stedman, Roy Gray Sr., now ninety-four years old, who formerly served as a Marine aviator, flying combat missions in World War II, Korea, and Vietnam, grew up almost in sight of Elkhorn. The Gray family farm lies on the southwest intersection of Peaks Mill Road and Steadmantown Lane, a quarter mile or so from what remains of Innes's residence. When asked about his boyhood fishing, he pulled a brown paper bag out of a recessed cubbyhole in an antique family desk. It contained two reels, a No. 3 B. C. Milam and a No. 1 Meek and Milam, both badly tarnished and in need of repair. He said that he always kept the No. 1 at the farm. An adult cousin, who grew up in Frankfort and knew that Mr. Gray loved to fish, interviewed him. When asked, Gray gave an account of the way he believed every serious fisherman who fished Elkhorn and other streams in the region in the 1800s and early 1900s used the early Meek and Milams:

> Every spring we went to the local hardware store and bought two cane poles out of a barrel. These barrels were plentiful around the area outside of shops. We bought #3 cotton line and wire eyes. The eyelets were secured to the poles with thread and glue. The reel seat was attached with black tape. We walked across the farm to the creek and always fished around Church's Grove, a large rock next to the bank where there were deep pools and riffles. . . . We used a seine to catch six-inch steelback minnows that we would store in a minnow bucket. We walked along the creek and cast into pools and riffles. A good fisherman did not get backlash and cast a smooth line so that the minnow landed gently. We let it sit and then did slow retrieves. Occasionally a smallmouth would run and break off the line on a ledge. They would fight! It was great fun to catch them. A good day yielded three or four smallmouth big enough to take home to eat. There was a large rock in the stream that always held sunfish. We'd catch some of them and fry them right on the bank in a cast iron skillet. We seldom saw another fisherman. We'd stay out all day. We would go home and take the line off to let it dry. We strung it from the henhouse to the smokehouse. Otherwise it would rot.[38]

Young Kentucky Fisherman. (Painting by Paul Sawyier.
Courtesy of Bill Coffey.)

It is not too great a stretch to imagine the young Gray as Paul Sawyier's subject in the portrait of the young fisherman posing by the sunlit Elkhorn a generation later, a kind of frozen pastoral homage to idyllic days on Elkhorn, past and present. Now, though the equipment may be more sophisticated, anglers can be found along its banks, in boats or wading in the shallows, during almost any weekend when the weather moderates.

Not all was idyllic. Gray also referred to the massive fish kill from the distilleries upstream when he was a young teen (about 1935), early evidence of the industrial degradation of the stream: "The water was so polluted that there were large numbers of dead fish in the big pools. It was a big deal."[39] Though this fish kill was not an isolated incident, much more aquatic life has been slowly poisoned or smothered by effluents and wastewater that pour out of Lexington and Georgetown as well as the run-off of fertilizers and farming pesticides along the way that infiltrate the creek. Yet we paint Elkhorn almost always in the most sanguine light, largely because it appears unspoiled when everything around it has been altered, not always for the better.

For some, fishing on the Elkhorn becomes a pilgrimage. My neighbor and friend Steve Wilson—"Brother" Wilson among members of the Church of Elkhorn—told me that one day, as he was working on the farmhouse he has been rehabbing as a bed and breakfast, a stranger knocked on his front door. Opening it, Steve met a diminutive elderly man carrying a pole and tackle box. Steve immediately guessed his mission. The man had an elf-like way about him, something in the eyes that assured my friend that here was a good man come to ask a simple favor. After introducing himself and saying that he had fished Elkhorn since he'd come to Frankfort from western Kentucky in the 1940s, he asked if he could cut across Steve's field to reach the creek. Steve saw no sign of the vehicle he had come in. For all my friend knew, he had trekked out the several miles from town. The story rang a bell, and I asked if the name he'd given was Hub Perdew, a man I knew and had long admired in the local Rotary. Steve said he believed it was. Hub had long ago told me that one of the secrets of his longevity turned on stealing off to Elkhorn as often as he could to fish. He cherished his hours on Elkhorn, though he didn't measure his success as a fisherman by the number of filets he'd packed in the freezer. Hub lived to be over a hundred, an elder in his church, a small man that people instinctively looked up to. He also carved wood as a hobby, and I treasure the hound he carved me out of cedar that sits on its haunches behind glass on a shelf in my bookcase.

Elkhorn's best stories perhaps remain unrecorded, shelved in the memories of residents who take the past as a given and see little need to share it beyond those within earshot. Many are irretrievably lost. A few highlighted memories trickle down through family stories, moments of pride in blood or instances of tragedy. Locals take their locales for granted, and few seem motivated or equipped to mine the dark recesses of the community's past, gathering the particulars that constitute its history, something larger and more significant than minute and seemingly unrelated particulars. Those outside the locale must rummage the court records and a handful of local histories, sometimes uncovering a trove of letters or a diary like Nicholas Cresswell's long-buried travel journal to Kentucky or packets of letters by Ebenezer Stedman. But such sources are almost as rare as a Rosetta stone. The available written record is lamentably scant in such places since increasingly we do not often value the past beyond the reach of our own perishable recollections.

The French symbolist poet Stéphane Mallarmé said, "Everything in the world exists to end up in a book." What he doesn't tell us, as the Greek philosopher discovered, is that "Nature likes to hide." So does history, the bulk of which is anonymous and unrecorded, some of it specious, comfortably berthed in the lodgings of myth. Elkhorn guards its secrets. It seldom announces, though it leaves clues—the vestiges of a millrace at the site of Stedman's mill, brachiopods in certain shelves of limestone, a bird point with serrated edges and grooved tail that is a synecdoche for an entire culture of Woodland Indians. I have tried to include every relevant thing I could find about the eight-mile stretch of the main stem of Elkhorn Creek, knowing that time erodes just as water erases whole valleys and displaces its rich soils. But one thing leads to another almost endlessly. The past, like silt, is carried away and finally cancels memory, which is equally fragile and changing. It does, however, leave little deposits—natural signs, bits of paper, stories, memories of those who have lived a long time in one place: yellow jonquils in the wilderness. These resources can profitably be retrieved like fossils at the bottom of the old departed sea, and in them we find mirrors of ourselves—our fears, our triumphs, our hopes, our failures. They tell us, finally, who we are.

Church of Elkhorn kayakers, 2011. (Photograph by Gene Burch.)

EPILOGUE

The real difference between a creek and a river is memories. A creek has memories. A river has large boats and barges and pollution, but never memories. Elkhorn Creek is a treasury of memories for me.
—**George Lusby,** *Of Woods and Waters,* 2005

Most streams appear to travel through a country with thoughts and plans for something beyond.
—**John Muir,** *A Thousand-Mile Walk to the Gulf,* 1916

A creek pays less mind to man than to geography.
—**James Still,** *The Wolfpen Poems,* 1986

On a Sunday in mid-July seven friends, including my daughter, Julia, and Mike Larimore, set off with a party of us from another friend's private entry to the creek. The water was low and green, ruffling white in some places and crowned by larger rocks but setting a mood more placid than troubled. The sounds of flowing water hung in our ears, a constant, amplifying as we entered the riffles between pools. At one of the pools we heard the distinct clucking of a rain crow, the yellow-billed cuckoo that visits seasonally to hatch its broods somewhere in the woods bordering the creek. Around one of the bends we saw a half-submerged fisherman a few feet from one bank, his pole as he moved it in the distance reflecting a needle of white light that seemed more visible than any part of him. We floated along the aisle of greenness under leafless limbs of dead ash trees, victims of the emerald ash borer that threatens the entire species. In the treeline along the creek, they stood bleached and shorn of foliage, limbs shucked off periodically as dead weight giving in to gravity. At one notoriously dangerous spot, a sharp ell with a projecting root ball where most of us had capsized at least once, we spotted the enormous wad of roots from a fallen sycamore into which the current inexorably pulls the unwary paddler, driving home to us that water is not our servant but often our master, and that we must be vigilant and active to survive what threatens us. Newcomers at such spots learned that passivity fathers its own perils, the wrong strategy for survival. The docility of the lamb has no place around fixed obstacles and swirling water. Underneath, a snarl of roots clasped remains of a flashy red kayak, its hull cracked in the grasp of a claw-like skein. Most of us let go of our heroic instincts to prevail and instead chose to portage.

When we reached the section where the highest palisades rise two hundred or so feet above the creek, Larimore had us scan the upper rocks. "See that ledge by the black rock?" he said, pointing. We looked up. "Just below it is the ledge where a red-shouldered hawk nested this spring." He explained that he'd seen the female carry a stick into the dark slit over a hundred feet above the stream, safe from almost any predator. He'd then watched the ledge each time he floated by—which was often— finally spotting small spats of white droppings on the rock facing below the suspected nest. Finally came the reward, seeing five hawks that circled in the sky above the formations. Fledgings. Proof that wildness, at least in this portion of the creek, was flourishing, that things were as they should be, or at least as nearly as they could be. Downstream, we passed a local casualty in the middle of the stream, a large, crooked elbow of a sycamore that had obviously fallen from the parent tree, hollow, its dark mouth swarmed with honeybees. Larimore back-paddled and came as close as he dared, promising to return with a mask and proper clothing as well as a smoker to harvest some of the doomed honey. Such instances made us realize that we share the creek with others, both below and above its surface, that Elkhorn provides a habitat vital to uncountable plant and animal lives, and that we bear a major responsibility for its health and well-being. Its future, in more ways than we can understand, is our future.

The greatest revelation came at the site of the Stedman paper mill, where we stopped to rest, drain excess water from our kayaks, and drink an India Pale Ale on the wide shelf of limestone adjacent to what remained of one of the three mills, a wall stoutly laid with enormous chunks of lime- stone napped into nearly perfect rectilinear blocks. Wading out into the shallow water, Larimore told us he'd spotted submerged timbers of what must have been the dam we knew had barricaded and channeled the creek 180 years ago. Most of us had read the Stedman book. As I waded into the water, I could see at least two dark submerged forms a couple of feet below the surface. Their straightness and regularity identified them as beams, probably white oak. We surmised that they had been spiked to the solid shelf of limestone extending across the creek, serving to anchor the base of the dam. Beneath the surface, we felt metal spikes that had been driven into holes drilled by the team of workers, thirty or so hands, that Ebenezer had hired to build the crib into which the workers poured fill to form the dam, one of the two or three incarnations that eventually succumbed to the unrelenting force of water, spring freshets, and flash floods. We felt pretty confident that we were among the first to rediscover them. To the best of our recollection, they had not been mentioned in the archaeological report that accompanied the most recent edition of *Bluegrass Craftsman*, Ebenezer Stedman's memoir. Investigating on shore, we found another spike, this one exposed and bent, and it took little effort to imagine the ghost beam it fastened to the creek bottom, at least temporarily. In the water we could see another ghost of the cribbing, a beam that was perpendicular to the first and running with the current. We imagined the tapering wall that rose there only to vanish in swollen floodwaters.

Discovering the phantom beams humbled us. The dam's absence, the spilling and dispersal of the stones that had filled it, reminded us that Stedman and our kind have no lasting claim on the creek, that we are interlopers, and that no human construction could ultimately withstand the forces that shape the natural world, on which our hold is at best temporary, tenuous, and ultimately illusory. Water chafes and eventually overcomes every physical obstacle, every human pretense. We also realized limits on what we can expect of it. Fish, recreation, irrigation, beauty, an appreciation for what remains unspoiled—we must respect and cherish Elkhorn, for finally it sustains the invisible scaffolding of our spirits.

All the runs I've made on Elkhorn—well over a hundred along its various segments—merge into one—spring, summer, fall, even winter. After the preliminaries—getting my trailer to the take-out spot, organizing who is in what kayak equipped with paddle and lifejacket—there comes that moment when one steps gingerly into the plastic shell, pushing or being pushed into the stream, and entering another element, one that quickly takes dominance. Water. That creek world forms its own mini-environment, its own microcosm of flowing water encapsulated by trees and air generally a few degrees cooler than the thermals above what borders the creek. This water world plays by its own rules. A careless or willful move can cause a flip in which contents and kayak often get away from the kayaker who tries to get free of its confining interior as it fills with water or is pinned against an immovable object—protruding roots or a tree girdled in flooding water.

Climbing into a kayak, a paddler experiences the sensation of giving oneself over to the power of currents, feet all but useless, arms lengthened by an extended artificial plastic fin that can propel or rudder the pod in which you sit in another direction and in riffles pry you off a rock on which you have foundered. Not following the dictates of water can cost your pride—or your life. Most of us become accustomed to unexpected drenchings, holding on as the current carries us to shallows where the kayak can be upturned on one end and drained. I think of these as recurrent baptisms in the Church of Elkhorn.

Giving oneself to the current is to acknowledge an extension of possibilities. Entering the water, we confess to a greater power, one that is indifferent, amoral, and unforgiving. On a wild river in Chile I once lost a kayak that didn't belong to me, allowing it through poor reckoning to lodge itself against a tree in fast-moving water that inundated the boat and made the kayak unbudgeable, water weighing eight pounds a gallon. Rushing water's pressure against a broad object is almost impossible to overcome, even with the help of two young guides who resorted, finally and futilely, to block and tackle from the nearby bank, the kayak by this time crimped like wadded aluminum foil. Caught in a strong current, one goes with it, not against it, maneuvering as best one can toward shore. Water humbles. It requires us to adapt to it, not it to us.

Water instructs us. Before I had my dangerous spill, the guide whose kayak at one point sidled next to mine asked if I'd had much experience kayaking. Yes, I told him, proud that I hadn't overturned in two or three summers on either Elkhorn or the Kentucky River. He nodded his head and looked apprehensively up at the sky, saying in effect that one does not tempt the gods. And he was right, for not a half mile later the swift current pulled me into the forked tree. Climbing out as the insides filled, I was met by the quick-acting guide, who saw me to safety and must have been thinking, as I did later, about the price of overconfidence, of boasting, of defying the powers that rule the natural world. The lesson was lost on neither of us, knowing things could have been much worse, a trip to some distant hospital accessible from there only by helicopter.

The creek reintroduces us to a natural world we've done our best elsewhere to domesticate or banish. Much of it is bordered by pastureland or inaccessible inclines almost immune from our intrusions and our trash. For a quarter mile or so, spectacular palisades flank this stretch of Elkhorn. They record the creek's history in rippled patterns and scallops engraved along its facings. Dwarfed trees cling to its crevices in meager soils, a study in roans and beiges that suggests their great age as well as their aloofness. At its apex these rocky structures reach as high as 250 feet. Each foot of this sedimentary rock represents approximately a million years of geological time in its formation, now etched and exposed by burrowing water. The creek itself unrolls in scrolls. Light filtered through trees on moving water creates an expanse of flitting silvery commas, constantly appearing and reappearing. Where the water has not been muddied by runoff and excessively churned, it has a sepia clarity in which you can make out objects on its bottom—a rock, a crawfish, a sunken can, a lost flip-flop. And fish, some quite large, cigar their way below your kayak, often darting in nervous schools. Elkhorn displays its order in undisturbed randomness, the fallen tree that has not been parceled into firewood, places where no trails dent the vegetation, beds of undisturbed ferns in elegant repose, ground that even the ubiquitous all-terrain vehicles cannot violate.

The creek stands as an emblem of constancy in change. Never does it flow at the same level, exactly the same temperature, the same velocity. It ranges from torrents to stammers. During droughts it stops just short of isolating itself in stagnant pools in which much of the fish population becomes imprisoned, hostages to rain. Many appear lucky enough or guided by the mandate of survival to find refuge in the deepest channels or pockets of the creek. Between runs, especially after storms or flooding, more trees have toppled, deadfalls that pose new obstacles and points of peril for anything afloat. The rock-strewn shorelines undergo frequent makeovers as they progress on their intermittent journeys downstream. In certain stretches, downed trees accumulate and tangle like pick-up sticks, interspersed with fence posts and beams from ill-placed barns and outbuildings, topped with plastic milk jugs. Elkhorn Creek is always under construction, answering to the imperatives of weather and flowing water.

The creek is also a monument to wildness: the graceful and regal heron, only its head visible above the scrubby margins of an inlet, poised to spear its dinner in the shallows. Or the deer skull whitening into oblivion a few yards into the woods, antlers intact. Or the mud turtles that on sunny days platter themselves on rocks or logs by the creek, sliding into obscurity as their alarm systems prompt them as we pass. Elkhorn is a museum in which we are strangers witnessing the complex cycles of life, great and small, as they are enacted there, the anonymous lives of mammal, amphibian, avian, insect, and microscopic aquatic life. Humans here are secondary, having little to contribute and much to degrade. We find much of Elkhorn's allure in its dissimilarity to the overwhelming bulk of territory we have reshaped with earthmovers, tamed with asphalt, domesticated into golf courses, shorn into submission with lawn mowers. Somewhere recently I read that not one square mile of America east of the Mississippi remains untouched by human presence. Recently, one of my biologist friends who lives farther downstream excitedly announced a pair of eagles nesting in his section of the creek, rebounding from the brink. In wildness, as Thoreau and John Muir so eloquently noted, we rediscover wonder. Our health and the eagles' comeback are inseparably one.

Those most familiar with hellgrammites are either smallmouth bass fishermen or environmental biologists. Popularly, especially in the South, people call these pincher-bearing creatures go-devils. Known as dobsonflies in their second life, they surface and sprout wings. A subfamily of insects, hellgrammites have two names because they essentially live two lives. In their larval stage with their wormlike forms and oversized mandibles that can clutch their prey or an angler's finger, they resemble militant centipedes. They use their jaws as defenses against what disturbs them. They live underwater for up to five years, feeding on other macro-invertebrates. In addition to serving as coveted though expensive bait, these larvae function more importantly as test tubes, living for a lengthy time under rocks in streambeds. Like thermometers, their presence registers what's normal, their absence what's not. Invisibility often masks the environmental health of the creek. What the creek can host accounts for much of the diagnosis. Hellgrammites serve as barometers of sickness or well-being. Either you see them or you don't. Healthy and swift-moving creeks flow over a carpet of macro-invertebrate aquatic life, creatures that can be seen without the aid of a microscope. Anglers love to use hellgrammites as bait because they attract fish the way beef-eaters queue up for filet mignon. They grow large and lively, also belligerent. Sadly, they cannot survive in polluted waters. Though Elkhorn at one time teemed with them, they struggle now, often entering the casualty lists as first victims of fish kills. Every freshwater biologist longs for the resurgence of hellgrammites. Unfortunately, too often the rest of us ignore what we cannot readily see. Because humans cause most pollution, hellgrammites, with a name like one of the lost tribes of the Old Testament, serve also as a mirror of our character and our moral worth. Divert the wastewater and the creek is rejuvenated, resurrected.

Elkhorn Creek should be listed in the local yellow pages as a therapy center, not so much a hospital for treating the injured but as a place where the spirit may be nurtured, healed, and reconfirmed. Ask the scores of fisherfolk, kayakers, and baskers who bring lawn chairs to its cobbled banks. Pushing off into the current for kayakers becomes a reunion with the eternal, a way to leave the daily concerns that occupy most of our waking hours and submit to a greater force, a physical challenge that draws us closer to our hereditary roots in our efforts to make nature serve our will. Elkhorn remains a place where human signs are few and trees still outnumber people, a place where we recognize something larger, more long-lived than ourselves. It invites us to become part of something bigger than self, to reenter the world of our ancestors and our ancestors' ancestors. It is an avenue of discovery, including the hidden and often undiscovered continent of the self. To visit it is to revisit our former evolutionary selves with whom we still bear an indissoluble connection. It is to reawaken our former selves as we confront the enormity of nature. Elkhorn serves as a museum in the sense of a place to muse, a place in which the muses, the gods of inspiration, can inspire. It is a place to recreate ourselves, to reflect and simply relax as our moods blend with those of the water before us—challenging among the white caps in flood stage, languid at low water at the end of summer, starkly beautiful in winter. The creek offers complexities as deep as the moods of any of us—turbulent, placid, luminescent, mopey, contemplative. Elkhorn reminds us that we are part of the stream of history.

Among my friends, after a week in the world of work, nothing seems more restorative than visiting the "Church of Elkhorn," my friends' farm off Peaks Mill Road. From the modified farmhouse fronting the roadway one passes through the side yard, past the barn, and down the long narrow strip of land that leads to a wooded strip bordering the creek. The woods end at a stony beach on a gradual bend in the creek. Across from it a wooded incline rises several hundred feet, tiers of trees like a stadium of green rising out of the steepness. A wall of lushness in summer, a pincushion in winter. The combination of woodscape, flowing water, and sky punctuated by birds floating the thermals make it a place of placid grandeur, a refuge, a cathedral of serenity with no human signs—no houses, no refuse, no motors, no visible power lines. At night, except for the lights of one distant house perched atop a bluff a mile away, one can see the unobstructed stars. Though we know the water carries its freight of carcinogens and is charged with effluents from Georgetown and Lexington upstream, it appears pristine. Here, one, three or four, or six or ten of us bring our coolers and lawn chairs, to marvel at the peacefulness and relax. Though the Church of Elkhorn contains no liturgy, no priests, no hierarchies, no ritual of bread breaking, no tithes, all of us in our way recognize these moments as spiritual, as communal in the best sense. Often a dog or two, a resident black lab or an aging walker hound, fetches tossed sticks from the water. Sometimes the Church has a cookout, sometimes snacks and confections in addition to beer or wine from one of the coolers. All of us sense that something renews us here, though no one feels a great need to prattle about it. Nature, flowing water, has no need to analyze or announce itself.

If the creek serves as a sanitarium to restore us, we have done too little to restore the creek. Elkhorn remains integral to the Bluegrass region's plumbing system, its drain, a means to convey human waste and chemicals that pollute the water, gradually intoxicating and smothering the lifeforms that make the creek distinctive. Fertilizers, pesticides, herbicides, and other potentially toxic substances have displaced oxygen in the creek to a dangerous degree, wreaking havoc on life-forms it has hosted for millennia. In its pristine state the creek became a theater for a natural pageant of water life, both plant and animal. Now it resembles a kind of exclusive country club with hierarchies and accommodations for only a few, shutting out the diverse many. In 1970 a feature in Frankfort's *State Journal* publicized the idea that the creek was dying, mostly from sewage pollution emanating from Lexington.[1] The writer based his story in part

on a study conducted by the Kentucky Department of Fish and Wildlife, making reference to the 16 million to 16.5 million gallons of treated
sewage pouring into the creek per day, amounting to about 24.8 to 25.5
cubic feet of treated sewage per second.[2] Those numbers probably have
not decreased. The stream so famous for smallmouth fishing before the
1950s has been degraded by sewage to the extent that the species must
struggle to survive. According to the study, "the dissolved oxygen content is one of the main obvious limiting factors of the fish population in
the polluted area of the south fork." We are suffocating our water life.
The two-year study tested water quality, bottom fauna (animal life), and
fish populations, concluding that water quality improved the farther it
flowed from Lexington's Town Branch, its main source of pollution. The
North Fork, less subject to massive pollution, suffered fewer effects than
the South Fork. As a result, it contained larger fish populations. Water
below the Forks in the main stem suffered less pollution, but fish populations, including the smallmouth, had obviously been affected. The rugged
corridor through which Elkhorn threads the Bluegrass should make it a
sanctuary for wildlife, not a dead zone.

The study outlined solutions, one of which was undertaking a means
for Lexington to convey its effluents to the Kentucky River, a costly solution but one morally justified since, in addition to whatever moral argu-
ments can be made, degradation of Kentucky's waterways violates state
law, an offense punishable by fine under the statutes. The volume of flow
in the Kentucky River, itself a conduit for pollutants, can withstand waste
more readily than South Elkhorn, the lesser of two evils. The theme of
the statute holds that each of us, including municipalities, should clean
up our own mess. Kentucky's stated but too-seldom practiced policy
regarding water pollution leaves little room for equivocation: "It is hereby
declared to be the policy of this Commonwealth to conserve the waters
of the Commonwealth for public water supplies, for the promulgation
of fish and aquatic life, for fowl, animal wildlife and arborous growth,
and for agricultural, industrial, recreational and other legitimate uses; to
provide a comprehensive program in the public interest for the preven-
tion, abatement and control of pollution; to provide for cooperation with
agencies of other states or of the Federal government carrying out these
objects."[3] Solutions, other than practicing a new ethic, are few, though
the technology that has exacerbated pollution may yet help us find a way

out. Solutions in large part depend on public will and political pressure to force industry and individuals to regard themselves as complicit in fouling the environment.

Few would contest the reality of pollution. The problem lies in seeking solutions and pushing enforcement. The prospect of a key waterway as a mortuary in which all the aquatic life has been strangled or poisoned is unthinkable. Too often, what we cannot see or feel immediately does not concern us, and the alarm bells' sounding comes too late for remedies. They too often serve as a death knell. Despite signs warning swimmers of dangers of drinking or eating what comes out of it, Elkhorn retains much of its original character and appearance, though in a diminished form. Beneath the shimmering water life-forms fight a desperate struggle for simple survival, a struggle aggravated by toxic influences. The creek's future beyond serving as a convenient drainage ditch depends on the public will to preserve a historic waterway and everything that makes it unique as well as necessary for our physical and spiritual health. The good guys do not appear to be winning.

What is the current health of Elkhorn? What kind of oversight protects it? The Kentucky Division of Water works in conjunction with the U.S. Environmental Protection Agency to restore and maintain the physical, chemical, and biological integrity of Kentucky's waters. Authority comes from the Federal Water Pollution Control Act, which was amended in 1972 and is now commonly known as the Clean Water Act (CWA). The act's broad goals are to make our waters drinkable, swimmable, and fishable by preventing point and nonpoint pollution. The CWA grew as a response to the crisis of polluted lakes and streams belatedly recognized in the late 1960s and early 1970s. Since its enactment, there have been substantial environmental gains. Heavy metal mercury and PCBs in our waterways have somewhat abated. The legislation regulated waste from industrial sources and sewage-treatment plants that release through pipes (point sources) into waterways. Nonpoint sources of pollution include run-off from farms and urbanized areas, the former often carrying fertilizer that feeds algae and diminishes oxygen and increases sediments that clog normal water flow, harming plants as well as imperceptible life forms that contribute to a body of water's well-being. These sources of pollution are more difficult to control. Many of these important but modest gains have been offset by the growth and increased development that gnaw at the heart of the Bluegrass, placing additional stress on its overworked water-ways. It is an inescapable geographical fact that both burgeoning George-town and Lexington with its sprawl are upstream of Main Elkhorn.

To determine progress in meeting the goals of the CWA, the Kentucky Division of Water regularly monitors water bodies in river basins state-wide. Kentucky has 90,961 miles of streams running through a gamut of habitats, from mountains to the Bluegrass of central Kentucky.[4] Division personnel use standardized methods to assess the physical, chemical, bio-logical, and habitat conditions of waterways to determine their suitability for designated uses such as primary contact recreation (e.g., swimming), warm water aquatic life, and fishing for consumption. As required under the CWA, assessment results are submitted to the EPA and Congress every even-numbered year. In 2018, the Division of Water reported 2016 assess-ment results for the Kentucky River basin, which includes Elkhorn Creek.[5]

In response to my query about the condition of Elkhorn Creek, Katie McKone, Kentucky's water-quality assessment coordinator, provided a more specific report about its overall health:

Elkhorn Creek from river mile 0.0 to 18.2, where the North and South Forks come together, was found to fully support the aquatic life designated use and fully support the secondary contact recreation designated use [i.e., boating]. However, it was found to not support the primary contact recre-ation designated use due to levels of bacteria exceeding the water quality standard that seeks to protect human health. It was also found to [only] partially support the fish consumption designated use due to methylmer-cury. Therefore, the Elkhorn Creek is on the list of impaired waters.[6]

McKone went on to explain that though the Elkhorn is designated as "impaired" for primary contact recreation, this assessment doesn't mean that the creek is unsafe for swimming all the time. She notes that Elkhorn meets the water-quality standard during times of "low flow." Bacteria lev-els are higher after rain events, when the flow increases and the water is brown. Though Elkhorn is listed as impaired for fish consumption, this designation does not mean that one should never eat fish taken from its waters. Currently, it is recommended that women of childbearing age and children six years and younger eat no more than six meals per year of predatory fish and no more than one meal per month of panfish and bottom-feeder fish. The general public is advised to eat no more than one meal per month of predatory fish and no more than one meal per week of panfish and bottom-feeder fish. Asked about how conditions could be improved, McKone noted that all human activities have an impact on the creek. As a first step, she recommended awareness of how our everyday activities have a direct impact on local water quality. She also stressed the importance of watershed planning.[7]

The sad truth is that our species has altered the Elkhorn Creek watershed by a variety of land uses that degrade water quality. Ebenezer Stedman and A. W. Macklin are nineteenth-century examples. We build our towns along waterways because we recognize the immediate value of water but not its enduring worth. In addition to two sizable cities, there are small subdivisions, farms, and remnant woodlands along the two forks and main stem of Elkhorn. Many of the surviving woods grow on steep slopes along the creek's erosive course. The mix of land use in the Elkhorn Creek watershed is about 5 percent residential, 45 percent rural, and 50 percent agricultural.[8] The 2016 assessment revealed that stream segments throughout the watershed do not consistently support use for primary contact recreation, warm water aquatic life, or fish consumption. The main causes of stream-use impairment are related to agriculture—specifically, pollutants such as sediment, harmful bacteria, and nutrients (e.g., fertilizers and animal waste) that wash from farmland into streams. Less common causes include water-chemistry impairment (e.g., elevated specific conductance, phosphorus, nitrogen, chlorine) from nonpoint sources, package sewage-treatment plants, transportation construction or site runoff, and urban runoff. For example, package sewage-treatment plants at subdivisions—locally, at Ridgeview Estates or the trailer camp below the Forks—often work inadequately, and their effluents can enrich receiving waters. Patterns of erratic weather create storms that push local sewers beyond their capacity and create additional pollution. Heavy rainfall in Lexington washes pollutants from impervious urban surfaces such as roads and vast mall parking lots into bodies of water. These inconsistent weather effects are often difficult to measure because sampling occurs only at designated points along the creek. As a result, pollution levels vary from place to place and time to time, reaffirming Heraclitus's observation that no person steps into the same river twice. Nothing in Elkhorn remains uniform or constant.

As noted above, one other significant impairment is the methylmercury that bioaccumulates in fish tissue. This contaminate derives from a source that is officially unknown but probably related to the burning of coal in power plants. The Kentucky Division of Water periodically issues advisories regarding the consumption of fish from Lower Elkhorn, including specific guidelines for children and nursing women.

Ronald R. Cicerello, a freshwater biologist who recently retired from the Kentucky State Nature Preserves Commission, is the author of numerous monographs and coauthor of a book on the distribution of mussels in Kentucky.[9] His study of mussels is a microcosm of the health of almost all the life in our waterways. It notes the extinction of a number of species of mussels in Kentucky's rivers and streams, including Elkhorn. Concerned about the health of our waterways, he affirmed the role of conservation in state government: "Rest assured, all state conservation agencies want to work with landowners and businesses to improve conditions, but they usually have their own agendas, and governments want growth more than conservation. Improvements are difficult to achieve, even when politics are more favorable than today. Improvements are only possible if the citizenry wants them. You can lead a horse to water, but you can't make him drink." According to Cicerello, we have failed to meet the goals of the federal legislation: "The original goal of the Clean Water Act was to have zero discharge by 1985 and for water bodies to be fishable and swimmable by 1983. Laudable deadlines passed long ago."[10]

In our interactions with the natural world, of which humans undeniably are a part, we seldom heed what we cannot see and what does not blatantly confront us. We conduct ourselves on the principle that what lies before us is there for our exclusive use and benefit. The net effect is a world that has been degraded significantly, yet we operate as though we are still living in the nineteenth-century world of laissez-faire expansion, with little governmental hindrance or regulation. In Macklin and Stedman's time, we lacked the scientific means to record degradation. Now, we have no excuse. According to the Kentucky Division of Water's formula, the Elkhorn watershed "ranks in the group with the highest need for protection and/or restoration."[11]

This ranking is based on averages, which suggests that the quality of particular sites can vary greatly. Though some conditions have improved, the population continues to increase, creating so many demands that natural systems are overwhelmed. If agriculture and larger population centers were removed from the watershed, conditions would rapidly improve. Currently, it's as though we are documenting the slow burning of a home without the will or the means to fight the fire.[12]

Tourism has had a lighter effect on the well-being of the Elkhorn. Because it is difficult to locate official figures on tourist activity in the Elkhorn, most of the evidence is visual and anecdotal. With each passing year, I encounter more traffic on the creek and see more kayaks atop cars and in the beds of pickups. Recently, I spoke with Caleb Bentley, the manager of Canoe Kentucky in Peaks Mill, the business most directly connected to the creek. He and his staff estimate that twenty to thirty thousand people rent canoes or kayaks from their livery each year. Canoe Kentucky uses trailers and vans for transport, some of them carrying fifteen or twenty kayaks. They keep records of peak days each month during the season. Last year, on their greatest single business day, according to a member of the staff, they recorded 277 rentals, an impressive number. As one might expect, the highest volume of rentals occurs on weekends or holidays, especially when the weather is temperate. Canoe Kentucky augments its sales by stocking accoutrements such as life jackets and creek shoes as well as new and (sometimes) used kayaks.

Add to this the number of individuals—enthusiasts—who bring their own kayaks or canoes, and the number grows considerably. On summer weekends I routinely spot scores of kayak-ladened cars and trailers threading toward put-in spots or take-out points along the creek—sometimes whole caravans along Peaks Mill Road. Because most kayakers are nature lovers and come to the creek in part to enjoy its scenic beauty, few litter. Sport fishermen likewise tend to clean up after themselves. However, a few who come to fish—sometimes whole families—deposit picnic leavings, bottles, and diapers along the shoreline at places with access to the road and parking. To its credit, Canoe Kentucky conducts two or three volunteer clean-ups each year along sections of the creek. Out-of-state visitors, some from as far away as California or New York, sometimes rent rooms in motels and hotels around Frankfort. In addition, the American Whitewater Association holds an annual weekend conference in Frankfort, drawing kayakers from near and far.

Canoe and kayak rentals easily account for the greatest economic benefit from Elkhorn Creek. On Memorial Day each year, I've floated with friends in a grand flotilla numbering up to thirty canoes and kayaks. No one yet has had the foresight to set up a bed-and-breakfast in the area, though at least one is in the works. Tourism on the creek is in its infancy and will only grow as more and more of the surrounding region is developed, fueling the desire to find a sliver of pristine nature—or, at least, the appearance of it. The risk is that interest in the area may unleash development that ultimately spoils what drew visitors to the Elkhorn Valley in the first place.

Water is family. Though it lacks form, it is protean, shaped by what resists it, endlessly enacting the cycles of nature and reflecting the turn of seasons. It changes, and is changed by, what it touches. It shapes valleys and watercourses, following its conspiracy with gravity to descend. In part it also shapes our destinies as it nourishes our spirits. Even when it stands and pools, it contains motion. It also reflects our natures. Elkhorn stands as a reservoir of the spirit just as it is a reservoir of history, its records scrawled into the adjacent hills as well as the lives of those who lived along it. Formless, it shapes and draws us to it as a seat of mystery, home of the invisible forces that shape our minds and spirits, from Jack Birchfield's father hunting along its marshy fringe, to Ebenezer Stedman harnessing its power to produce paper, to Judge Innes musing on a legal brief in his poster bed and hearing the water's incessant murmur outside his cabin window.

Creeks, like other organisms, age. They move from birth to maturity to a kind of aqua senility. The only death they know is deserts. Their braiding currents carry the paradox of constancy and change. Constancy lies in a persistent flow that varies from flood to trickle within, or a little beyond, its customary bed. Change may be witnessed in the relentless etching of water into landscape, creasing and gouging it like wrinkled skin. As the twentieth century has painfully learned, streams serve as the earth's arteries, its lifeblood, part of the larger cycle of condensing vapors and rain that make life sustainable, an increasingly critical element in the planet's prospects for a future. Elkhorn and its tributaries when displayed on paper resemble an anatomical chart of the human circulation system. With age, they bend and wander. When exposed to humans, they clog with impurities that have poisoned its life-forms almost to the point of extinction over the last two hundred years. They meander and dry up in places, always seeking new channels, following the ancient imperative of descent. They rush, they linger, they pool. Creeks have lives affected by the forces that permeate them, the plant and animal life that inhabit them and contribute to their character and well-being. Water is both conduit and witness. The metaphor of water as life seems strained because we cannot grasp an existence so long, so changeable, so seemingly timeless. The lives of people who live along it, past, present, and future, seem minuscule by any measure.

As for pollution, a creek functions in cycles as water runs repeatedly through a filter of clouds, a vast hydraulic recycler. It heals itself when what threatens does not overwhelm it. Over the years, Elkhorn has shown a resilience that models adaptability despite the threats of toxins and a prevailing mind-set of neglect that too often ignores what does not visibly confront us. Except for a few biologists and whistle-blowers—nature's neighborhood watch—we live mostly in a region of ostriches, a country of ostriches. We become silent witnesses, silent participants in the desecration of a key waterway that for many is invested with spiritual immanence. Elkhorn is more than a playground. It is a reserve, one of those last places that merit defense. Rejuvenating the creek would be a fundamental recognition of our kinship to every living thing—the smallmouth, hellgrammites, the water in which we and our relatives swim. In rejuvenating Elkhorn, we rejuvenate ourselves.

ACKNOWLEDGMENTS

At the end of Thoreau's *Walden,* a butterfly or other winged insect emerges after decades of being entombed in a farmer's applewood table, its egg once set in the living tree. The farmer could hear the bug inside gnawing before it dug its way out. Gestation is longer for some things than others. I've wanted to write this book since the mid-seventies, though the impulse took its time announcing itself, longer to translate into research and writing. I've been asking questions about the Elkhorn neighborhood since 1975, scissoring out articles and scrawling annotations in books, and keeping files relating to the area for over thirty years. In December of 2015 the time finally came to write, and I began at my doorstep, enlarging my range as far upstream as the Forks and as far downstream as Knight's Bridge, an area whose surface I've only scratched over decades of living by and floating on Elkhorn Creek, listening to stories about it, drawn by its beauty and what visibly remains of its history. Most of it was written in a year, though new chapters kept suggesting themselves, new butterflies appearing. Reading a landscape is as demanding and elusive as reading a book, and the Elkhorn Valley is an abbreviation of the history of this region whose full story will never be told because so much of it, like the highlands out of which it was carved, has vanished. Like the land below from the perspective of a turkey buzzard, the view constantly changes though the terrain itself remains much the same.

Just as the rivers derive from contributions of creeks, and creeks from the puddles and rivulets that begin at our gutter spouts, there are many persons whose knowledge and insights have fed this narrative. I am indebted to many friends and well-wishers whose knowledge of Elkhorn has both a greater depth and breadth than mine, especially in their knowledge of the science that undergirds it.

Among the contributors a few stand out as being especially generous and helpful: Gwynn Henderson, Katherine Mueller, Joseph Jones, Ron Cicerello, Jim and Martha Birchfield, John Gray and Roy Gray Sr., Betty Barr, John and Carol Palmore, Squire Williams, John Baughman, Chuck Dickinson, Jessica Schuster, Katie McKone, Hank Hancock, Russell Harris, Jeff Ellis, Steve and Christine Wilson, Bill Coffey, Mike Larimore, Mary Belle Harwich, Scottie Sams, Ron Ellis, Venita Bright, Ann Macklin Peel, Rob McCoy, Tim Schell, Mike Waford, B. J. Gooch, Kandie Adkinson, James Holmberg, Tom Fiehrer, Marc Evans, and my daughter, Julia Taylor. My good friend Pat Kennedy provided me with a copy of his uncle's fishing map and the story behind it. Gene Burch has helped mightily with the visuals, scanning images and giving good advice and applying his technical skills as well as supplying some of his photographs made to order. He also gave permission to use images from *Bluegrass Craftsman* (2006). Bob Lanham also offered much help with design and advice about visuals. Thanks, too, to Sallie Clay Lanham for permission to use images from *Portrait of Early Families: Frankfort before 1860* (2009). Gray Zeitz, of Larkspur Press, permitted me to reprint my poem "The Feast of Silence," from the 2017 collection of the same name, as well as a part of "In Praise of Sycamores" from *In the Country of Morning Calm* (1998). Dr. Richard Medley graciously extended permission to reproduce a Paul Sawyier painting that was under consideration for the cover.

Charles Hockensmith critiqued the chapter on the Stedman mills, as did Stedman descendant Mary Nash Cox. My good friend and mentor Neal Hammon read the surveyors chapter and provided much assistance. Russ Hatter of the Capital City Museum, who knows more local history than anyone I know, alive or dead, read the whole manuscript, offering suggestions and corrections as well as giving encouragement and opening his files and his personal library. Michael Moran also read it and offered many helpful suggestions. I want especially to thank Ron Cicerello and Katie McKone for their technical understanding of Elkhorn's health and for helping me weave language relating to water quality into the larger narrative. Thanks to Leila Salisbury and Tasha Ramsey at the University Press of Kentucky, who offered encouragement and exercised patience at every step of the process to publication. I would also like to recognize the more indirect support of members of the "Church of Elkhorn," my kayaking friends with whom I have spent untold hours on and by the creek, adding to the reservoir of associations and memories about this small portion of the world that is much larger than its mapped boundaries.

And special thanks goes to Beth Van Allen, who edited the manuscript with an unfailing eye for both missing and superfluous details, who possesses an almost instinctive sense of how a sentence should work and a great eye for spotting flaws in the writing as well as the writer, including incomplete citations and a penchant for repeating details about the pelvic girdles of Pleistocene mammoths, qualities that make her the editor we all wish for in making language work at its optimum.

APPENDIX A

A Visit to the Farm of Harry Innes Todd

Frankfort Commonwealth, October 20, 1871

A casual ride a few days ago through Brown's Bottom and up the winding and picturesque road that girts the deep-wooded ravine, heading toward the famous and fertile Innes valley brought us in the neighborhood of the farm owned by Capt. Harry I. Todd, our representative elect. The pleasant day and the proximity to a place about which we had heard so much, led us to drive in the gate and down to the farmhouse of Capt. Todd—about a half mile distant from the Peaks Mill Pike.

Nearly the entire farm of Capt. Todd is enclosed by a stout and compactly built stone fence, while many of the cross fences and enclosures are of the same material. This gives the farm an appearance equal to the best bluegrass homesteads of our central Kentucky agriculturalists, not in the least diminished by the broad, undulated fields of rich grass or mown crops. Much of the soil is of a deep, dark loam that gives ample assurance of beautiful harvest, well attested by the plethoric barns and well-fed stock. The timber is ash, oak, walnut, sugar tree, hickory, &c common to thrifty and fertile soils. No place could be better watered, for near the farm house, burst out the famous Innes Spring, gushing with its large volume of water that succumbs to no drowth while other springs, ponds, and brooks are scattered about the tract. Several well-built stables, finely arranged and commodious, form shelter for some excellent specimens of harness and trotting stock, and for other purposes.

Our limited stay prevented a thorough inspection of the premises, and hence deprived us of a survey of the fine breeds of Alderney and other cattle, horse stock, &c, for which the Todd farm is noted. The dwelling house is a large handsome frame, cottage style, with a fine view of the valley from its front porch, and surrounded with all the modern conveniences. Underneath is a cool, and airy milk cellar, whose floor was paved with brimming pans of the lacteous fluid, which he daily converted into pound on pound of rich butter that brings the highest price in the market.

Capt. Todd does not reside on his farm, preferring his elegant and costly city residence, leaving the farm in the care of his son Harry, and his overseer, Mr. Hockensmith. The Harry Todd farm is not only of general modern notoriety, but is a locality famous in Kentucky pioneer history, as the scene of fierce Indian attacks, embracing as it does the territory covered by the Innes Settlement. Of the cabins nested near the Innis [*sic*] Spring, by the Cooks, the Martins, the Dunns, the Bledsoes, and the Innises, [*sic*] only the latter remains, and that is in a crumbling and decaying condition. Its port-holes are still visible from the interior, though boarded up on the outside. Erelong, it too, will pass away, leaving naught to mark the spot save the Spring and the older memories that will long hang in the moss-clad garniture about its salient features. It was here that a party of Indians made an attack in April of 1792, killing one of the Cooks and mortally wounding the other, who fled to his cabin ere yielding his life. Martin, two of the Dunns, and a negro at the Innis cabin, were killed, while McAndré, Dunn, and one of the Martins' children escaped. The two Cook widows with three children were collected in one cabin, whose doors they barred. The Indians attacked it, when one of the women, biting a musket ball in two with her teeth, loaded a rifle and shot dead one of the assailants, as he sat on a log near the house. The Indians then mounted the roof and sought to set it on fire, but with Spartan courage the women again and again extinguished the flames from the loft with water, broken eggs, the bloody waistcoat of the dead husband, and by other expedients. Fearing pursuit, the Indians finally gave up the assault and retreated, leaving the brave defenders uninjured.

APPENDIX B

Reinterment of Judge Innes and Family Members

Louisville, Ky., Nov 13th, 1891

In the fall of 1890 I promised my father, Harry Innes Todd, that I would at some future time remove the remains of certain parties buried on the old Innes Place, which is located on the Peaks Mill road five miles from Frankfort.

On November 9th, 1891, I, with John Hammond and John Nelson, (col.) secured a spring wagon in Frankfort, Ky., and drove to Cedar Hill farm, (which was settled by Judge Harry Innes in 1790) for the purpose of removing the remains of Judge Innes and wife, Justice Thomas Todd, his son John H. Todd, and his grandson, Thomas Todd, to the Frankfort Cemetery. The first grave opened was that of the Hon. Thomas Todd. The following was inscribed on the flat marble slab, which was three by six feet, and rested upon a stone foundation three feet high.

Sacred to the
Memory of
Hon. Thomas Todd.
Died Feb. 7th, 1826
Aged 61 years.

After removing the stone and eighteen inches of earth, we came to three large flag stones, which covered the entire grave, and in order to get them out of the way, we were compelled to break them. After digging about two feet deeper, we came to two layers of large flag stones which rested upon the brick vault which contained the coffin. These stones, like the others, had to be broken to be moved. The vault was the shape and size of a coffin, the bricks being laid with mud mortar. After removing the flag stones, we found the bones in good condition, and the head indicated more than ordinary intelligence. There was very little left of the coffin, but enough to show that it was made of cedar, and was covered with dark green velvet. The handles of the coffin were brass, very small and delicate, but well preserved.

The next grave opened was that of Judge Harry Innes. The tomb that surmounted the grave was of the same character as that of Justice Todd, with the following

The Noble
Harry Innes
OB 20 Sept. 1816
AE 64

We experienced the same trouble in removing the large flag stones, and found the brick vault the same as that of Justice Todd. The coffin was made of walnut and the handles brass, and very light and small. The bones were well preserved. The skull is in a remarkable state of preservation, and indicated extraordinary ability. Upon close examination I found every tooth perfect and in its proper place; something remarkable, taking into consideration the person being sixty-four years old and having been buried over seventy-five years.

Mrs. Ann Innes, the wife of Judge Innes was buried some thirty years later than her husband. The grave was not marked, nor was she buried like the others. The grave was modern, and the bones were almost gone.

We opened the grave by mistake, taking it to be that of John H. Todd, but upon examination we found that his remains were directly beneath the monument erected by his son, H. I. Todd. In order to get at the brick vault, we had to break up the monument first, and then the stone slabs. The bones were well preserved. The following was inscribed on the monument:

Sacred to the memory of
John H. Todd
Youngest son of
Thomas and Elizabeth Todd
Born Oct. 30, 1795
Died Aug. 31 1824

Thomas
Infant son of
John H. and Maria K. Todd
Born May 15th, 1822
Died Oct. 10th, 1823

We did not complete the work of exhuming on the 9th, owing to darkness coming on so soon. The remains of Justice Todd and Judge Innes and wife, were kept in my house in Frankfort over night.

On the morning of the 10th, the rain came down in torrents, and I sent Hammond and Nelson after the remains of John H. Todd and son. Above twelve o'clock they returned, and with the others they were deposited in the Frankfort Cemetery vault.

On Friday, the 18th, of Nov., 1891, the remains were interred in the Frankfort cemetery; those of Justice Todd and Judge Innes in the Todd lot, and Mrs. Innes, John H. Todd and son in the Genl. T. L. Crittenden's lot.

SIGNED; Geo. D. Todd

APPENDIX C

The Responsibility of Owners of Historic Buildings

In researching this project, I came across an op-ed piece I wrote that was published in the local newspaper, the *Frankfort State Journal,* on June 2, 1982. I had lost my own copy and was pleased to find it because the demolition of the old Stedman "Hotel" did much to push me toward preservation of old buildings:

The character of a community in large part is shaped by its past, the composite lives and actions of those who make up its cumulative history. Long after the generations pass, long after the events of people's lives are forgotten or footnoted in a few local histories, the buildings in which they lived and worked remain as testaments to their daily living, their values, their aspirations. Old buildings reflect the lives of those who lived in them. As the state's capital and one of its oldest settlements, Frankfort and Franklin County are especially rich in such places, some concentrated in the historic districts of downtown and south Frankfort, others scattered through the smaller communities and farms comprising the county. They range from clapboard cabins and modest outbuildings to more substantial brick and stone farmhouses.

Unfortunately, much of the county's past is hard to define because only a fraction of these structures still stand. Weather and fires have taken their toll. The 1974 tornado was particularly devastating. These are losses that must be accepted because they cannot be prevented. The majority, however, have been victims of human neglect and indifference. Many have been victims of the attitude that the old is impractical and inconvenient, even though the materials and design of many new "practical" buildings ensure that they will not outlive the generation that built them.

Old buildings are an endangered species. As with the loss of a snail darter, a passenger pigeon, or a rare plant, extinction or loss of an old house diminishes our knowledge of the past as well as possibilities for the future. Like nature, cultures thrive on diversity and succession. Old buildings give us the necessary reminder that we are not the first to occupy this place just as the ginkgo tree reminds us that we exist in a continuum spanning millions of years of geological time. To forget or deny this is to be shortsighted. Few would deny the troubling uniformity and narrowness of much that is praised and justified as new.

For these reasons, the demolition of another county landmark is cause for community concern. The Stedman "Hotel," as it is called, is probably the most significant and attractive structure on Steadmantown Lane. It belonged to the family that gave the road its name, even though somehow the road name acquired an additional "a." The house was the seat of the Stedman family who in the decades before the Civil War established a whole community around the papermaking mill that ultimately supplied all of the paper for state government and much of the newsprint for Frankfort publishers. In 1959 the reminiscences of Ebenezer Hiram Stedman (1808–1885) was printed in Bluegrass Craftsman, a book published by the University Press of Kentucky, now out of print. The reminiscences are an account of the Stedman family's migration to Franklin County in the early decades of the last century [19th]. In 1833 the Stedmans acquired a millsite on Elkhorn Creek where Stedmantown gradually formed as the papermaking business flourished. Several times Ebenezer Stedman mentions the Stedman house, the site of which he refers to as "Old Mount Pleasant": "We arrived at home and as always is the Case 'home Sweet Home' is Best of all Homes Old mt. pleasant home Begins this year to show what industry will do for a place. A new home is on the hill whare stood the old sheep Ranch. A new fence is around the house. The pasture that had so long Remainded [sic] a commons for all the cattle hogs, and sheep now is fenced in. Sam Stedmans log cabbin is still there (Bluegrass Craftsman, 174)." Until recently, anyone passing along Steadmantown Lane during the last hundred years could recognize the same house on the bluff above Elkhorn Creek.

The rights of property owners to do with their property as they wish is a cherished precept in Anglo-American law. With few exceptions, a person can use or abuse his land and the structures on it any way he sees fit. Reluctant to infringe on the rights of property owners, lawmakers have been slow to recognize the interest of the community in preserving its landmarks. It's true that the federal government awards some tax relief to individuals who wish to rehabilitate old buildings. It's also true that persons who tear down historic structures can claim no tax credits for the cost of demolition. Still, more positive incentives are needed to persuade owners that they and the community stand to profit by preserving their common heritage.

The problem is not new. Chaumiere du Prairies, the garden showplace of the Bluegrass during the early years of the last century [19th], was virtually wrecked by a spiteful owner who acquired the property at auction and used one of the main buildings as a cowbarn. White Hall, the home of Cassius M. Clay and now a state shrine, suffered similar abuse.

A person may act freely so long as he doesn't injure the life or property of others. The law provides protection against measurable hurts. Unfortunately, the extent to which a county, a city, or a neighborhood is damaged by the destruction of its historic buildings is not so easily measured. Though the community has a valid interest in the preservation of the landmarks that define it, there is no legal remedy. But we all know the difference between communities in which the past has been lovingly and usefully preserved and those in which the past has been destroyed, or those that are too recent to have one. And we all sense, I hope, the terrible sterility of an area in which its connections to the past are erased or emasculated, the standardized blandness that describes too much of our modern landscape where things look just about the same everywhere.

With so much of our past passing, we need to develop new attitudes about ownership. Owning property, especially historical landmarks like the Stedman "Hotel," is a kind of trust in which the entire community are beneficiaries. The terms of this trust are that ownership entails responsibility to improve or at least maintain the property so it may be passed intact to others. There is a corollary duty not to reduce its material, historical, or aesthetic value. At present there is no penalty for violation of this trust, nor perhaps, given the tradition of ownership our society, should there be. The emphasis should be on inducements and positive incentives for the owners to preserve their property. Make preservation pay.

Owning property is a responsibility as well as a privilege. If the owner does not wish to maintain or utilize the property he owns, it should be sold or leased to those who will. Owners should enlist the advice and aid of organizations like the state Heritage division, Franklin County Trust, or Historic Frankfort. It is probably too late to save the Stedman house, but it is not too late for interested individuals and local government, through regulation or informal consultation, to prevent other such losses. The passing of the Stedman "Hotel" diminishes all of us, but the greatest loss is to generations to come who will know the place only through books and records or a pile of foundation stones strewn on the hillside.

APPENDIX D
An Elkhorn Poem

In *The Macklins of Frankfort and Franklin County* there is a poem about Elkhorn Creek that was probably never published for the public eye. It was written by the unnamed brother of Joseph Quilling, husband of Mary Frances "Fannie" Macklin, after a visit to Franklin County.

DISTANT VIEW
Written aboard the steamer Yorktown, September 25, 1854

There is on Elkhorn's rippling stream
    A green and pleasant spot
Which, though I ne'er can near it live
    Shall never be forgot.
On this I love to stand and gaze
    For scenes so grand are few,
And from its prospect o'er the land,
    They call it "Distant View."
A rough and craggy clift winds 'round
    This high and healthy place;
And Elkhorn's gentle Stream flows down
    Along its rugged base.
Flowers of every hue are culled
    Some sweet as ever grew
From the shady hill and locust grove
    Near lovely Distant View.

The balmy breeze floats 'round so free
   O what can be more true,
Than my remembrance of that scene
   Thou lovely Distant View.
No, not while life itself shall last
   What ever else I do
Will I forget thy sweet retreat
   Through pleasant Distant View

NOTES

Introduction

1. Betty Lee Mastin, *Lexington Herald-Leader*, 1977, undated clipping in author's personal files.

2. Harry Innes, 1752–1816, Social Networks and Archival Content, http://socialar chive.Iath.virginia.edu/ark:/99166/w6ok2c1f.

3. W. H. Perrin, *Kentucky: A History of the State* (Chicago and Louisville: F. A. Battey, 1887), 810.

4. Todd Family File, Kentucky Historical Society, Frankfort, Kentucky.

5. Advertising flyer for James A. Holt farm, 1905, in possession of the author.

6. Ibid.

7. Heraclitus (535–475 B.C.), also spelled Herakleitos, was a pre-Socratic Greek philosopher who was famous for his contention that the universe was in a state of constant change, as in his saying, "No man steps into the same river twice." Guy Davenport, trans., *Herakleitos and Diogenes* (San Francisco: Grey Fox Press, 1990), 14.

8. David Orr, *Earth in Mind: On Education, Environment, and the Human Prospect* (Washington, D.C.: Island Press, 2004).

9. John Betjeman, with an introduction by W. H. Auden, *Slick but Not Streamlined: Poems and Short Pieces* (New York: Doubleday, 1947).

10. Mike Cronin, "Enshrined in Blood: The Naming of Gaelic Athletic Association Grounds and Clubs," *Sports Historian* 18 (1998): 90–104.

11. Yi-Fu Tuan, *Topophilia* (New York: Columbia Univ. Press, 1974), 93.

12. Orr, *Earth in Mind*, 137.

13. Scott Sanders blurb in Erik Reece, ed., *Field Work: Modern Poems from Eastern Forests* (Lexington: Univ. Press of Kentucky, 2008).

14. William Blake, *The Marriage of Heaven and Hell* (London: Self-published, 1790). Of the original copies of Blake's most influential work, only nine still exist. All extant copies of this illuminated book are available online through the Blake Archive, https://blog .blakearchive.org/2016/08/30/the-marriage-of-heaven-and-hell-copy-a/.

1. Elkhorn

1. Carolyn Murray Wooley, *The Founding of Lexington: 1775–1776* (Lexington, Ky.: Lexington-Fayette County Historic Commission, 1975), 9.

2. Jedidiah Morse, *The American Geography* (London: John Stockdale, 1792), 404.

3. John Filson, *The Discovery and Settlement of Kentucky,* facsimile (1784; reprint, New York: Readex Microprint Corporation, 1966), 24.

4. A. K. Moore, *The Frontier Mind* (Lexington: Univ. Press of Kentucky, 1957).

5. Father Lalement, *Voyage au Kantoukey et sur les bords du Genesee* (Paris, 1821), 156–57.

6. Elijah Craig, quoted in Isaac Reed, *The Christian Traveller: In Five Parts: Including Nine Years and Eighteen Thousand Miles* (New York: J. and J. Harper, 1828), 47–48.

7. Bill Meyers, "Massacre of Hosea and Jesse Cooke," *Bred in Old Kentucky,* July 18, 2014, https://familysearch.org/photos/artifacts/8888995.

8. Norman F. Maclean, *A River Runs Through It, and Other Stories* (Chicago: Univ. of Chicago Press, 1976).

9. Allan Gurganus, *Oldest Surviving Confederate Widow Tells All* (New York: Knopf, 1989).

10. In 1991, Los Angeles police officers brutally beat Rodney King following a high-speed car chase. Thirteen months later, when a mostly white jury acquitted the police officers, riots broke out in the streets of the city. King's plea, quoted here, became famous, and he became a civil rights icon. King died in June 2012, the same year that his memoir about his experiences was published. Rodney King, with Lawrence J. Spagnola, *The Riot Within: My Journey from Rebellion to Redemption* (New York: HarperOne, 2012).

2. A Glimpse into the Distant Past

1. Like the mammoths, Jillson came to Kentucky from the north, though not pursued by ice sheets. Born in Syracuse, New York, Jillson studied geology at Syracuse University, earning his master's degree in 1915 from the University of Washington. He later continued his studies at the University of Chicago and Yale. First working as a petroleum geologist in the South and West, opportunities in oil, gas, and coal brought him to Kentucky, where he made business deals that permitted him to live quite comfortably. His Queen Ann-style house in South Frankfort—just a few blocks from the state capitol—still stands, passed every day by neighbors who have no idea that an important and prolific scholar lived and worked there. Someone familiar with his reputation for productiveness told me that Jillson had a long worktable on which the papers for multiple projects were placed for easy access until they headed for a local printing establishment, Roberts Printing of Frankfort. He had a close association with the Kentucky Historical Society, an organization with an extensive library of Kentucky materials to which he had privileged access. Seemingly inexhaustible, he had an appetite for new challenges, teaching at the University of Kentucky and Transylvania College, curating the Kentucky State Museum, and serving as a

consultant for the gas, coal, and oil industries after his resignation as state geologist in 1932. From 1947 until 1951, he taught geology at Transylvania and chaired a department, serving as first vice president of the Kentucky Historical Society. He had a wide range of interests: paleontology, mining, regional history, biography, bibliography, the history of Kentucky newspapers, and Kentucky literature. He wrote monographs on virtually every subject that caught his eye. Collectors avidly seek his books, especially those relating to Kentucky history.

2. Big Bone Lick State Park, Kentucky State Parks, n.d. (brochure), in the author's possession.

3. Willard Rouse Jillson, *The Elkhorn Mammoth: An Account of the Discovery of Elephas Columbi in Franklin County, Kentucky, Coupled with Geological and Paleontological Notes*, (Frankfort, Ky.: Roberts Printing, 1947).

4. Willard Rouse Jillson, *Big Bone Lick: An Outline of Its History, Geology, and Paleontology* (Louisville: Standard Printing, 1936).

5. *Frankfort State Journal*, August 10, 1945.

6. Stanley Hedeen, *Big Bone Lick: The Cradle of American Paleontology* (Lexington: Univ. Press of Kentucky, 2011), xvii.

7. Jillson, *Big Bone Lick.*

8. John Mack Faragher, "Foreword," in Hedeen, *Big Bone Lick*, xii.

9. Big Bone Lick State Park, Kentucky State Parks, n.d. (brochure).

10. J. Simpson, "Word Stories: 'mammoth,'" *Oxford English Dictionary Online*, http:// public.Oed.com/aspects-of-english/word-stories/mammoth/.

11. *Frankfort State Journal*, August 10, 1945.

12. Jillson, *The Elkhorn Mammoth.*

3. The Ones Who Came Before

1. Federal Writers' Project, *Lexington and the Bluegrass Country*, American Guide Series (Lexington, Ky.: E. M. Glass, 1938), 99.

2. Nettie Henry Glenn, *Enda Lechaumanne: Legend of the Forks of Elkhorn* (Frankfort, Ky.: Roberts Printing, 1981).

3. More recently, Mike Waford, a kayaking friend and member of the Church of Elkhorn, composed a song called "Wapiti" based on the legend.

4. A. Gwynn Henderson and Eric J. Schlarb, *Adena, Woodland Period Moundbuilders of the Bluegrass* (Lexington, Ky.: Kentucky Geological Survey, 2007), 14–15.

5. Bennett H. Young, *The Prehistoric Men of Kentucky: A History of What Is Known of Their Lives and Habits* (Louisville, Ky.: John P. Morton, 1910), 68–69.

6. Ibid., 69.

7. Willard Rouse Jillson, *Sketches of Early Frankfort, Kentucky* (Frankfort, Ky.: Roberts Printing, 1950), 1.

8. Ibid.

9. Ibid.

10. A. Gwynn Henderson, "Dispelling the Myth: Seventeenth- and Eighteenth-Century Indian Life in Kentucky," *Register of the Kentucky Historical Society* 90, no. 1 (1992): 1–25.

11. John E. Kleber, ed., *The Kentucky Encyclopedia* (Lexington: Univ. Press of Kentucky, 2000), s.v. "Archaeology."

12. Henderson, "Dispelling the Myth," 2–3.

13. Ibid.

14. Ibid., 6.

15. R. Barry Lewis, *Kentucky Archaeology* (Lexington: Univ. Press of Kentucky, 1996), 60.

16. Ibid., 62.

17. Amy Carman, "The Beginning," in *Franklin County, 1795–1995* (Frankfort, Ky.: Frankfort State Journal, 1995), 47.

18. Henderson, "Dispelling the Myth," 7.

19. Ibid., 7–8.

20. A. Gwynn Henderson, "Capitol View: An Early Madisonville Horizon Community in Franklin County," in *Current Archaeological Research in Kentucky*, vol. 2, ed. David Pollack and A. Gwynn Henderson (Frankfort, Ky.: Kentucky Heritage Council, 1992), 223.

21. Ibid., 224.

22. Ibid.

23. Henderson, "Dispelling the Myth," 7.

24. Henderson, "Capitol View," 231.

25. Ibid., 232.

26. Ibid., 238.

27. Ted Belue, *The Long Hunt: Death of the Buffalo East of the Mississippi* (Mechanicsburg, Pa.: Stackpole Books, 1996), 163.

4. Compass and Chains

1. According to Neal Hammon, the grave lies 4,500 feet east-southeast of where Kentucky Route 52 crosses Taylor's Fork (Neal O. Hammon to the author, June 14, 2016). Next morning the survivors started the trek southeast across the mountains as quickly as they could, carrying Taylor's precious record book as well as their own. Taylor's will was the first recorded in Kentucky, his surveys among the earliest of Louisville, Frankfort, and the Central Bluegrass. His was also the earliest identified grave of a Euro-American. When I saw it a few years ago, it was marked only by a pile of stones hurriedly gathered by survivors of the surveying parties, though a highway marker a quarter mile away served as Taylor's cenotaph.

2. According to Neal O. Hammon in an unpublished manuscript in possession of the author, others in Taylor's party included Willis Lee, John Willis, John Ashby, John Green, and John Bell. Counting Strother, Heponstall, and Taylor himself, it was a surveying party of eight men.

3. Neal O. Hammon, ed., *John Floyd: The Life and Letters of a Frontier Surveyor* (Louisville, Ky.: Butler Books, 2013), 10.

4. Hammon, ed., *John Floyd*, 5.

5. Ibid., 8.

6. Ibid., 9.

7. Ibid., 27.

8. James Douglas, deputy surveyor of Fincastle County, is remembered in connection with another tributary of the Kentucky River, Jessamine Creek, which in turn gave the name to the county. Though Collins's *History* claims that Douglas settled at the head of the creek and named it in honor of his daughter, Bennett Young's *A History of Jessamine County* states that someone else in fact settled at the head of the creek and that others named it for the profusion of jessamine flowers growing along its banks. Young refers to the "romance" that grew up around the naming of the creek. Sitting on a rock by a spring at the head of the creek, the legend goes that a prowling Indian tomahawked Jessamine as she sat daydreaming, gazing at the stream. In 1773, Douglas had been one of the first whites to visit Big Bone Lick, noting the bones he found there and employing the skeletal ribs of a mammoth as poles to spread his tent. Charles Kerr, *History of Kentucky*, vol. 11 (Chicago: American Historical Society, 1922), 1107; Lewis Collins, *History of Kentucky* (Cincinnati: J. A. and U. P. James, 1847), 1:181, 377; Bennett H. Young, *A History of Jessamine County, Kentucky* (Louisville, Ky.: Courier-Journal Job Printing, 1898), 67–68.

9. Wilson Miles Cary, "The Dandridges of Virginia," *William and Mary Quarterly* 5. no. 1 (July 1896): 33.

10. Neal O. Hammon to the author, August 16, 2002.

11. Ibid., May 11, 2016.

12. Ibid.

13. Ibid.

14. Thomas Hanson, "Tom Hanson's Journal," April 7–August 9, 1774, in Hammon, ed., *John Floyd*, 226.

15. Hammon to author, n.d.

16. Hanson, "Tom Hanson's Journal," typed transcription by Neal O. Hammon in possession of the author.

17. Ibid.

18. Hammon, *John Floyd*, 272.

19. Ibid., 11.

20. Willis Lee, Hancock Taylor's cousin, was killed at the fort he established at what became Leestown, a settlement later absorbed by Frankfort. Of the original surveyors in the party that came in 1774, only James Douglas and Isaac Hite, who had been seriously wounded, died natural deaths.

21. Kleber, ed., *The Kentucky Encyclopedia*, s.v. "Floyd, John."

22. Ibid.

23. John Floyd to William Preston, March 28, 1783, quoted in Hammon, ed., *John Floyd*, 45.

24. Ann Bevins, *The Royal Spring of Georgetown, Kentucky* (Georgetown, Ky.: Scott County Historical Society, 1970), 11.

25. Lyman C. Draper, "Sketch of John Floyd," in Hammon, ed., *John Floyd*, 244.

26. Two of the others came during a raid on the Innes settlement nearly nine years later, when members of the raiding party murdered two of Innes's slaves.

5. Judge Harry Innes

1. Thomas Marshall Green, *Historic Families of Kentucky* (Baltimore, Md.: Genealogical Publishing, 1975), 192.

2. Mary K. Bonsteel Tachau, *Federal Courts in the Early Republic: Kentucky, 1789–1816* (Princeton, N.J.: Princeton Univ. Press, 1978), 32.

3. Green, *Historic Families of Kentucky*, 193.

4. Innes Family File, Kentucky Historical Society, Frankfort, Kentucky.

5. Lewis Collins, *History of Kentucky*, 1:314–15.

6. Edna Talbott Whitley, *Kentucky Ante-Bellum Portraiture* (Paris, Ky.: National Society of the Colonial Dames of American in the Commonwealth of Kentucky, 1956), 388.

7. William H. Averill, *A History of the First Presbyterian Church, Frankfort, Kentucky, with the churches in Franklin County, in Connection with the Presbyterian Church in the United States of America* ([Frankfort, Ky.?], 1901), 67, 243, 248.

8. Thomas D. Clark, *A History of Kentucky* (Lexington, Ky.: John Bradford Press, 1960), 89.

9. Averill, *A History of the First Presbyterian Church*, 66.

10. Jillson, *Sketches of Early Frankfort, Kentucky*, 110.

11. *Dictionary of American Biography*, s.v. "Innes, Harry."

12. Judicial Conference of the United States, Bicentennial Committee, *History of the Sixth Circuit* (Washington, D.C.: The Committee, [1977?]), Innes Family File, Kentucky Historical Society, Frankfort, Kentucky.

13. Harry Innes to Thomas Jefferson, August 27, 1791, Harry Innes Papers, 1772–1890s, Kentucky Historical Society, Frankfort, Kentucky.

14. Ibid., 2.

15. Malcolm J. Rohrbough, *The Trans-Appalachian Frontier: People, Societies, and Institutions, 1775–1850* (New York: Oxford Univ. Press, 1978), 381.

16. *History of the Sixth Circuit*, 38.

17. George A. Lewis, "The Old Innes Fort on Elkhorn Creek," *Register of the Kentucky Historical Society* 19 (1921): 29.

18. Ibid., 31.

19. Willard Rouse Jillson, *Early Frankfort and Franklin County* (Louisville, Ky.: Standard Printing Company, 1936), 47.

20. Neal O. Hammon and Richard L. Taylor, *Virginia's Western War: 1775–1786* (Mechanicsburg, Pa.: Stackpole Books, 2002), 206.

21. Indian troubles were to persist in Franklin County at least until 1794, when a young woman, Mary Downey, was sent to the spring at Peaks Mill to fetch water. When she didn't return, her father went to the spring and found signs that she had been taken. Mary, the account goes, had two suitors, one an Irishman, the other a native of England.

When the father called for help, the Irishman joined the rescue party. They came upon the Indians, four of them, to the north at Six Mile Creek, killing two and wounding two, who managed to escape. Unharmed, Mary in gratitude married the Irishman. This was said to have been the last invasion of Indians into the county. When Franklin County was formed in 1795, its increased settlement made it too risky for raiding parties to reach it without detection. Charles F. Hinds, "The Pioneers," in *Franklin County, 1795–1995* (Frankfort, Ky.: Frankfort State Journal, 1995), 57.

22. George A. Lewis, "A Relic of Indian Days," *Register of the Kentucky Historical Society* 19 (1921): 30.

23. Ibid.

24. Ibid.

25. *Frankfort Roundabout* 10, no. 1 (September 28, 1886), A1.

26. "Know all men by these presents that I Robert Andrews of ye city of Williamsburg hath by these presents bargained and sold & do herby bargain and sell unto Harry Innis of yet County of Bedford one mulattoe man slave named Peter for & in consideration of the quantity of 8000 punds weight of nett tobacco, which said slave is vested in the Heirs of Robert Ballard deceased late of York County, to have & to hold ye s'd slave to the s'd Harry Innis his Heirs and Assignes forever and yet s'd Robert Andrews for himself & his Heirs the s'd slave to the s'd Harry & his Heirs shall a & will warrant & forever defend firmly by these presents, In witness whereof I have hereunto set my hand & seal this 13th day of November 1779. [Robert Andrews (seal), Witness Fielding Lewis, James Thompson.]" *Frankfort Roundabout* 10, no. 1 (September 28, 1886), A1.

27. C. E. James, *A Short History of Franklin County* (Frankfort, Ky.: Frankfort Roundabout Office, n. d.).

28. Jillson, *Early Frankfort and Franklin County*, 71.

29. Frontier historian Neal O. Hammon cites a letter of Harry Innes as evidence that Innes did not live at Innes Station until 1793. It is possible that after he purchased the land he simply delegated its building to others. Letter to William Fleming, December 15, 1793, quoted in Neal O. Hammon, "Kentucky Pioneer Forts and Stations," *Filson Club Quarterly* 76 (fall 2002): 572.

30. Nancy O'Malley, *Stockading Up: A Study of Pioneer Stations in the Inner Bluegrass Region of Kentucky*, Archaeological Report 127 (Frankfort, Ky.: Kentucky Heritage Council, 1987), 222

31. Originally a part of Harry Innes's holdings, the Joe Bradburn farm is also identified with Henry Giltner, who built a house in 1859 on the bluff above Innes's Bottom. Interestingly, Giltner is said to have lived in Innes Station while his own house was under construction. Which house is not clear—the one by the creek or the reputed structure to the north off Holt Lane. Certainly, the Holt Lane location would have been more convenient since it was in sight of the construction.

32. Tachau, *Federal Courts in the Early Republic*, 60.

33. Richard Collins, *History of Kentucky*, vol. 2 (Covington, Ky., 1874), 273.

34. Patricia Watlington, *The Partisan Spirit: Kentucky Politics, 1779–1792* (Chapel Hill: Univ. of North Carolina Press, 1972), 57.

35. Ibid., 57–58.

36. Nettie Henry Glenn, *Early Frankfort, 1786–1861* ([Frankfort, Ky.?]: N. H. Glenn, 1986), 9.

37. Ibid., 26.

38. Tachau, *Federal Courts in the Early Republic,* 42.

39. Ibid., 140.

40. Ibid., 141.

41. Ibid., 145.

42. Harry Innes and Humphrey Marshall, Memorandum of Understanding, February 17, 1816, Harry Innes Papers.

43. Ibid.

44. One of the earliest biographies of Wilkinson is Royal Ornan Shreve's *The Finished Scoundrel* (Indianapolis, Ind.: Bobbs-Merrill, 1933). The title gives a sense of how contemporaries regarded Wilkinson, being drawn from a statement of John Randolph of Roanoke, a prominent if erratic and outspoken U.S. senator from Virginia: "Wilkinson is the most finished scoundrel that ever lived; a ream of paper would not contain the proofs," 11. This assessment is confirmed more recently in a subsequent biography: Andro Linklater, *An Artist in Treason: The Extraordinary Double Life of General James Wilkinson* (New York: Walker, 2009).

45. There is evidence that in 1795 Wilkinson's Spanish contact and governor of Louisiana, Baron Hector de Carondelet, authorized Wilkinson to guarantee pensions of $2,000 to Innes, Sebastian, and George Nicholas, men whose cooperation was sought in effecting Kentucky's secession. There is no evidence that Harry Innes either accepted or received any monies under this authorization. He consistently recoiled from the proposition that Kentucky become a part of the Spanish empire. Linklater, *An Artist in Treason,* 93, 153.

46. Water must have been poured into it for bathing, then scooped back out since drain pipes and other plumbing would not have been available at the time. Larger than most coffins, the tub survives as a rare example of an eighteenth-century bathing convenience—a mode of ablution for the privileged in a time when few people, beyond periodic dips in local ponds, streams, or rivers, bothered to bathe regularly, if at all.

47. "Harry Innes' 1785 Book Order," in Tachau, *Federal Courts in the Early Republic,* 208.

48. Thomas Jefferson to Harry Innes, September 18, 1813, Innes Family File, Kentucky Historical Society, Frankfort, Kentucky.

49. Notebooks, Harry Innes Papers.

50. Ibid.

51. Ibid.

52. *Dictionary of American Biography,* s.v. "Innes, Harry."

53. Christopher L. Leadingham, "To Open 'the Doors of Commerce': The Mississippi River Question and the Shifting Politics of the Kentucky Statehood Movement," *Register of the Kentucky Historical Society* 114 (summer/autumn 2016): 344.

54. Tachau, *Federal Courts in the Early Republic,* 59.

55. Like his uncle, Thomas Todd, a fellow Jeffersonian, sued the editor of the *Western World,* feeling he had been libeled by Humphrey Marshall (Tachau, *Federal Courts in the*

Early Republic, 60). Though a Republican at heart, he upheld the constitutional principles promoted by Chief Justice John Marshall, Humphrey's kinsman.

56. *The Biographical Encyclopaedia of Kentucky* (Cincinnati: J. M. Armstrong, 1878), s.v. "Todd Hon. Thomas."

57. Russ Hatter, *A Walking Tour of Frankfort* (Frankfort, Ky.: Frankfort Heritage Press, 2002), 8.

58. Whitley, *Kentucky Ante-Bellum Portraiture,* 392.

59. Estill Curtis Pennington, *Lessons in Likeness, Portrait Painters in Kentucky and the Ohio River Valley, 1802–1920* (Lexington: Univ. Press of Kentucky, 2011), 172.

60. The grandson of John J. Crittenden and Maria Knox Innes was John Jordan Crittenden Jr., commissioned a lieutenant and killed at the Battle of the Little Bighorn with Custer's 7th Cavalry. His gold pocketwatch apparently made its way north with the Sioux, who withdrew into Canada after the battle. Some Samaritan traced it to the maker in New England, who returned it to the family in Frankfort, identifying them by the watch's serial number. A watch with a story, it can be seen on exhibit at the Thomas D. Clark Center for Kentucky History in Frankfort.

61. Whitley, *Kentucky Ante-Bellum Portraiture,* 392.

62. *The Encyclopedia of Arkansas History and Culture,* s.v. "Robert Crittenden (1797–1834)," http://www.encyclopediaofarkansas.net/encyclopedia/entry-detail. aspx?entryID=2270.

63. Will of Harry Innes, Franklin County Courthouse, Frankfort, Kentucky.

64. E. F. Ellet, *Pioneer Women of the West* (Philadelphia: H. T. Coates, [1852?]), 60. Ellet misidentified her as "Anna" Innes in her text.

65. Undated obituary of Anna [Ann] Innes from the *Frankfort Commonwealth,* quoted in ibid.

66. John Francis McDermott, ed., "The Western Journals of Dr. George Hunter, 1796–1805," *Transactions of the American Philosophical Society* 53 (1963): 52.

67. Ibid. A respected man of science, George Hunter was born in Edinburgh, Scotland, on March 14, 1755. He came to Philadelphia with his family in 1774. He fought in the Revolution and, like so many of his generation, was a man of many parts—an apothecary, land speculator, soldier, and businessman—who associated with the scientific elite of Philadelphia as well as Thomas Jefferson and John James Audubon. Perhaps with speculative land interests, Hunter made several trips to the western frontier. In 1796 he traveled from Philadelphia to Pittsburgh and then southwest, making it as far as Saint Louis. In 1802 he set out for Kentucky and Illinois. Perhaps having a desire to invest in property for mining, he took a special interest in investigating Kentucky land that had deposits of saltpeter, potash, lime, iron, silver, and lead. In 1804 Jefferson appointed him to accompany William Dunbar, another respected scientist, on an expedition to the southern portion of the Louisiana Purchase, designed to parallel that of Lewis and Clark to the northwest. Although less-known, Hunter and Dunbar made important early scientific contributions in their explorations of the Old Southwest. Hunter returned to Kentucky in 1809 and then resettled in New Orleans in 1815, where he was a druggist and operated a rolling mill on the side. He died in New Orleans in 1832. Audubon identified Hunter as one of the people he

most desired to meet when he traveled to New Orleans. Ibid., 5–7, 123–24; George Hunter Journals, 1796–1809, American Philosophical Society, http://www.amphilsoc.org/collections/view?docId=ead/Mss.B.H912-ead.xml.

68. Mary E. Wharton and Roger Barbour, *Trees and Shrubs of Kentucky* (Lexington: Univ. Press of Kentucky, 1973), 482.

69. Tachau, *Federal Courts in the Early Republic,* 53.

6. The Cook Massacre

1. Harry Innes to John Brown, December 7, 1787, "From the Archives," *Register of the Kentucky Historical Society* 54 (October 1956): 369.

2. William G. Scroggins, comp., *Leaves of a Stunted Shrub: A Genealogy of the Scrogin-Scroggin-Scroggins Family,* vol. 1 (Cockeysville, Md.: Nativa, 2009), 13, https://books.google.com/books?id=bt99KfyjpFUC&pg=RA7-PA13&lpg=RA7-PA13&dq=jesse+and+betsy+bohannon+cook&source=bl&ots=n14CzKM25d&sig=A-iNyoK#v=onepage&q=jesse%20and%20betsy%20bohannon%20cook&f=false.

3. *Frankfort State Journal,* November 28, 1971.

4. Carl E. Kramer, *Capital on the Kentucky: A Two Hundred Year History of Frankfort and Franklin County* (Frankfort, Ky.: Historic Frankfort, 1986), 29.

5. Nancy O'Malley, *Stockading Up: A Study of Pioneer Stations in the Inner Bluegrass Region of Kentucky,* Archaeological Report 127 (Frankfort, Ky.: Kentucky Heritage Council, 1987), 214.

6. R. T. Dillard, "A Fragment of Kentucky History," *Frankfort Commonwealth,* November 14, 1843; *Frankfort Commonwealth,* October 20, 1871, Innes Family File, Kentucky Historical Society, Frankfort, Kentucky; Scroggins, *Leaves of a Stunted Shrub,* 16.

7. Scroggins, *Leaves of a Stunted Shrub,* 16–18.

8. Ibid., 10–11.

9. Dillard, "A Fragment of Kentucky History."

10. Scroggins, *Leaves of a Stunted Shrub,* 13.

11. O'Malley, *Stockading Up,* 214.

12. Chester Raymond Young, ed., *Westward into Kentucky: The Narrative of Daniel Trabue* (Lexington: Univ. Press of Kentucky, 2004), 137.

13. Ibid., 138.

14. Ibid.

15. Ibid., 139.

16. Lewis Collins, *History of Kentucky,* 1:307.

17. Ted Belue, *The Long Hunt: Death of the Buffalo East of the Mississippi* (Mechanicsburg, Pa.: Stackpole Books, 1996), 124.

18. Leonna Jett Shyrock, "Jared De Mint," *Register of the Kentucky Historical Society* 14 (May 1916): 57–61.

19. Ibid.

20. J. Clement, ed., "Heroism at Innis [*sic*] Settlement," *Noble Deeds of American Women* (Boston: Lee and Shepard, 1869), 120–23.

21. William W. Fowler, *American Women on the Frontier* (Hartford, Conn.: S. S. Scranton, 1880).

22. Dillard, "A Fragment of History."

23. Nettie Glenn, "Original Cook Cabin in Good Condition," *Frankfort State Journal*, June 18, 1978.

7. Milltown on the Elkhorn

1. Nancy O'Malley, *Stockading Up: A Study of Pioneer Stations in the Inner Bluegrass Region of Kentucky*, Archaeological Report 127 (Frankfort, Ky.: Kentucky Heritage Council, 1987), 223.

2. Mary Nash Cox, Sallie Clay Lanham, Bob Lanham, and Gene Burch, *Portrait of Early Families: Frankfort Area Before 1860* (Frankfort, Ky.: Early Families, 2009), 78.

3. Ibid.

4. Carl E. Kramer, *Capital on the Kentucky: A Two Hundred Year History of Frankfort and Franklin County* (Frankfort, Ky.: Historic Frankfort, 1986), 26.

5. State Journal Staff Report, "The River," in *Franklin County, 1795–1995* (Frankfort, Ky.: Frankfort State Journal, 1995), 33.

6. Neal O. Hammon and Richard L. Taylor, *Virginia's Western War: 1775–1786* (Mechanicsburg, Pa.: Stackpole Books, 2002), 17.

7. Cox, Lanham, Lanham, and Burch, *Portrait of Early Families*, 79.

8. Ibid. Mount Pleasant, first known as Gomer Baptist Church, is one of Franklin County's earliest churches.

9. M. C. Darnell, "Kentucky More Hunting Ground Than Residence for Indians," *Frankfort State Journal*, May 12, 1960.

10. Livingston Taylor, "Spiritual Values," in *Franklin County, 1795–1995* (Frankfort, Ky.: Frankfort State Journal, 1995), 68.

11. Dard Hunter, *Papermaking: The History and Technique of an Ancient Craft*, 2nd ed. (New York: Knopf, 1967), 175.

12. Charles Kerr, *History of Kentucky*, vol. 5 (New York: American Historical Society, 1922), 352.

13. Leonard N. Rosenband, "The Many Transitions of Ebenezer Stedman," in *Reconceptualizing the Industrial Revolution*, ed. Jeff Horn, Leonard W. Rosenband, and Merritt Roe Smith (Cambridge, Massachusetts: M.I.T. Press, 2010), 203.

14. Ibid., 202.

15. Ibid., 204.

16. Ebenezer Hiram Stedman, *Bluegrass Craftsman* (Lexington: Univ. Press of Kentucky, 1959; reprint, Frankfort, Ky.: Frankfort Heritage Press Kentucky, 2006). Citation page numbers refer to the 2006 Frankfort Heritage Press edition.

17. Stedman, *Bluegrass Craftsman.*

18. Charles D. Hockensmith, "Ebenezer Stedman's Mills: A Nineteenth Century Paper, Grist, and Lumber Milling Complex Near Frankfort, Kentucky," in Stedman, *Bluegrass Craftsman,* 225–53.

19. Dard Hunter, *Papermaking,* 184.

20. Stedman, *Bluegrass Craftsman,* 57.

21. Ibid., 120.

22. Ibid., 115.

23. Ibid., 42.

24. Ibid., 136.

25. Ibid., 108.

26. Lyman Hiram Weeks, *A History of Paper Manufacturing in the United States, 1690–1916* (New York: Lockwood Trade Journal, 1916), 169.

27. Hockensmith, "Ebenezer Stedman's Mills," 227.

28. Stedman, *Bluegrass Craftsman,* 111–12.

29. Ibid., 148.

30. John E. Kleber, ed., *The Kentucky Encyclopedia* (Lexington: Univ. Press of Kentucky, 2000), s.v. "Cholera Epidemics."

31. Stedman, *Bluegrass Craftsman,* 164.

32. Cox, Lanham, Lanham, and Burch, *Portrait of Early Families,* 159.

33. Stedman, *Bluegrass Craftsman,* 167.

34. George Lewis, "Industries of Other Days in Franklin County," unidentified newspaper article, Capital City Museum, Frankfort, Kentucky.

35. Stedman, *Bluegrass Craftsman,* 167.

36. Ibid., 154.

37. Ibid., 152.

38. Ibid., 159.

39. Ibid., 156.

40. Ibid., 157.

41. Ibid., 159. This turn of phrase references a Scotch proverb that "alludes to the former practice of making spoons out of the horns of cattle or sheep." It means "to make a determined effort to achieve something whatever the cost." *Oxford Dictionary of English Idioms* (Oxford: Oxford Univ. Press, 2010), s.v. "spoon." Sir Walter Scott uses the phrase in chapter 22 of his historical novel *Rob Roy,* published in 1819, and Lord Byron uses it in a letter to John Murray dated April 23, 1820. George Gordon Byron, *The Works of Lord Byron,* vol. 5, ed. Rowland E. Prothero (London: John Murray, 1904), 16.

42. Stedman, *Bluegrass Craftsman,* 158.

43. Ibid., 161.

44. M. C. Darnell, "History of the Stedmantown Section Can Be Traced to Pre-Historic Times," *Frankfort State Journal,* May 12, 1960.

45. Russell Hatter, "Here's the Story of a Man, a Mill, and Nearby Waters that Transcended History," *Frankfort State Journal,* November 5, 2006.

46. Charles Bogart interview, by the author, January 30, 2016.

47. The population of the county in 1830 was 9,234. L. F. Johnson, *The History of Franklin County, Ky.* (Frankfort, Ky.: Roberts Printing Company, 1912), 90. In the 1820s, Frankfort newspapers included the *Argus*, the *Patriot*, the *Spirit of '76*, the *Commentator*, and the *Constitutional Advocate*. State Journal Staff Report, "Making a Living," in *Franklin County, 1795–1995* (Frankfort, Ky.: Frankfort State Journal, 1995), 20.

48. Edmund Morgan, *The Genuine Article: A Historian Looks at Early America* (New York: Norton, 2004), 169–70, as quoted in Rosenband, "The Many Transitions of Ebenezer Stedman," 204.

49. Stedman, *Bluegrass Craftsman*, 230.

50. The "forty-year-old female" was probably Isabella. Census information provided by John Gray.

51. Stedman, *Bluegrass Craftsman*, 168.

52. Ibid., 35.

53. Rosbenband, "The Many Transitions of Ebenezer Stedman," 209.

54. Stedman, *Bluegrass Craftsman*, 123.

55. Rosbenband, "The Many Transitions of Ebenezer Stedman," 215.

56. Stedman, *Bluegrass Craftsman*, 165–66.

57. Rosbenband, "The Many Transitions of Ebenezer Stedman," 210.

58. Stedman, *Bluegrass Craftsman*, 202.

59. Ibid., 179.

60. Rosbenband, "The Many Transitions of Ebenezer Stedman," 218.

61. Stedman, *Bluegrass Craftsman*, 178.

62. Ibid., 138.

63. Hockensmith, "Ebenezer Stedman's Mills," 228.

64. Stedman, *Bluegrass Craftsman*, 181.

65. Ibid., 188.

66. The Backbone is the sharp spine of timber that rose out of the bottom between the mill site and Innes Station. Stamping Ground was a gathering place for buffalo to wallow and lick salt. Salt licks refers to more distant sites to the north, such as Blue Licks in Nicholas County, Drennon's Lick in Henry County, and Big Bone Lick in Boone County.

67. Stedman, *Bluegrass Craftsman*, 142.

68. This is another name for the sugar maple, one of the dominant trees of the region.

69. Stedman, *Bluegrass Craftsman*, 206.

70. This was the name of the mill when Amos Kendall owned it.

71. Stedman, *Bluegrass Craftsman*, 203.

72. Ibid., 197.

73. Ibid., 201.

74. Ibid.

75. Ibid., 207.

76. Ibid.

77. Ibid.

78. Ibid., 20.

79. Ibid., 148.

80. M. C. Darnell, "Kentucky More Hunting Ground Than Residence for Indians," *Frankfort State Journal,* circa 1960.

81. Ann Macklin Peel, ed., *To Become a Texian: The Letters and Journeys of Caroline Cox Morgan and Her Family, 1839–1857* (Frankfort, Ky.: Kentucky Color Publishing, 1997), 42.

82. Hockensmith, "Ebenezer Stedman's Mills," 228.

83. Ibid.

84. Ibid., 231.

85. Robert M. Rennick, *Kentucky Place Names* (Lexington: Univ. Press of Kentucky, 1984), 283.

86. Hockensmith, "Ebenezer Stedman's Mills," 230.

87. Ibid., 231.

88. Ibid., 221.

89. Nelly Stedman Cox, *Leaves from History* (unpublished manuscript, n.d.), Capital City Museum, Frankfort, Kentucky.

90. Cox, Lanham, Lanham, and Burch, *Portrait of Early Families,* 157.

91. George Stedman to Mary Steffee Stedman and Ebenezer Hiram Stedman, January 5, 1865, quoted in Jim Prichard, *Embattled Capital: Frankfort, Kentucky in the Civil War* (Frankfort, Ky.: Frankfort Heritage Press, 2014), 162.

92. Cox, *Leaves from History.*

93. Prichard, *Embattled Capital,* 251.

94. Kramer, *Capital on the Kentucky,* 171.

95. Stedman, *Bluegrass Craftsman,* 221.

96. Cox, *Leaves from History.*

97. Frances L. S. Dugan and Jacqueline P. Bull, "Introduction," in Stedman, *Bluegrass Craftsman,* x–xi.

98. Nelly Stedman Cox, *Leaves from History.*

99. Stedman, *Bluegrass Craftsman,* 224.

100. Ibid.

101. Hockensmith, "Ebenezer Stedman's Mills," 237.

102. In "The Deserted Village" (1770), Oliver Goldsmith blended "recollections of the Irish village of his boyhood, Lissoy," with his more recent travels through the villages of England. At the time, they were undergoing the process of depopulation. "The Deserted Village" is a descriptive poem and a powerful polemic. The "shapeless ruin" that Goldsmith "sees in the landscape reflects the decadence produced by the pursuit of luxury." Carol Rumens, "Poem of the Week: The Deserted Village by Oliver Goldsmith," *Guardian,* May 31, 2010, https://www.theguardian.com/books/booksblog/2010/may/31/poem-week-goldsmith-deserted-village.

103. Russ Hatter, "Here's the Story of a Man, a Mill, and Nearby Waters that Transcended History" *Frankfort State Journal,* November 5, 2006.

104. Cox, Lanham, Lanham, and Burch, *Portrait of Early Families,* 159.

105. John Palmore interview, by the author, fall 2016.

106. See Appendix C.

107. Notes of Nelly Stedman Cox, Stedman File, Capital City Museum, Frankfort, Kentucky.

8. Entrepreneur of the Elkhorn

1. Jim Richards, "Historic Landmark Passes 100th Anniversary Almost Unnoticed," *Frankfort State Journal*, circa 1976, Capital City Museum, Frankfort, Kentucky.

2. Ann Macklin Peel, *The Macklin Family of Frankfort and Franklin County* (Frankfort, Ky.: Ann Macklin Peel, 2006), 1.

3. Ibid., 25.

4. Ibid.

5. Ibid., 26.

6. Ibid.

7. One ex-slave in particular, listed in Macklin's will as Jim Macklin, must have raised some concerns within the Macklin family and the larger law-abiding community. He was a slave when the will was made, but a free man when Jim died. Jim Macklin was thirty-six when the will was drawn up. Next to his name in parentheses, A. W. Macklin added the inexplicit adjective "delicate," probably a reference to some debilitating illness or disability that kept him from working. Other slaves listed in the will had similar notations, "crippled" or "diseased," to justify their lower valuations. In late January of 1868, Jim Macklin allegedly assaulted a young Irish woman and threw her body over the river embankment near the railroad tunnel below the old State Arsenal, close by the Macklin slaughterhouse where he probably worked. On the evening of January 30 an angry mob, consisting mostly of Irishmen, gathered at the jail and attempted to remove him. Trying to prevent a lynching, the commonwealth attorney enlisted the aid of Father Lambert Young, priest of the Church of the Good Shepherd. On reaching the jail, Father Young pleaded unsuccessfully with his parishioners to let the law take its course. The mob dragged Macklin to the site of the crime and hanged him. At least one later Macklin descendant believed that Jim Macklin had been a scapegoat for some drunken revelers who had committed the crime. His "delicate" condition, as noted in Macklin's will, probably does not support the notion that he was physically robust enough to assault the victim (Peel, *The Macklin Family*, 49).

U.S. marshals later arrested thirteen of the mob members for alleged violation of civil rights statutes, transferring them to Louisville, where a grand jury weighed the evidence. The prosecuting attorney called Father Young to testify, but he refused on the grounds that he could not violate the confidences of his office as a priest. In fact, many of the accused were his parishioners. The court jailed him for a time under a contempt charge, but eventually all of the defendants were released for lack of evidence (Carl E. Kramer, *Capital on the Kentucky: A Two Hundred Year History of Frankfort and Franklin County* [Frankfort, Ky.: Historic Frankfort, 1986], 175). One wonders how A. W. Macklin would have acted or reacted had he been alive. Notably, at least one of the slaves listed in his estate, George Owens, aged forty-four, joined the Union Army, enlisting in the 119th U.S. Colored Infantry and dying of smallpox in 1866. (Jim Prichard, *Embattled Capital: Frankfort, Kentucky in the Civil War* [Frankfort, Ky.: Frankfort Heritage Press, 2014], 181).

8. Peel, *The Macklin Family of Frankfort and Franklin County*, 40–41.

9. John Taylor, *Baptists on the American Frontier: A History of Ten Baptist Churches*, ed. Chester Raymond Young (Macon, Ga.: Mercer Univ. Press, 1995), 165.

10. L. F. Johnson, *History of Franklin County* (Frankfort, Ky.: Roberts Printing Company, 1912), 140.

11. Mary Nash Cox, Sallie Clay Lanham, Bob Lanham, and Gene Burch, *Portrait of Early Families: Frankfort Area Before 1860* (Frankfort, Ky.: Early Families, 2009), 79.

12. *The Biographical Encyclopaedia of Kentucky* (Cincinnati: J. M. Armstrong, 1878), s.v "Macklin, A. W."

13. Hank Hancock to Russ Hatter, January 8, 2013, Capital City Museum, Frankfort, Kentucky.

14. Charles D. Hockensmith, "Elkhorn Water Mills and Elkhorn Roller Mills: Franklin County, Kentucky," *Millstone* 9, no. 2 (2010): 3.

15. Hockensmith, "Elkhorn Water Mills," 18.

16. Peel, *The Macklin Family*, 27.

17. *The Biographical Encyclopaedia of Kentucky*, s.v. "Macklin, A. W."

18. Hockensmith, "Elkhorn Water Mills," 4.

19. Richard Taylor, "A Self-Guided Tour of Selected Historic Landmarks of the Georgetown Road, Forks of Elkhorn and Peaks Mill Areas" (unpublished manuscript, circa 1978), Capital City Museum, Frankfort, Kentucky. A copy is in the author's possession.

20. Russ Hatter and Nicky Hughes, *Frankfort Cemetery: The Westminster Abbey of Kentucky* (Frankfort, Ky.: Frankfort Heritage Press, 2007), 35.

21. Prichard, *Embattled Capital*, 231.

22. Cox, Lanham, Lanham, and Burch, *Portrait of Early Families*, 103.

23. Prichard, *Embattled Capital*, 231.

24. *Merriam Webster*, 16th ed., s.v. "erysipelas."

9. Whistlerian Blue

1. Willard Rouse Jillson, *Paul Sawyier and His Paintings: Centennial Exhibition (1865–1965)* (Louisville, Ky.: J. B. Speed Memorial Museum, 1965), 8.

2. James D. Birchfield, "Thomas S. Noble: 'Made for a Painter,'" *Kentucky Review* 6, no. 1 (winter 1986): 39.

3. "Duveneck, Frank, American, 1848–1919," The National Gallery of Art, https://www.nga.gov/content/ngaweb/Collection/artist-info.1258.html.

4. Arthur F. Jones, *The Art of Paul Sawyier* (Lexington: Univ. Press of Kentucky, 1976), 7.

5. It also is no coincidence that Sawyier's teacher Frank Duveneck's paintings have been mistakenly identified as works by famous American painter James McNeill Whistler, "whom Duveneck knew in Venice." "Duveneck, Frank, American, 1848–1919."

6. William Donald Coffey, *Paul Sawyier, Kentucky Artist: An Historical Chronology of His Life, Art, Friends and Times from Old Frankfort to the Catskills* (Frankfort, Ky.: Frankfort Heritage Press, 2010), 64.

7. Jillson, *Paul Sawyier and His Paintings*, 11.

8. Jones, *The Art of Paul Sawyier*, 26.

9. Ibid., 22.

10. Ibid.; John E. Kleber, ed., *The Encyclopedia of Louisville* (Lexington: Univ. Press of Kentucky, 2001), s.v. "K. Norman Berry Associates."

11. Jones, *The Art of Paul Sawyier*, 27.

12. Ibid., 67.

13. Ibid., 68.

14. Ibid., 31.

15. Ibid., 28.

16. Jillson, *Paul Sawyier and His Paintings*, 46.

17. Nettie Henry Glenn, *"Love to All, Your Paul"* (Ephrata, Pa.: Science Press, 1974); Coffey, *Paul Sawyier, Kentucky Artist.*

10. Remnants, Ghosts, and Ciphers

1. George Crutcher Downing, "Where Santa Anna Was a Prisoner," *Register of the Kentucky Historical Society* 6, no. 16 (January 1908): 13, 15–16; Willard Rouse Jillson, *Early Frankfort and Franklin County* (Louisville, Ky.: Standard Printing Company, 1936), 101.

2. Martha Anne Turner, *The Yellow Rose of Texas: The Story of a Song* (El Paso, Tex.: Texas Western Press, 1971), 107; "Santa Anna Almost Hanged in Kentucky," *Lexington (Ky.) Herald-Leader*, July 21, 1974.

3. Allan M. Trout, "Forks of Elkhorn," *Louisville (Ky.) Courier-Journal*, September 27, 1964.

4. Willard Rouse Jillson, *Literary Haunts and Personalities of Old Frankfort* (Frankfort, Ky.: Kentucky Historical Society, 1941), 82, 86.

5. Ebenezer Hiram Stedman, *Bluegrass Craftsman* (Lexington: Univ. Press of Kentucky, 1959; reprint, Frankfort, Ky.: Frankfort Heritage Press Kentucky, 2006), plate 4. Citation page numbers refer to the 2006 Frankfort Heritage Press edition.

6. Richard Taylor, "A Self-Guided Tour of Selected Historic Landmarks of the Georgetown Road, Forks of Elkhorn and Peaks Mill Areas" (unpublished manuscript, circa 1978), 10, Capital City Museum, Frankfort, Kentucky. A copy is in the author's possession.

7. B. N. Griffing, *An Atlas of Franklin County, Kentucky: From Actual Surveys* (Philadelphia: D. J. Lake, 1882).

8. Taylor, "A Self-Guided Tour."

9. M. C. Darnell, "Church Family Prominent in Early Days at Stedmantown," *Frankfort State Journal*, May 12, 1960.

10. Ibid.

11. Clem J. O'Connor, "An Automobile Ride through History" (Frankfort, Ky.: Historic Frankfort, Inc., circa 1975) (unpublished 8-page manuscript, in possession of the author).

12. Johnson, *History of Franklin County*, 154, 278.

13. Russell Hatter interview, by the author, May 2017.

14. Urey Woodson, *The First New Dealer* (Louisville, Ky.: Standard Press, 1939), 121.

15. Correspondence to *Louisville Courier-Journal*, n.d., Innes Family File, Kentucky Historical Society, Frankfort, Kentucky.

16. Knight-Taylor-Hockensmith House, National Register of Historic Places Registration Form, Kentucky Heritage Council, Frankfort, Kentucky.

17. Stedman, *Bluegrass Craftsman*, 187.

18. John E. Kleber, ed., *The Encyclopedia of Louisville* (Lexington: Univ. Press of Kentucky, 2001), s.v. "Covered Bridges."

19. Melissa C. Jurgensen, *Through Their Eyes: Covered Bridges of Franklin County, Kentucky* (N.p.: Due Belli Autrici Books, 2013), 9.

20. Kleber, ed., *The Kentucky Encyclopedia*, s.v. "Covered Bridges."

21. Jurgensen, *Through Their Eyes*, 67.

22. Ibid.

23. Jurgensen, *Through Their Eyes*, 21.

24. Peel, *The Macklin Family*, 109–10.

25. Ibid., 110.

26. Ibid.

27. Ibid.

28. Patrick Kennedy correspondence with the author, September 27, 2016.

29. O'Connor, "An Automobile Ride through History," 5.

30. Charles H. Bogart and William M. Ambrose, *The Whiskey Route: The Frankfort and Cincinnati Railroad, Frankfort, Kentucky* (Frankfort, Ky.: Yellow Sparks Press, 2012), 13.

31. Bogart and Ambrose, *The Whiskey Route*, 13.

32. E. Lucy Braun, *Deciduous Forests of Eastern North America* (1950; reprint, Caldwell, N.J.: Blackburn Press, 2001).

33. Greg Abernathy, Deborah White, Ellis. L. Lauderback, and Marc Evans, *Kentucky's Natural Heritage: An Illustrated Guide to Biodiversity* (Lexington: Univ. Press of Kentucky, 2010), 114.

34. Ibid., 123.

35. Deborah White email correspondence with the author, November 9, 2016.

36. Capital City Museum, Frankfort, Kentucky.

37. Carl E. Kramer, *Capital on the Kentucky: A Two Hundred Year History of Frankfort and Franklin County* (Frankfort, Ky.: Historic Frankfort, 1986), 93.

38. Roy Gray Sr. interview, by Betty Barr, in possession of John Gray, Frankfort, Kentucky.

39. Ibid.

Epilogue

1. Ron Herron, "Can a Dying Creek Be Saved?" *Frankfort State Journal*, July 19, 1970.

2. Ibid.

3. Kentucky Revised Statutes 220.590.

4. Kentucky Division of Water, *Kentucky's Water Health Guide*, 1st edition, http://water.ky.gov/watershed/Documents/Kentucky%27s%20Water%20Health%20Guide%20-%20Online%20Version.pdf.

5. *Integrated Report to Congress on the Condition of Water Resources in Kentucky, 2016* (Frankfort, KY: Kentucky Division of Water, 2018), http://water.ky.gov/waterqual ity/Integrated%20Reports/2016%20Integrated%20Report.pdf.

6. Katie McKone, email to author, April 16, 2018

7. Ibid.

8. Kentucky River Basin Assessment Report, http://www.uky.edu/WaterResources/ Watershed/KRB_AR/elkhorn_creek.htm

9. Wendell R. Haag and Ronald R. Cicerello, *A Distributional Atlas of the Freshwater Mussels of Kentucky,* Scientific and Technical Series, No. 8 (Frankfort, KY: Kentucky State Nature Preserves Commission, 2016).

10. Ronald Cicerello, email to author, April 2018.

11. Kentucky Water Research Institute, *Kentucky River Basin Assessment Report,* 2000, http://www.uky.edu/Watershed/KRB_AR/elkhorn_creek.htm.

12. I am grateful to Katie McKone and Ronald R. Cicerello for much of the technical information relating to the ecological health of the Elkhorn. Both are dedicated professionals.

INDEX